CLYMER®

HONDA

FOURTRAX 90 • 1993-2000

D1601786

The world's finest publisher of mechanical how-to manuals

INTERTEC PUBLISHING

P.O. Box 12901, Overland Park, Kansas 66282-2901

Copyright © 2000 Intertec Publishing

FIRST EDITION
First Printing July, 2000

Printed in U.S.A.

CLYMER and colophon are registered trademarks of Intertec Publishing.

ISBN: 0-89287-749-9

Library of Congress: 00-105285

MEMBER

MOTORCYCLE INDUSTRY COUNCIL, INC.

Technical photography by Ron Wright

Cover: Photographed by Mark Clifford, Mark Clifford Photography, Los Angeles, California. TRX90 courtesy of Rice Motorsports, La Puente, California.

INTERTEC BOOK DIVISION

President Cameron Bishop
Executive Vice President of Operations/CFO Dan Altman
Senior Vice President, Book Division Ted Marcus

EDITORIAL

Director of Price Guides
Tom Fournier

Senior Editor
Mark Jacobs

Editors
Mike Hall
Frank Craven
Paul Wyatt

Associate Editors
Robert Sokol
Carl Janssens
James Grooms

Technical Writers
Ron Wright
Ed Scott
George Parise
Mark Rolling
Michael Morlan
Jay Bogart
Ronney Broach

Inventory and Production Manager
Shirley Renicker

Editorial Production Supervisor
Dylan Goodwin

Editorial Production Coordinator
Sandy Kreps

Editorial Production Assistants
Greg Araujo
Dennis Conrow
Shara Meyer
Susan Hartington

Technical Illustrators
Steve Amos
Robert Caldwell
Mitzi McCarthy
Michael St. Clair
Mike Rose

MARKETING/SALES AND ADMINISTRATION

General Manager, Technical and Specialty Books
Michael Yim
General Manager, AC-U-KWIK
Randy Stephens
Advertising Production Coordinator
Kim Sawalich
Advertising Coordinator
Jodi Donohoe
Advertising/Editorial Assistant
Janet Rogers
Advertising & Promotions Manager
Elda Starke
Senior Art Director
Andrew Brown
Marketing Assistant
Melissa Abbott
Associate Art Director
Chris Paxton
Sales Manager/Marine
Dutch Sadler
Sales Manager/Manuals
Ted Metzger
Sales Manager/Motorcycles
Matt Tusken
Sales Coordinator
Paul Cormaci
Telephone Sales Supervisor
Joelle Stephens
Telemarketing Sales Representative
Susan Kay
Customer Service/Fulfillment Manager
Caryn Bair
Fulfillment Coordinator
Susan Kohlmeyer
Customer Service Supervisor
Terri Cannon
Customer Service Representatives
Ardelia Chapman
Donna Schemmel
Dana Morrison
April LeBlond

The following books and guides are published by Intertec Publishing.

CLYMER SHOP MANUALS
Boat Motors and Drives
Motorcycles and ATVs
Snowmobiles
Personal Watercraft
ABOS/INTERTEC/CLYMER BLUE BOOKS AND TRADE-IN GUIDES
Recreational Vehicles
Outdoor Power Equipment
Agricultural Tractors
Lawn and Garden Tractors
Motorcycles and ATVs
Snowmobiles and Personal Watercraft
Boats and Motors
AIRCRAFT BLUEBOOK-PRICE DIGEST
Airplanes
Helicopters

AC-U-KWIK DIRECTORIES
The Corporate Pilot's Airport/FBO Directory
International Manager's Edition
Jet Book
I&T SHOP SERVICE MANUALS
Tractors
INTERTEC SERVICE MANUALS
Snowmobiles
Outdoor Power Equipment
Personal Watercraft
Gasoline and Diesel Engines
Recreational Vehicles
Boat Motors and Drives
Motorcycles
Lawn and Garden Tractors

CONTENTS

QUICK REFERENCE DATA

Table 1 GENERAL TORQUE SPECIFICATIONS

	N•m	in.-lb.	ft.-lb.
5 mm bolt and nut	5	44	–
6 mm bolt and nut	10	88	–
8 mm bolt and nut	22	–	16
10 mm bolt and nut	35	–	26
12 mm bolt and nut	55	–	41
5 mm screw	4	35	–
6 mm screw	9	80	–
6 mm flange bolt (8 mm head)	9	80	–
6 mm flange bolt (10 mm head) and nut	12	106	–
8 mm flange bolt and nut	27	–	20
10 mm flange bolt and nut	40	–	29

Table 2 TIRE INFLATION PRESSURES

	Front psi (kPa)	Rear psi (kPa)
Recommended operating pressure	2.9 (20)	2.9 (20)
Maximum pressure	3.3 (23)	3.3 (23)
Minimum pressure	2.5 (17)	2.5 (17)
Bead seating pressure	36 (250)	36 (250)

Table 3 FUEL, LUBRICANTS AND CAPACITIES

Engine fuel	Unleaded gasoline; 86 octane minimum
Fuel tank capacity	6.0 liters (1.58 U.S. gallons)
Fuel tank reserve	1.3 liters (0.34 U.S. gallon)
Engine oil[1]	SAE 10W-40; SF/SG rated or newer
Engine oil capacity	0.9 liter (1.0 U.S. quart)
Drive chain	O-ring type chain lubricant or SAE 80 or 90 weight gear oil
Control cables[2]	Cable lube
Air filter	Foam air filter oil
Steering kingpins	Molydisulfide grease

1 See text for oil recommendations for various riding conditions.
2 Do not use drive chain lubricant on control cables.

Table 4 TUNE-UP SPECIFICATIONS

Compression ratio	9.2:1
Cylinder compression	178 psi (1226 kPa)
Idle speed	1600 ± 100 rpm
Ignition timing F mark	
1993-1998	7° @ 1600 rpm
1999-2000	7° @ 1500 rpm
Ignition timing full advance	30° BTDC @ 3050 rpm
Valve clearance	
Intake and exhaust	0.05 ± 0.02 mm (0.002 ± 0.0008 in.)

Table 5 SPARK PLUG SPECIFICATIONS

Spark plugs	
Standard plug (mixed-speed riding)	NGK CR7HSA or Denso U22FSR-U
Hot plug (extended slow-speed riding)	NGK CR6HSA or Denso U20FSR-U
Cold plug (extended high-speed riding)	NGK CR8HSA or Denso U24FSR-U
Spark plug gap	0.6-0.7 mm (0.024-0.028 in.)

Table 8 DRIVE CHAIN MEASUREMENTS

Drive chain free play	20-30 mm (3/4-1 1/4 in.)
Drive chain length, 21-pin span	
Service limit	268 mm (10.6 in.)

CHAPTER ONE

GENERAL INFORMATION

This manual covers the 1993-2000 Honda Fourtrax 90. The text provides complete information for the maintenance, tune-up, repair and overhaul of the vehicle. Photographs and drawings guide the owner through every job.

As in all Clymer books, the chapters are thumb-tabbed. Major headings are indexed at the back of the manual. All procedures, tables and illustrations in this manual are for the reader who may be working on the vehicle or using this manual for the first time. Frequently used specifications are listed in the *Quick Reference Data* pages at the front of the book.

Refer to the manual before making adjustments or repairs. The manual provides information on how the vehicle operates, when maintenance procedures are required, and how to lower repair costs.

The following tables are included at the end of this chapter.

Table 1 lists general dimensions.
Table 2 lists weight and load capacities.
Table 3 lists windchill factors.
Table 4 lists technical abbreviations.
Table 5 lists general tightening torques.
Table 6 lists conversion factors.

Table 7 lists metric tap drill sizes.
Table 8 lists decimal and metric equivalents.

MANUAL ORGANIZATION

This chapter provides:
1. Information for using the manual.
2. General information about the vehicle.
3. Shop safety practices and service standards.
4. Standards for commonly used fasteners.
5. Tools and test equipment, and their usage.
6. Techniques for removing damaged fasteners.
7. Techniques for removing and installing bearings and seals.
8. Recommendations for riding and operating the vehicle.

Chapter Two provides troubleshooting information and lists the typical symptoms of potential problems. Appropriate tests for this vehicle are also included in the chapter.

Chapter Three details the periodic maintenance, lubrication and tune-up procedures necessary to keep the vehicle operating at peak performance. Occasionally, the reader will be directed to a specific chapter in order to perform a maintenance procedure. This usually occurs when the maintenance procedure is also part of completing a more complex repair.

Subsequent chapters describe in step-by-step detail how to remove, repair and install specific systems, such as the engine, fuel system, transmission and brakes. If a repair requires special equipment usually found only in a machine shop, or if the repair is impractical for the home mechanic, it is indicated as such. It is usually faster, more practical and less expensive to have some repairs done by a dealership or machine shop. When necessary, tables are provided at the end of the chapters that specify torque values, service limits, measurements and capacities.

PERFORMING THE PROCEDURES

Note the following:

1. All dimensions and capacities are expressed in United States Customary (USC) and metric units (SI, Standard International Units).

2. *Front*, as described in this manual, refers to the front of the vehicle. The front of any component is the end closest to the front of the vehicle. The *left* and *right* sides refer to the position of the parts as viewed by the operator sitting on the vehicle, facing forward (**Figure 1**).

3. In the procedures, *replace* means to discard a defective part and replace it with a new or exchange unit. *Overhaul* means to remove, disassemble, inspect and replace parts as required to recondition a major system or component.

4. Some repairs require special hand tools. In most cases, the tool is shown in use and the part number is provided so it may be purchased from a dealership. Experienced mechanics may find they can substitute tools they have on hand, or they can fabricate the special tool or fixture.

5. Some repairs require tools usually found only in a machine shop. Unless the home mechanic has this equipment and the skill to operate it, these operations should be performed by a dealership or machine shop. Attempting to do this type of work with makeshift equipment can result in personal injury or damage to the vehicle. The cost of the repair can be minimized by removing the defective part, then taking it in for repairs.

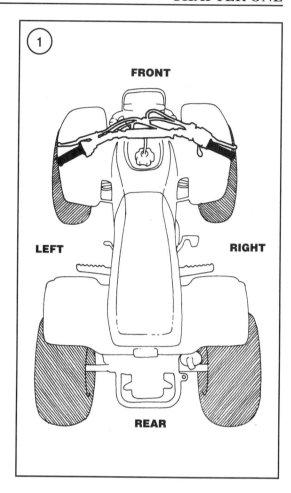

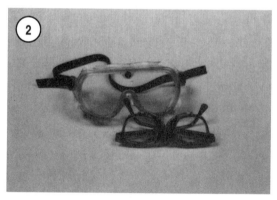

NOTES, CAUTIONS AND WARNINGS

The terms NOTE, CAUTION and WARNING have specific meanings in this manual. A NOTE provides additional information to make a step or procedure easier or clearer. Disregarding a NOTE could cause inconvenience, but would not cause damage or personal injury.

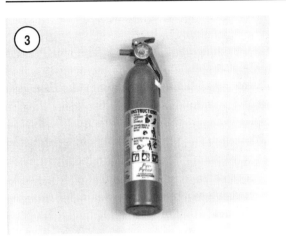

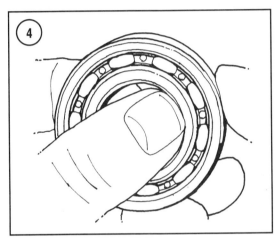

5. Never smoke or use a torch in the vicinity of gasoline or solvent that is in an open container.

6. If welding or brazing is required on the machine, remove the fuel tank and take it a safe distance away from the vehicle.

7. Use jackstands or other stable supports when raising the vehicle or removing suspension components. Always apply the parking brake.

8. Use properly-sized wrenches to avoid personal injury and damage to the fasteners.

9. When loosening a tight nut or bolt, protect the hands in case the wrench should slip.

10. If replacing a fastener, the new fastener should have the same measurements and strength as the old fastener. Incorrect or mismatched fasteners can result in vehicle damage and personal injury. Fastener kits that contain ungraded nuts, bolts, washers and cotter pins should be avoided.

11. Keep all hand and power tools clean and in good condition. Replace or repair damaged tools and power cords.

12. Keep the work area clean and uncluttered.

13. Wear safety goggles (**Figure 2**) during all operations involving drilling, grinding, hammering and spraying, or *anytime* eye safety is questionable. Safety goggles should also be worn when handling battery electrolyte and whenever solvent or compressed air is used to clean parts.

14. Keep an approved fire extinguisher (**Figure 3**) in the work area. It should be rated for gasoline (Class B) and electrical (Class C) fires.

15. When drying bearings or other rotating parts with compressed air, never allow the air jet to rotate the bearing or part. The air jet is capable of spinning them at speeds greater than their intended speeds. The unlubricated spinning bearing or part can damage easily, and could disassemble and cause serious injury. To prevent injury and bearing damage when using compressed air, grasp both the inner and outer bearing races with the fingers (**Figure 4**).

A CAUTION emphasizes an area where equipment damage could occur. Disregarding a CAUTION could cause permanent mechanical damage; however, personal injury is unlikely.

A WARNING emphasizes an area where personal injury or even death could result from negligence. Mechanical damage may also occur. WARNINGS *are to be taken seriously.*

SHOP SAFETY

When working on the vehicle, there are many potential hazards that could cause personal injury and property damage. Always observe the following shop and safety practices:

1. Work in a well-ventilated area.

2. Never work on a hot engine.

3. Wipe up fuel and solvent spills immediately.

4. Never use gasoline as a cleaning solvent.

SERIAL NUMBERS

Since the manufacturer may make changes to the vehicle during its production run, the serial numbers are used to verify which parts are fitted to the vehicle. Therefore, it is important to know the serial numbers and their location on the vehicle. Additionally, the model year of the vehicle is printed on a decal attached to the frame. For 1999 and 2000 models, another decal provides PAIR (Pulse Secondary Air Injection System) emission control information.

Record the frame, engine and model year numbers and keep them in a safe place. They are necessary for ordering replacement parts, insurance and registration purposes, and product recalls. The following are the locations of the serial numbers and reference stickers:

1. The frame number is stamped into the frame behind the front lift bar (**Figure 5**).

2. The engine number is stamped into the crankcase on the left side of engine (**Figure 6**).

3. The model year decal is located on the left frame member above left shock absorber (**Figure 7**).

4. The PAIR decal is located on the right frame member above right shock absorber (**Figure 8**).

NOTE
The original Honda ignition key is stamped with an ignition number. Record this number as well. Replacement ignition keys can be made if this number is available.

PARTS REPLACEMENT

When ordering parts, always provide the engine and frame numbers. Whenever possible, take the old part to the dealership. Minor differences in the new part may not be evident unless the parts are compared and examined closely.

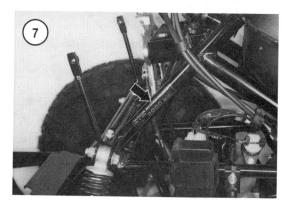

SERVICE TIPS

Most of the service procedures in the manual can be performed by anyone reasonably handy with tools. Before starting a job, read each procedure *completely* while looking at the actual parts. Consider the skill and equipment required before attempting any procedure involving major disassembly. In order to properly complete a repair, be patient, methodical and organized. The following shop tips will help the home mechanic perform a thorough job.

1. When disassembling major components, label the parts so their order of assembly and orientation is known. Keep the parts of major assemblies organized on the workbench in their order of removal. Make drawings, or use a video or Polaroid camera to keep parts and assemblies organized and identified. This is particularly useful if the job will be completed at a later date.

2. Small parts can be identified by placing them in labeled plastic bags (**Figure 9**). If reassembly will take place immediately, organize small parts for each assembly in a cupcake pan, egg carton or similar container.

3. Protect finished surfaces from tool and chemical damage. Gasoline and cleaning solvents can damage plastic, painted surfaces and decals.

4. Use penetrating oil on frozen or tight nuts, bolts and screws. Avoid the use of heat whenever possi-

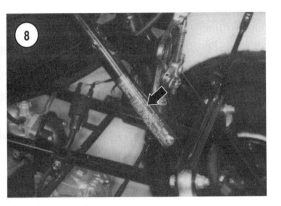

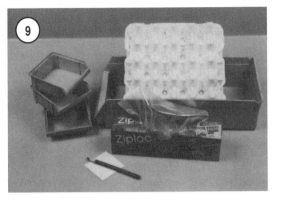

ble, as it can warp, melt or affect the temper of parts. Heat also damages plastic and painted finishes.

5. No parts, other than bushings and bearings, in the procedures should require unusual force to remove or assemble. If difficulty is encountered, inspect the part for possible oversights before choosing alternative methods.

6. Prevent small objects and dirt from entering the engine by covering openings as parts are removed.

7. Clean the vehicle before beginning repairs. The job will go faster and there is less likelihood of dirt entering the engine. Special cleaners are available for washing the engine and related parts. Follow the manufacturer's directions for use and limitations of the products.

8. If special tools are required to do a job, have the tools available before starting the work. When the job is started, it can be completed in a timely manner.

9. Wherever a rotating part contacts a stationary part, a shim or washer should be between the two parts.

10. Use new gaskets or O-rings on all components that are subjected to pressure or require an airtight seal, such as cylinder heads and oil passageways.

When old, non-pressure type gaskets are reused, a thin coat of silicone sealant can help them seal effectively. If it is necessary to make a cover gasket and the old gasket is not available to use as a guide, use the cover as a template. Apply oil to the sealing surface of the cover, place it squarely on the gasket material and press down on the cover. The oil will transfer to the gasket material and leave an outline of the cover and bolt hole locations.

> *CAUTION*
> *When purchasing material to make a gasket, measure the thickness of the old gasket at an uncompressed point so new gasket material of the approximate thickness can be purchased. Some components rely on the gasket thickness to maintain clearance between parts.*

11. If small parts tend to fall out of place during assembly, use grease to hold the part in place. If working on electrical components, use dielectrical grease. Do not use conventional grease on electrical components.

12. Clean carburetors by disassembling and washing the parts in hot soapy water. Never soak gaskets and rubber parts in solvents. Swelling or disintegration of the part can occur. Never use wire to clean jets or air passages, since they are affected by gouges and scratches. Use compressed air to blow out passages after the carburetor has been disassembled.

LUBRICANTS

Periodic lubrication is necessary to ensure the long life of the vehicle. The *type* of lubricant used is just as important as the lubrication service itself.

Generally, all liquid lubricants are called *oil*. They may be mineral-based (including petroleum bases), natural-based (vegetable and animal bases), synthetic-based or emulsions (blends). *Grease* is oil suspended in a thickening base so the end product is semisolid. Grease is often classified by the type of base, such as lithium.

The following paragraphs describe lubricants that are commonly used on ATVs. Follow the manufacturer's recommendations for lubricant application and limitations.

Engine Oil

The oil used in four-stroke engines must have several qualities in order to be an effective lubricant.

1. Circulate quickly at startup.
2. Provide adequate lubrication between engine parts at a wide range of operating temperatures.
3. Cool the engine and dissipate heat.
4. Provide a sealing action between piston rings and the cylinder wall.
5. Suspend and hold contaminants so they can be removed by the filter and by draining.

To meet these qualities, engine oil is tested and graded by the Society of Automotive Engineers (SAE) and the American Petroleum Institute (API). Two specifications are important to know when selecting an engine oil that is appropriate for the engine: *viscosity* and *service classification*.

The viscosity or *weight* of the oil is indicated by its SAE number, such as 10W-40. The *service classification* is indicated by the API rating, such as SF/SG. Both of these specifications are on the oil container (**Figure 10**). Do not use oil that is not graded and classified.

The weight, or thickness, of oil used depends on the temperature range in which the vehicle will be operated. As the weight number increases, the thickness of the oil also increases. Use a heavy grade of oil in hot weather and a lighter oil in cold weather. Oil is available in a single weight, such as SAE 30, or a multigrade, such as SAE 10W-40. The multigrade oil contains additives that allow it to vary its viscosity and be used over a wider temperature range. The *W* in the grading indicates approval for cold weather operation.

The service classification indicates that the oil meets certain lubrication standards specified by engine manufacturers. The first letter in the classification, *S*, indicates that the oil is for gasoline engines. As engine designs change, so do the lubricating standards for the engines. Therefore, the second letter in the classification, *G*, indicates which revision of the standards the oil satisfies. The classification began at the letter A and is currently at the letter J. Always use an oil with the classification recommended by the manufacturer or an oil with a newer classification. Engine damage can occur by using an oil with a classification that is older than that recommended by the manufacturer.

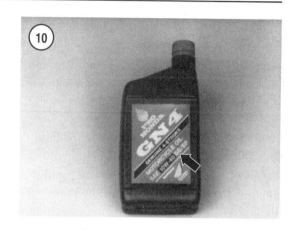

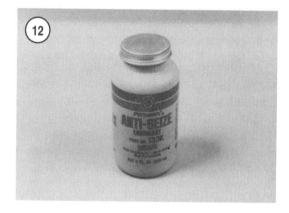

Grease

Grease (**Figure 11**) is graded by the National Lubricating Grease Institute (NLGI) and assigned a number according to the consistency of the grease. The grades range from No. 000 to No. 6, with No. 6 being the most solid. A typical multipurpose grease is NLGI No. 2.

Grease with a modifier such as molybdenum disulfide (MOS2) is required for some components.

plied to the threads of a fastener prior to installation. After the fastener is tightened, the compound remains squeezed between the threads. This prevents corrosion of the threads and allows the fastener to be easily removed in the future.

Threadlocking Compound

Threadlocking compound (**Figure 13**) is applied to the threads of the fastener prior to tightening. The compound prevents fasteners from loosening due to vibration and helps seal against leaks. Threadlocking compounds are available in different strengths. Parts subjected to an average vibration that are disassembled often should use a low-strength compound. This will allow the parts to remain secure, but still allow disassembly with hand tools. Parts that are subjected to severe vibration should use a high-strength compound. This type of compound will make disassembly difficult and heat may be required to loosen the fastener.

RTV Sealant

A common sealant used in the shop is RTV (room temperature vulcanizing) sealant (**Figure 14**). This sealant requires several hours to cure, which allows time for adjusting parts during the assembly process. Gaskets are not damaged when parts are disassembled before the sealant is cured. When the sealant is cured, it remains flexible and waterproof. RTV sealants are available for a variety of applications, including high-temperature applications. When choosing a sealant, follow the manufacturer's recommendations and application instructions.

Cleaners and Solvents

A variety of cleaners and solvents are available to help keep the vehicle clean and to recondition parts (**Figure 15**). These products are often used for special purposes, such as dissolving heavy accumulations of grease from the exterior of the engine, dissolving varnishes in the carburetor, cleaning electrical contacts, or cleaning brake components.

As with any solvent, care must be taken when using the product. Painted parts, rubber, plastics and decals can be damaged by these cleaners. Read the

This grease provides lubricating qualities when subjected to extreme pressure or when long intervals between lubrication occur. Swing arm bushings and steering components are usually lubricated with this type of grease. Always use the appropriate grease for each application.

SEALANTS AND CLEANERS

Antiseize Compound

Antiseize compound (**Figure 12**) contains fine particles of aluminum, brass or copper and is ap-

label to determine the limitations and possible hazards of the product.

As with any petroleum-based product, be aware of any ordinances that require special procedures for disposing of these products in an environmentally-safe manner.

> *WARNING*
> *When using these products, protect the arms, hands and eyes from possible splashing and backspray. Many of these products can ignite, irritate the skin, and contain vapors that should not be inhaled.*

TORQUE SPECIFICATIONS

When installing fasteners, the correct torque and tightening sequence is necessary to prevent damage, leakage and components loosening due to vibration. Use an accurate torque wrench and then tighten components to the proper value.

Torque specifications throughout this manual are listed in foot-pounds (ft.-lb.) and Newton-meters (N•m). Torque wrenches that are calibrated in meter kilograms can be used by performing a conversion. Simply move the decimal point one place to the right. For example: 3.5 mkg = 35 N•m. The exact mathematical conversion is 3.5 mkg = 34.3 N•m.

Table 5 lists general torque specifications for fasteners used on the vehicle. Use these values unless specified otherwise.

FASTENERS

Many types of fasteners are used to assemble the vehicle. The majority of these are nuts, bolts, screws, cotter pins and circlips (also called snap rings or retainers). In order for the vehicle to remain safe and trouble-free, threaded fasteners must be torqued properly, and cotter pins and retainers must be installed properly. Anytime fasteners are damaged, replace them with a fastener of identical size and strength.

Measuring Systems

Two standards are currently used to specify most threaded fasteners, the standard or the metric system. Since each system is based on a different mea-

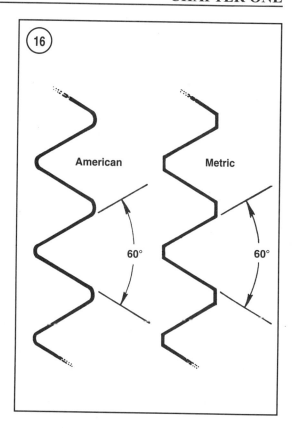

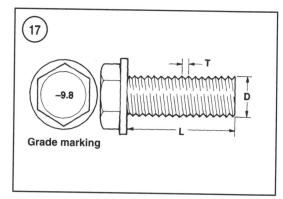

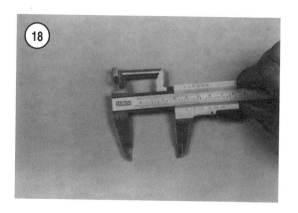

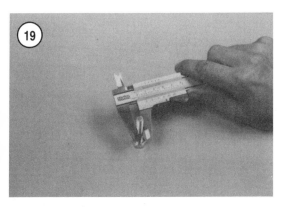

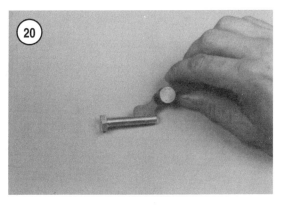

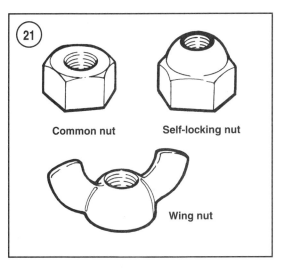

Common nut   Self-locking nut

Wing nut

Thread Pitch, Diameter and Length

Metric bolts and screws are classified by length (L, **Figure 17**), diameter (D) and distance between thread crests (T). A typical bolt might be identified by the numbers 8–1.25 × 130. This indicates that the bolt has a diameter of 8 mm, the distance between thread crests is 1.25 mm, and bolt length is 130 mm.

Use a caliper to accurately check the length (**Figure 18**) and diameter (**Figure 19**). If thread pitch is unknown, use a thread pitch gauge (**Figure 20**) to determine the pitch.

Fastener Strength

The strength of a fastener is determined by its size and by the quality of the steel. To identify the various strengths of fasteners, a grade number (**Figure 17**) is stamped into the head of the fastener. The higher the number, the stronger the fastener.

> *CAUTION*
> *Using a fastener of a lower grade than the one installed by the manufacturer can cause equipment failure and personal injury.*

Nuts

Nuts are manufactured in a variety of shapes and sizes to fit specific design requirements. Three commonly used nuts are shown in **Figure 21**. The common hex nut is generally used with a lockwasher and is used extensively throughout the vehicle.

Self-locking nuts create interference in the threads and prevent the nut from loosening. Therefore, no lockwasher is required. Interference is achieved by distorting the threads, coating the threads with dry adhesive or nylon, distorting the top of an all-metal nut, or using a nylon insert in the center or at the top of a nut. Replace self-locking fasteners during reassembly.

Wing nuts are designed for installation and removal by hand. These nuts are often used for convenience on components that are disassembled often.

Nuts are sized the same as bolts and screws, but without the length dimension. To determine wrench size for tightening a nut, measure across two flats on the nut (**Figure 22**).

suring standard (inches versus millimeters), the fasteners are not compatible with one another. Any attempt to join mismatched threads, even though they appear similar, will damage both threads. **Figure 16** shows the difference in the cut of the threads.

The fasteners used on the Honda Fourtrax vehicle have metric threads. The information in the following paragraphs applies to metric fasteners.

Washers

There are two basic types of washers: flat washers and lockwashers. Flat washers are simple discs with a hole to fit a screw or bolt. Lockwashers are designed to prevent a fastener from working loose due to vibration, expansion or contraction. **Figure 23** shows other types of lockwashers that may be found on the vehicle. Washers are also used for the following functions:
1. As spacers.
2. To prevent galling or damage to the equipment by the fastener.
3. To help distribute fastener load during torquing.
4. As seals.

Cotter Pins

Cotter pins (**Figure 24**) prevent nuts from loosening, usually in critical areas, such as axle nuts. They are also a simple retainer in noncritical, no-load applications. In order to use a cotter pin with a nut, the nut must be slotted or castellated. The shaft must be bored so the pin can pass through and then be spread. Do not reuse cotter pins or use a pin that is too short to be bent properly. To install a cotter pin:
1. Torque the nut. Finish the torque stroke so a slot in the nut aligns with the hole in the bolt. If necessary, continue to tighten the nut so the slot and hole align. Do not loosen a torqued nut to achieve alignment.
2. Insert the cotter pin through the nut and bolt. The diameter of the pin should just fit through the hole. Do not use an undersize pin, as shearing may occur.
3. Snug the pin in the hole, then bend the ends to secure the cotter pin tightly (**Figure 24**).

Circlips

Circlips (also called snap rings or retainers) can be internal or external in design (**Figure 25**). They retain items on shafts (external type) or within tubes (internal type). In some applications, circlips of varying thickness are used to control the end play of assemblies. These are often called selective circlips. Replace circlips during reassembly, as removal weakens and deforms them.

Two basic styles of circlips are available: machined and stamped circlips. Machined circlips can be installed in either direction (shaft or housing) be-

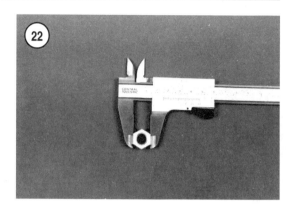

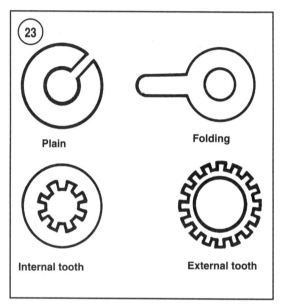

Plain   Folding

Internal tooth   External tooth

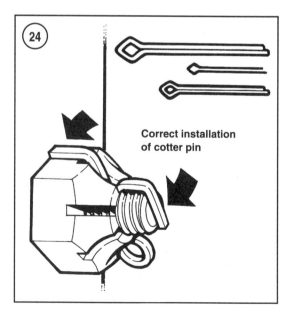

Correct installation of cotter pin

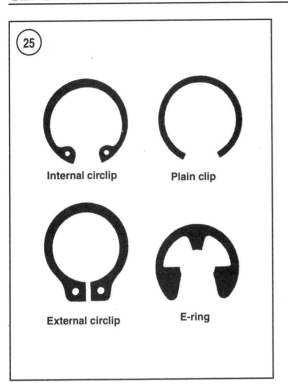

Internal circlip   Plain clip

External circlip   E-ring

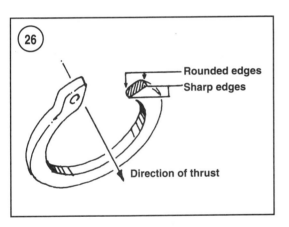

Rounded edges
Sharp edges
Direction of thrust

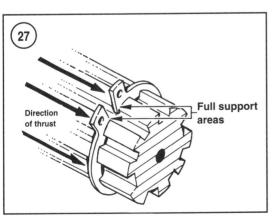

Direction of thrust   Full support areas

cause both faces are machined, which creates two sharp edges. Stamped circlips (**Figure 26**) are manufactured with one sharp edge and one rounded edge. When installing stamped circlips in a thrust situation, the sharp edge must face away from the part producing the thrust (**Figure 27**). Circlips become worn with use. Always use new circlips during reassembly. When installing circlips, observe the following:

1. Use circlip pliers to remove or install circlips.
2. Compress or expand circlips only enough to install them.
3. After installation, make sure the circlip is completely seated.

BASIC HAND TOOLS

Most of the procedures in this manual can be carried out with common hand tools and test equipment familiar to the home mechanic.

Obviously, top-quality tools are desired, as the fit and finish is superior to inexpensive tools. Additionally, they are more economical in the long run, since they are made of high-quality materials and often have a lifetime warranty.

Quality tools are made of alloy steel and are heat-treated for greater strength. They are lighter, better balanced, fit well and easy to keep clean. They are also a pleasure to use and help develop good work techniques. When building a tool collection, start with the basics. Buy high-quality tools in the common sizes. Additional tools can be purchased as they are needed.

Screwdrivers

The screwdriver is a basic tool that is often misused. The slot on a screw has a definite dimension and shape. Therefore, select the proper size and taper of screwdriver to conform to that shape (**Figure 28**). If the wrong size screwdriver is used, damage to the screw head will occur.

Two basic types of screwdrivers are required: *common* for slotted screws and *Phillips* for crosshead screws (**Figure 29**).

Screwdrivers are available in sets which often include an assortment of common and Phillips blades. The following sizes are used for common repairs:

    a. Common screwdriver—5/16 × 6 in. blade.

b. Common screwdriver—3/8 × 12 in. blade.

c. Phillips screwdriver—size 2 tip, 6 in. blade.

Use screwdrivers only for driving screws. Using a screwdriver for prying, chiseling or removing other types of fasteners will damage the tip.

Always keep the tip of a common screwdriver in good condition. If it becomes damaged or worn, grind the tip so it is symmetrical and has the profiles shown in **Figure 28**. Replace Phillips screwdrivers that have damaged tips.

Pliers

Pliers come in a variety of types and sizes. Pliers are useful for holding, cutting, bending and crimping. They should never be used to cut hardened objects, or to turn nuts or bolts. **Figure 30** shows several types used for common repairs.

Locking Pliers

Locking pliers (**Figure 31**) can be adjusted to hold objects like a vise. Because locking pliers can exert more pressure than regular pliers, their jaws can permanently scar, deform or crush the object that is held. Careful adjustment is required to prevent damage. Locking pliers are available in a variety of sizes and jaw configurations.

Circlip Pliers

Circlip or snap ring pliers (**Figure 32**) are used to remove and install circlips. External pliers spread the ends of the circlip so it can be removed from the outside of a shaft or other part. Internal pliers compress the ends of the circlip so it can be removed from inside a tube, gear or housing. Adjustable circlip pliers will remove both types of circlips.

Box-End, Open-End and Combination Wrenches

Open-end (A, **Figure 33**) and box-end (B) wrenches are available in sets or individually. The number stamped on open- and box-end wrenches refers to the distance between two parallel flats on a nut or bolt head. Combination wrenches (C) have a box-end wrench on one end and an open-end

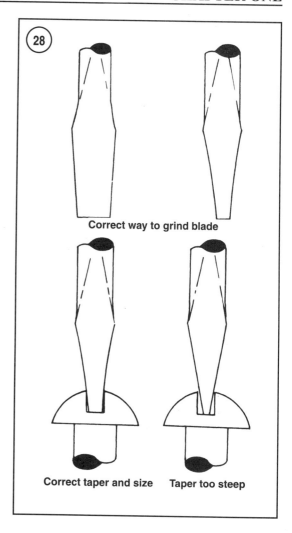

Correct way to grind blade

Correct taper and size   Taper too steep

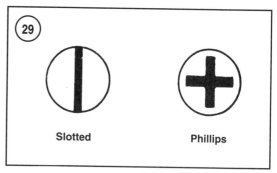

Slotted   Phillips

wrench of the same size at the other end. The size is stamped near each head.

A box-end wrench grips all six corners of a fastener for a very secure grip. However, the fastener must have overhead access to use a box-end wrench. Box-end wrenches are available in 6- or 12-point styles. A 6-point wrench provides superior

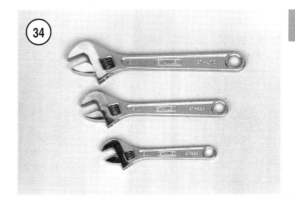

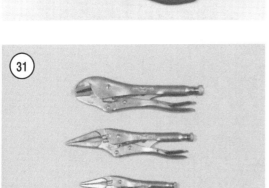

holding ability compared to a 12-point wrench, but requires a greater swinging radius. A 12-point wrench is more suitable when working in a confined area.

Open-end wrenches work best in areas with limited overhead access. Their wide jaws make them unsuitable for situations where the bolt or nut is recessed in a well or in close quarters. These wrenches only grip on two flats of a fastener. If either the fastener head or wrench jaws are worn, the wrench may slip off.

Adjustable Wrenches

An adjustable wrench (**Figure 34**) can adjust to fit nearly any nut or bolt head that has clear access around its perimeter. Use an adjustable wrenches as a backup wrench to keep a nut or bolt from turning while the other fitting is being loosened or tightened with a sized wrench.

Adjustable wrenches have two jaws with one designed to move. The large size of adjustable wrenches limits where they can be used. The adjustable feature also makes this type of wrench more apt to slip and possibly damage the fastener or part. When using an adjustable wrench, make sure the force is transmitted through the fixed jaw.

Adjustable wrenches come in several sizes, but a 6 or 8 in. size is recommended as an all-purpose wrench.

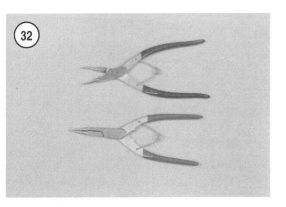

Socket Wrenches

The socket wrench is probably the fastest, safest and most convenient wrench to use. Sockets, which attach to the ratchet handle (**Figure 35**), are available with 6- or 12-point openings. Extensions allow

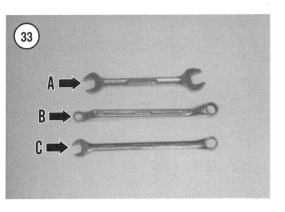

the socket to reach into tight places. Ratchet handles are made in 1/4, 3/8, 1/2 and 3/4 in. square drives. The drive size refers to the dimensions of the square coupling on the ratchet.

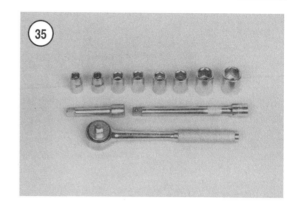

Impact Driver

The impact driver (**Figure 36**) aids in the removal of tight fasteners, and reduces the chance of damage to bolts and screw slots. Fit the correct bit into the driver. Adjust the driver to turn either clockwise or counterclockwise. Fit the tool on the fastener and strike with a hammer to loosen the fastener. Be careful when removing some fasteners, as the impact may break parts that are cast.

Sockets can also be used with hand impact drivers. However, the socket must be designed for impact use. Regular hand-type sockets can shatter during use.

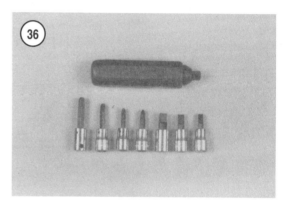

Hammers

The correct hammer (**Figure 37**) is necessary for certain repairs. A hammer with a face or head of rubber or plastic is usually necessary during engine disassembly. Sometimes these hammers have heads that are filled with metal shot and are called dead-blow hammers. The shot in the hammer head minimizes any rebounding of the hammer. Never use a metal-faced hammer on engine parts, or damage can occur. The same amount of force can be achieved with a soft-faced hammer. A metal-faced hammer can be used with an impact driver or cold chisel. In these cases, the shock of the hammer blow is necessary.

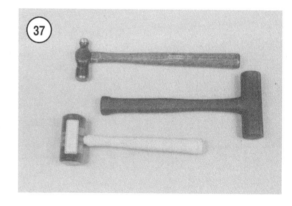

Torque Wrenches

Use a torque wrench (**Figure 38**) with a socket to install a nut or bolt to a specific tightness. The wrench is calibrated in ft.-lbs., in.-lbs. or N•m. Torque wrenches are available in 1/4, 3/8 and 1/2 in. drives. The drive size refers to the dimensions of the square coupling on the wrench.

A torque wrench is a precision tool and should be maintained and stored carefully. Keep it stored away from other tools when not in use.

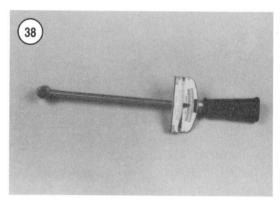

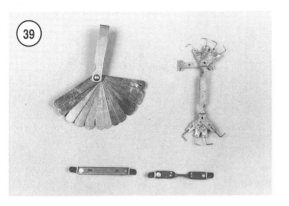

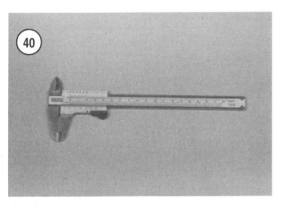

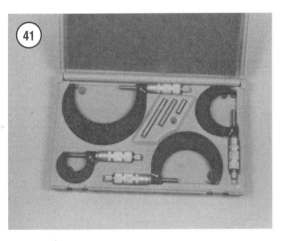

PRECISION MEASURING TOOLS

Accurate measurement is an important part of vehicle maintenance and repair. Measurements can be basic, such as setting spark plug gap, or they can be more complex, such as measuring crankshaft runout. In either case, the appropriate measuring tool is required to perform the measurement correctly. Purchase the commonly used gauges first, so routine measurements can be performed. As more complex repairs are attempted, purchase quality instruments to meet the needs of the repairs.

The following are measuring tools frequently used in vehicle maintenance and repair.

Feeler Gauge

Feeler gauges (**Figure 39**) are available in assorted sets and types. The gauge is made of either a flat blade or a round wire. Both are made of hardened steel and marked with their sizes. Use the round wires to check spark plugs, and the blades for most other measurements, such as checking valve clearances and cylinder head warp.

Vernier Caliper

The vernier caliper (**Figure 40**) is valuable in reading inside, outside and depth measurements. This type of caliper is typically accurate to 0.001 in. (0.025 mm). Common uses include measuring nuts, bolts, shims, bore depths and spring lengths. The traditional vernier caliper is marked with a scale along the bar. Some calipers are also fitted with a dial gauge. Digital vernier calipers are also available. These have an electronic readout instead of a dial gauge.

Outside Micrometer

Use outside micrometers (**Figure 41**) to make critical measurements of components, such as the piston, piston pin, rings and crankshaft. This micrometer is also used to measure the dimension taken by a small hole gauge or telescoping gauge. Since these gauges have no scale, they are first set to the dimensions of a bore, then removed and measured by the outside micrometer.

Micrometers may be purchased in sets or individually. They are available in metric or inch scales. The standard metric micrometer is accurate to one one-hundredth of a millimeter (0.01 mm). The standard inch micrometer is accurate to one-thousandth of an inch (0.001).

Dial Indicator

Use a dial indicator (**Figure 42**) to check dimensional variations, such as crankshaft runout or the

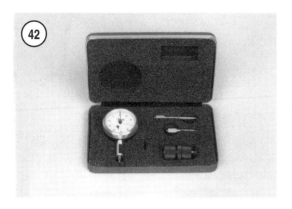

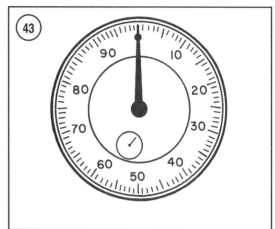

end play of shafts. For the home mechanic, select a dial indicator with a continuous dial (**Figure 43**). This gauge is usually used with a holding fixture, such as a magnetic stand or clamp.

Cylinder Bore Gauge

The cylinder bore gauge is a very specialized precision tool. The gauge set shown in **Figure 44** consists of a dial indicator, handle and a variety of adapters so the gauge can be fitted to different bore sizes. Use the bore gauge to make cylinder bore measurements such as bore size, taper and out-of-round. Of course, it can be used to measure other bores as long as the adapters allow it to be correctly fitted. Use an outside micrometer to calibrate the bore gauge to a specific dimension.

Small Hole Gauge

A small hole gauge set (**Figure 45**) measures small holes and slots up to 13 mm (0.5 in.) wide. The gauge is commonly used to measure small bushings, valve guides and piston pin bores. Since the gauge has no scale, measure it with an outside micrometer.

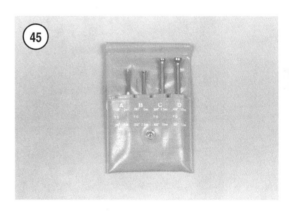

Telescoping Gauge

Telescoping gauges (**Figure 46**) measure holes from approximately 8-150 mm (5/16-6 in.). After the gauge is fitted and locked to the dimension of the bore, remove the gauge and measure it with an outside micrometer.

Compression Gauge

A compression gauge measures pressure in the cylinder as the engine is cranked. If pressure is not within specification, this indicates that further cylinder diagnosis is required. **Figure 47** shows two types of compression gauges. One type screws into the spark plug hole, while the other type is held tightly in place while the engine is cranked.

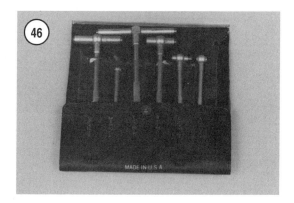

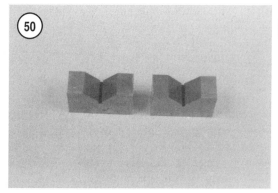

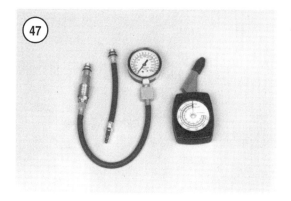

Thread Pitch Gauge

A thread pitch gauge (**Figure 48**) identifies the thread pitch of nuts, bolts and screws. The gauge is made up of several blades. Each blade has a specific thread pitch cut into one edge. To use the gauge, fit each blade into the fastener until the gauge and fastener threads seat together. Then read the blade to identify the thread pitch.

Magnetic Stand

A magnetic stand (**Figure 49**) holds a dial indicator securely when checking runout or end play.

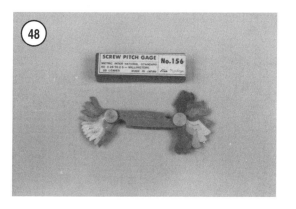

V-Blocks

V-blocks (**Figure 50**) are precision-ground steel blocks used to hold a round object, such as a crankshaft, when checking its runout or condition.

Strobe Timing Light

Use a strobe timing light (**Figure 51**) to check the adjustment of the ignition timing, or to determine if a cylinder is firing. When it is attached to the ignition system and cylinder, the timing light will flash each time the cylinder fires. When attached to the cylinder that times the engine, the light illuminates the timing marks stamped into the flywheel. Because of its stroboscopic effect, the marks will appear to stand still, and engine timing can be determined.

A light with a xenon tube and inductive pickup is recommended. The xenon tube is very bright and makes it easy to see timing marks, while the induc-

tive pickup allows it to be clipped around the spark plug wire.

Multimeter

A multimeter or VOM (volt and ohm meter) (**Figure 52**) is a valuable tool for all electrical troubleshooting. Use the voltage settings to determine the voltage applied or available to various electrical components. Use the ohmmeter settings to measure the resistance of a circuit or component. The ohmmeter can also check for continuity, or lack of continuity, in a circuit.

Analog and digital meters are commonly available. The analog meter has an indicator needle and a calibrated face. Digital meters have an electronic readout. The digital meter is generally easier to use and more accurate, particularly when making very small readings.

SPECIAL TOOLS

A few special tools are required to perform some maintenance or repair procedures of the vehicle. These tools are described in the appropriate chapters and, in some cases, shown in use. The part numbers are provided for the tools so they can be ordered from a Honda dealership.

MECHANIC'S TECHNIQUES

Since some repairs occur infrequently, fasteners can become corroded, seized, broken or stripped. This makes removal and replacement difficult and time-consuming.

Also, the home mechanic may not have much experience in removing and installing bearings and seals. These parts are more difficult to remove and install. If removed or installed improperly, damage to the part and other components could occur.

The following paragraphs provide instructions for working with broken fasteners, bearings and seals. As with any repair, if the appropriate tools are not available, take the part to a machine shop or dealership for repairs.

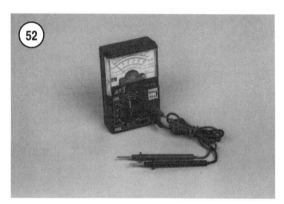

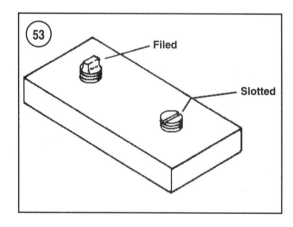

Removing Frozen Fasteners

1. Liberally apply penetrating oil, such as Liquid Wrench or WD-40. Let it penetrate for 10-15 minutes.

2. Tap the fastener several times with a small hammer. Do not strike it hard enough to cause damage to the head or any exposed threads. Attempt to carefully remove the fastener. Avoid damaging the fastener head or twisting the head off the fastener. If it cannot be loosened, continue to the next step.

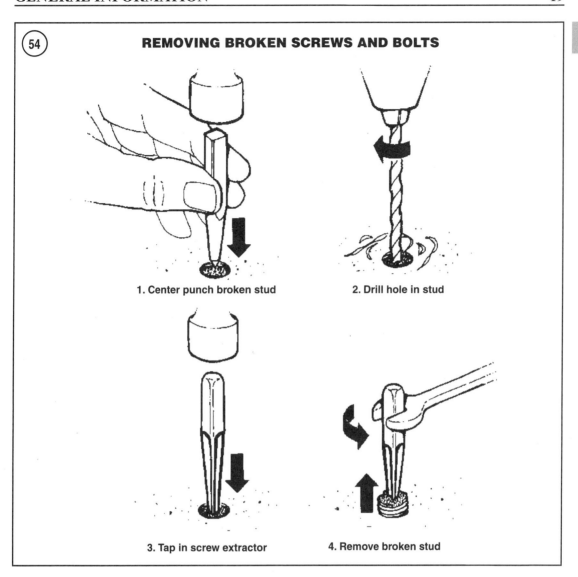

54 REMOVING BROKEN SCREWS AND BOLTS

1. Center punch broken stud

2. Drill hole in stud

3. Tap in screw extractor

4. Remove broken stud

3. To remove screws, insert a screwdriver into the slot and tap the screwdriver with a hammer. To remove nuts and bolts, use a wrench to apply pressure in both directions. This helps loosen the rust so the lubricant can penetrate. If available, use an impact driver to attempt removal. If it cannot be loosened, continue to the next step.

4. Grip the fastener with locking pliers and twist the screw out. If necessary, remove the fastener using the *Removing Broken Fasteners* procedure.

> *NOTE*
> *Avoid applying heat to aid in removal.*
> *Heat can melt, warp or remove the*
> *temper from parts.*

Removing Broken Fasteners

Follow these steps if the head breaks off a fastener, but a portion of the fastener is still projecting from the part:

1. Liberally apply penetrating oil, such as Liquid Wrench or WD-40. Let it penetrate for 10-15 minutes.

2. Grip the fastener with locking pliers. If the projection is too small, file it to fit a wrench or cut a slot to fit a screwdriver (**Figure 53**). Remove the fastener.

If the fastener head breaks off flush, use a screw extractor to remove the fastener (**Figure 54**) as follows.

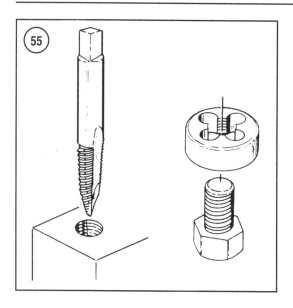

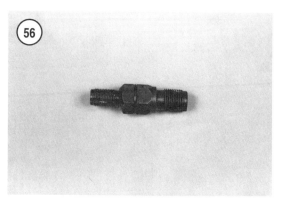

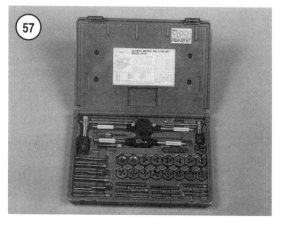

1. Centerpunch the fastener.

2. Drill a small hole in the fastener.

3. Tap the extractor into the hole.

4. Place a wrench on the extractor and back out the fastener. If the fastener does not come out easily, apply penetrating oil to the threads. Work the fastener back and forth as it is extracted. Avoid damaging the threads, if possible.

Repairing Damaged Threads

Damaged threads can often be repaired by running a tap, for internal threads, or die, for external threads, through the threads (**Figure 55**). Use a spark plug tap (**Figure 56**) to clean or repair spark plug threads.

NOTE
*Taps and dies can be bought individually or in a set as shown in **Figure 57**.*

If an internal thread is severely damaged, install a thread insert, such as a HeliCoil (**Figure 58**). Follow the manufacturer's instructions when installing the insert. If it is necessary to drill and tap a hole, refer to **Table 7** for metric tap drill sizes.

Seal Replacement

Seals are used to prevent leakage of fluids or grease from a housing. Seals also prevent dirt, water

and other contaminants from entering the housing. Usually, the seal protects a bearing.

Good technique is necessary to ensure that the housing is not damaged during seal removal and the new seal is not damaged as it is seated in the housing. Replace seals as follows:

1. Pry out the old seal with a seal puller or wide-blade screwdriver, as shown in **Figure 59**. Place a folded shop rag under the screwdriver to prevent damage to the housing.

2. If a new bearing will be installed, replace the bearing before installing the new seal.

3. Clean the seal bore. Inspect the contact area on the shaft for burrs or other defects. Lightly file and polish any defects that are detected. The shaft must be smooth so the new seal is not damaged.

4. Pack grease in the lip of the new seal (**Figure 60**).

5. Place the seal squarely in the bore, with the closed side of the seal facing out.

6. Use a seal driver or socket to seat the seal in the bore.

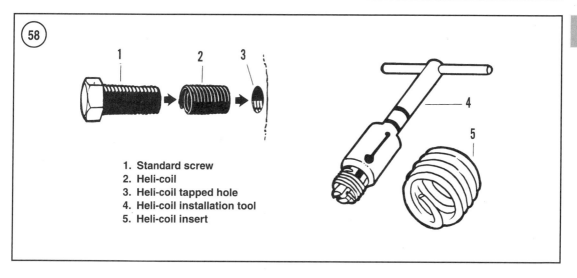

1. Standard screw
2. Heli-coil
3. Heli-coil tapped hole
4. Heli-coil installation tool
5. Heli-coil insert

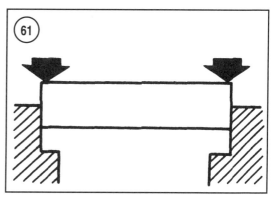

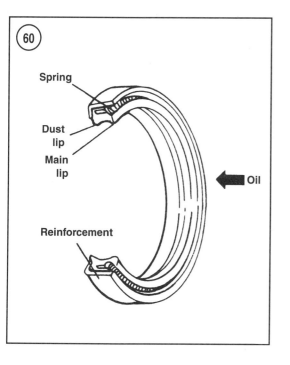

CAUTION
When driving seals, the driver must fit at the perimeter of the seal (Figure 61). If the driver presses toward the center of the seal, the seal can become distorted, and the internal garter spring can become dislodged and cause the seal to leak.

Bearing Removal

Procedures for removing specific bearings are described in the appropriate chapters. The following information describes the techniques for removing bearings from recesses or shafts. Improper removal can result in damage to the bearing, housing or shaft.

1. When using a puller to remove a bearing from a shaft:

  a. Place a metal spacer between the end of the puller screw and the shaft (**Figure 62**).

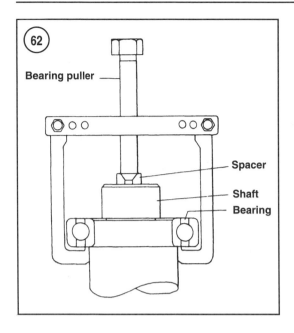

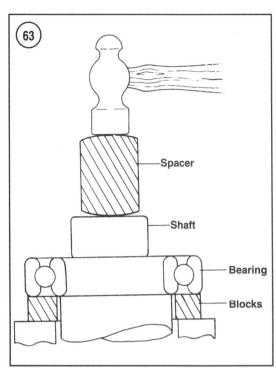

b. Fit the arms of the puller against the *inner* bearing race (**Figure 62**). Never pull on the outer bearing race, as the balls and races will jam and become damaged.

2. When using a hammer to remove a bearing from a shaft:

a. Support both bearing races with wooden or aluminum blocks (**Figure 63**). Allow some space under the shaft assembly so it may be driven from the bearing.

b. Place padding under the shaft assembly so it is not damaged after it is driven from the bearing.

c. Place a brass or aluminum spacer over the end of shaft that will be struck by the hammer (**Figure 63**).

3. When using a hydraulic press to remove a bearing from a shaft:

a. Support both bearing races with wooden or aluminum blocks (**Figure 64**). Allow some space under the shaft assembly so it may be driven from the bearing.

b. Place padding under the shaft assembly so it is not damaged after it is driven from the bearing.

c. Accurately align the press ram with the shaft before applying pressure (**Figure 64**).

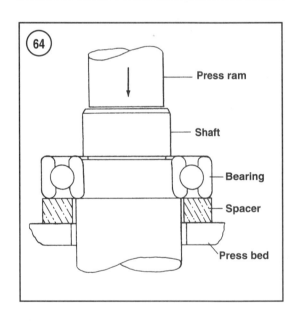

Bearing Installation

Procedures for installing specific bearings are described in the appropriate chapters. The following information describes the techniques for installing bearings in recesses or on shafts. Improper removal can result in damage to the bearing, housing or shaft.

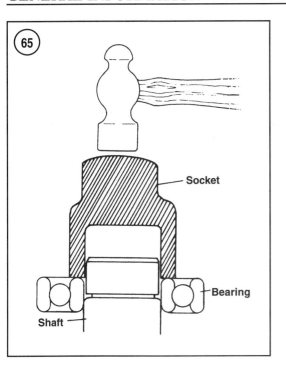

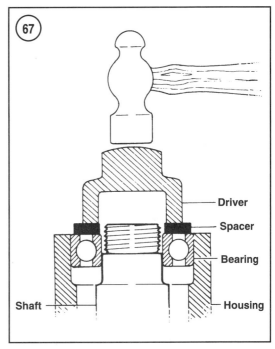

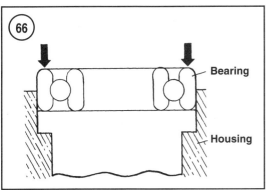

inner bearing race, as the balls and races will jam and become damaged.

3. When installing a bearing in a housing and over a shaft:

    a. Align the bearing squarely over the housing bore and shaft. The manufacturer's marks or numbers should face out.

    b. Use a bearing driver or socket that fits completely over *both* bearing races (**Figure 67**). Never press on one bearing race, as the balls and races will jam and become damaged.

Shrink-Fit Bearings

Some bearings are installed with an *interference fit*. The bearing is dimensionally larger or smaller than the shaft or housing in which it is installed. For shafts, the inside diameter of the bearing is smaller than the outside diameter of the shaft. For housings, the outside diameter of the bearing is larger than the bore in the housing. In either case, the bearings can only be installed by shrink-fitting.

For shafts, this requires heating the bearing so it will expand and fit over the shaft. For housings, the bearing is chilled to contract the bearing and the housing is heated to expand the bore. After the parts are assembled and return to room temperature, the parts fit tightly together.

1. When installing a bearing on a shaft:

    a. Align the bearing squarely over the end of the shaft. The manufacturer's marks or numbers should face out.

    b. Place a bearing driver or socket on the *inner* bearing race (**Figure 65**). Never press on the outer bearing race, as the balls and races will jam and become damaged.

2. When installing a bearing in a housing:

    a. Align the bearing squarely over the housing bore. The manufacturer's marks or numbers should face out.

    b. Place a bearing driver or socket on the *outer* bearing race (**Figure 66**). Never press on the

Shrink-fit bearings should never be hammered into position when both parts are at room temperature. The bearing, and possibly the shaft or housing, will be damaged.

Shrink-fitting a bearing on a shaft

Read the entire procedure in order to quickly and safely install the bearing. Have all tools ready for use when the bearing is ready to be installed.

1. Secure the shaft so the end receiving the bearing is vertical.
2. Clean the shaft so it is free of burrs and residue.
3. Fill a suitable container with enough mineral oil to cover the bearing. Heat the oil to 120° C (248° F). Suspend the thermometer so it measures actual oil temperature and not the pan temperature.
4. Attach a wire to the bearing, then submerge it in the hot oil. Maintain the 120° C (248° F) temperature for several minutes until the bearing has heated to the oil temperature.
5. Wearing heavy, heat-resistant gloves, remove the bearing from the oil and quickly place it over the end of the shaft. The manufacturer's marks or numbers should face out. If necessary, seat the bearing with a driver or socket that fits on the *inside* bearing race.
6. Allow the bearing to cool after it is installed on the shaft.

Shrink-fitting a bearing into a housing

Read the entire procedure in order to quickly and safely install the bearing. Have all tools ready for use when the bearing is ready to be installed. Always work with one housing at a time.

> *NOTE*
> *Old bearings can be removed by heating the housing as described in this procedure. After the housing and bearing are thoroughly heated, place the housing bearing-side down, so the bearing can be tapped out of the bore.*

1. Clean the housing so it is free of all oil and deposits. Wash the housing in hot soapy water.
2. Place the bearing(s) in a freezer for at least an hour, allowing it to contract.
3. Place the housing in an oven, then heat the housing to 100° C (212° F). The temperature is correct

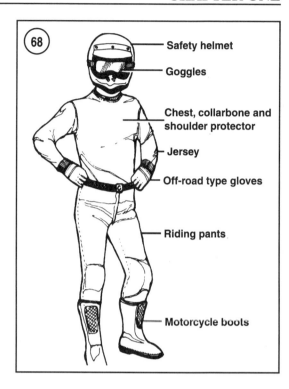

when water droplets splashed on the housing will evaporate immediately.
4. Wearing heavy, heat-resistant gloves, remove the housing from the oven. Quickly place the bearing over the bore in the housing and press into place. The manufacturer's marks or numbers should face out. If necessary, seat the bearing with a driver or socket that fits on the *outside* bearing race.
5. Allow the bearing to cool after it is installed in the housing.

RIDING SAFETY

Know The Vehicle

Read the owner's manual and understand:
1. The age, skills and physical size required of the rider for this vehicle.
2. The performance potential and limitations of the vehicle.
3. The locations of the controls and how they are used.
4. The techniques for safely handling stalls on hillsides, riding in slippery conditions, rolling backwards, skidding and other possible situations.
5. The location of the nearest training facilities for inexperienced riders.

WINTER PROTECTIVE CLOTHING

Inner layers — Outer layers

- Safety helmet
- Goggles
- Face mask
- Wool shirt
- Insulated suit
- Glove liners
- Leather gloves
- Thermal underwear
- Heavy pants
- Wool socks
- Motorcycle or snowmobile boots

Regular Checks and Maintenance

Keep the vehicle in safe and good working condition.

1. Perform a pre-ride check of the vehicle, as described in Chapter Three.

2. Perform the maintenance procedures, as described in Chapter Three.

3. Troubleshoot problems, as described in Chapter Two.

Operating Habits

Good operating habits will substantially reduce the risk of personal injury, and will extend the life of the vehicle.

1. Do not operate the vehicle without a flag. This is required in many riding areas.

2. Do not carry a passenger on the vehicle.

3. Do not operate the vehicle on public streets, highways or paved surfaces.

4. Operate the vehicle at speeds that are appropriate for the terrain and riding conditions.

5. Do not attempt to operate the vehicle in fast-moving water.

6. Do not attempt wheelies, jumps or stunt riding.

7. Keep a safe distance from other vehicles.

8. Check the fuel supply before traveling far from the loading point.

9. Keep both hands on the handlebars and both feet on the footpegs.

10. Do not allow individuals that are intoxicated to operate the vehicle.

11. Wear the proper riding gear to avoid injury.

12. Ride only in designated areas.

13. Protect the environment and maintain the designated riding area.

Riding Gear

Riding an ATV subjects the rider to many hazards that can cause personal injury if the rider is not properly protected. Regardless of the time of year or the location the vehicle is operated, proper riding gear is necessary. Refer to **Figure 68** for appropriate summer riding gear and **Figure 69** for appropriate winter gear. Note the following:

1. Wear a helmet and eye protection to prevent injury from falls and airborne debris.

2. Wear a long-sleeved shirt and riding pants to protect from falls, abrasions, burns and airborne debris.

3. Wear gloves to protect the hands.

4. Wear heavy boots, preferably without laces.

5. For winter riding, wear clothing that is well-insulated, but not so bulky as to impair operating the vehicle. Windchill is extremely dangerous and increases with the speed of the vehicle. Refer to **Table 3** for windchill factors and their affect on the body. Stop riding when windchill factors become dangerous.

Tables 1-9 are on the following pages.

Table 1 GENERAL DIMENSIONS

	mm	in.
Overall length	1489	58.6
Overall width	895	35.2
Overall height	917	36.1
Wheelbase	985	38.8
Front tread	701	27.6
Rear tread	700	27.6
Seat height	648	25.5
Footpeg height	239	9.4
Ground clearance	102	4.0

Table 2 WEIGHT AND LOAD CAPACITY

	kg	lb.
Dry weight	110	243
Curb weight	115	254
Maximum weight capacity	85	187

Table 3 WINDCHILL FACTORS

Estimated wind speed in mph	Actual thermometer reading (°F)											
	50	40	30	20	10	0	-10	-20	-30	-40	-50	-60
	Equivalent temperature (°F)											
Calm	50	40	30	20	10	0	-10	-20	-30	-40	-50	-60
5	48	37	27	16	6	-5	-15	-26	-36	-47	-57	-68
10	40	28	16	4	-9	-21	-33	-46	-58	-70	-83	-95
15	36	22	9	-5	-18	-36	-45	-58	-72	-85	-99	-112
20	32	18	4	-10	-25	-39	-53	-67	-82	-96	-110	-124
25	30	16	0	-15	-29	-44	-59	-74	-88	-104	-118	-153
30	28	13	-2	-18	-33	-48	-63	-79	-94	-109	-125	-140
35	27	11	-4	-20	-35	-49	-67	-82	-98	-113	-129	-145
40	26	10	-6	-21	-37	-53	-69	-85	-100	-116	-132	-148
*												

Little danger (for properly clothed person)	Increasing danger	Great danger
		• Danger from freezing of exposed flesh •

*Wind speeds greater than 40 mph have little additional effect.

Table 4 TECHNICAL ABBREVIATIONS

ABDC	After bottom dead center
ATDC	After top dead center
BBDC	Before bottom dead center
BDC	Bottom dead center
BTDC	Before top dead center
C	Celsius (Centigrade)
cc	Cubic centimeters
CDI	Capacitor discharge ignition
cu. in.	Cubic inches
F	Fahrenheit
ft.-lb.	Foot-pounds
gal.	Gallons
H/A	High altitude
hp	Horsepower
in.	Inches
kg	Kilograms
kg/cm^2	Kilograms per square centimeter
kgm	Kilogram meters
km	Kilometer
L	Liter
m	Meter
MAG	Magneto
ml	Milliliter
mm	Millimeter
N•m	Newton-meters
oz.	Ounces
PAIR	Pulse secondary air injection system
psi	Pounds per square inch
PTO	Power take off
pt.	Pint
qt.	Quart
rpm	Revolutions per minute

Table 5 GENERAL TORQUE SPECIFICATIONS

	N•m	in.-lb.	ft.-lb.
5 mm bolt and nut	5	44	–
6 mm bolt and nut	10	88	–
8 mm bolt and nut	22	–	16
10 mm bolt and nut	35	–	26
12 mm bolt and nut	55	–	41
5 mm screw	4	35	–
6 mm screw	9	80	–
6 mm flange bolt (8 mm head)	9	80	–
6 mm flange bolt (10 mm head) and nut	12	106	–
8 mm flange bolt and nut	27	–	20
10 mm flange bolt and nut	40	–	29

Table 6 CONVERSION TABLES

	Multiply by:	To get the equivalent of:
Length		
Inches	25.4	Millimeter
Inches	2.54	Centimeter
Miles	1.609	Kilometer
Feet	0.3048	Meter

(continued)

Table 6 CONVERSION TABLES (continued)

	Multiply by:	To get the equivalent of:
Length		
Millimeter	0.03937	Inches
Centimeter	0.3937	Inches
Kilometer	0.6214	Mile
Meter	3.281	Mile
Fluid volume		
U.S. quarts	0.9463	Liters
U.S. gallons	3.785	Liters
U.S. ounces	29.573529	Milliliters
Imperial gallons	4.54609	Liters
Imperial quarts	1.1365	Liters
Liters	0.2641721	U.S. gallons
Liters	1.0566882	U.S. quarts
Liters	33.814023	U.S. ounces
Liters	0.22	Imperial gallons
Liters	0.8799	Imperial quarts
Milliliters	0.033814	U.S. ounces
Milliliters	1.0	Cubic centimeters
Milliliters	0.001	Liters
Torque		
Foot-pounds	1.3558	Newton-meters
Foot-pounds	0.138255	Meters-kilograms
Inch-pounds	0.11299	Newton-meters
Newton-meters	0.7375622	Foot-pounds
Newton-meters	8.8507	Inch-pounds
Meters-kilograms	7.2330139	Foot-pounds
Volume		
Cubic inches	16.387064	Cubic centimeters
Cubic centimeters	0.0610237	Cubic inches
Temperature		
Fahrenheit	(F 32°) 0.556	Centigrade
Centigrade	(C × 1.8)	Fahrenheit
Weight		
Ounces	28.3495	Grams
Pounds	0.4535924	Kilograms
Grams	0.035274	Ounces
Kilograms	2.2046224	Pounds
Pressure		
Pounds per square inch	0.070307	Kilograms per square centimeter
Kilograms per square centimeter	14.223343	Pounds per square inch
Speed		
Miles per hour	1.609344	Kilometers per hour
Kilometers per hour	0.6213712	Miles per hour

Table 7 METRIC TAP DRILL SIZES

Metric	Drill size	Decimal equivalent	Nearest (mm) fraction
3 × 0.50	No. 39	0.0995	3/32
3 × 0.60	3/32	0.0937	3/32
4 × 0.70	No. 30	0.1285	1/8
4 × 0.75	1/8	0.125	1/8
5 × 0.80	No. 19	0.166	11/64

(continued)

Table 7 METRIC TAP DRILL SIZES (continued)

Metric	Drill size	Decimal equivalent	Nearest (mm) fraction
5 × 0.90	No. 20	0.161	5/32
6 × 1.00	No. 9	0.196	13/64
7 × 1.00	16/64	0.234	15/64
8 × 1.00	J	0.277	9/32
8 × 1.25	17/64	0.265	17/64
9 × 1.00	5/16	0.3125	5/16
9 × 1.25	5/16	0.3125	5/16
10 × 1.25	11/32	0.3437	11/32
10 × 1.50	R	0.339	11/32
11 × 1.50	3/8	0.375	3/8
12 × 1.50	13/32	0.406	13/32
12 × 1.75	13/32	0.406	13/321-7

Table 8 DECIMAL AND METRIC EQUIVALENTS

Fractions	Decimal in.	Metric mm	Fractions	Decimal in.	Metric mm
1/64	0.015625	0.39688	33/64	0.515625	13.09687
1/32	0.03125	0.79375	17/32	0.53125	13.49375
3/64	0.046875	1.19062	35/64	0.546875	13.89062
1/16	0.0625	1.58750	9/16	0.5625	14.28750
5/64	0.078125	1.98437	37/64	0.578125	14.68437
3/32	0.09375	2.38125	19/32	0.59375	15.08125
7/64	0.109375	2.77812	39/64	0.609375	15.47812
1/8	0.125	3.1750	5/8	0.625	15.87500
9/64	0.140625	3.57187	41/64	0.640625	16.27187
5/32	0.15625	3.96875	21/32	0.65625	16.66875
11/64	0.171875	4.36562	43/64	0.671875	17.06562
3/16	0.1875	4.76250	11/16	0.6875	17.46250
13/64	0.203125	5.15937	45/64	0.703125	17.85937
7/32	0.21875	5.55625	23/32	0.71875	18.25625
15/64	0.234375	5.95312	47/64	0.734375	18.65312
1/4	0.250	6.35000	3/4	0.750	19.05000
17/64	0.265625	6.74687	49/64	0.765625	19.44687
9/32	0.28125	7.14375	25/32	0.78125	19.84375
19/64	0.296875	7.54062	51/64	0.796875	20.24062
5/16	0.3125	7.93750	13/16	0.8125	20.63750
21/64	0.328125	8.33437	53/64	0.828125	21.03437
11/32	0.34375	8.73125	27/32	0.84375	21.43125
23/64	0.359375	9.12812	55/64	0.859375	22.82812
3/8	0.375	9.52500	7/8	0.875	22.22500
25/64	0.390625	9.92187	57/64	0.890625	22.62187
13/32	0.40625	10.31875	29/32	0.90625	23.01875
27/64	0.421875	10.71562	59/64	0.921875	23.41562
7/16	0.4375	11.11250	15/16	0.9375	23.81250
29/64	0.453125	11.50937	61/64	0.953125	24.20937
15/32	0.46875	11.90625	31/32	0.96875	24.60625
31/64	0.484375	12.30312	63/64	0.984375	25.00312
1/2	0.500	12.70000	1	1.00	25.40000

CHAPTER TWO

TROUBLESHOOTING

By approaching problems in a logical and methodical manner, the diagnosis of problems with the vehicle, either mechanical or electrical, can be relatively easy. Keep the fundamental operating requirements in mind.

1. Define the symptoms of the problem.
2. Determine which areas could exhibit those symptoms.
3. Test and analyze the suspect area.
4. Isolate the problem.

Quickly assuming a particular area is at fault can lead to increased problems, lost time and unnecessary parts replacement.

Performing the lubrication, maintenance and tune-up procedures described in Chapter Three is the easiest way to keep troubleshooting simple. This will aid in understanding the condition and functions of the vehicle.

Always start with the simple and obvious checks when troubleshooting. This includes engine stop switch position, fuel level, fuel valve position and spark plug cap tightness.

If the problem cannot be solved, stop and evaluate all conditions prior to the problem. If the vehicle must be taken to a dealership, the mechanic will want to know as many details as possible.

A variety of good-quality hand tools are required to troubleshoot. A multimeter is required for electrical troubleshooting. Patience and common sense are also important in resolving problems accurately and quickly.

For removal, installation and test procedures for some components, refer to the specific chapter in the manual that relates to that component. When applicable, tables at the end of each chapter provide specifications and wear limits.

OPERATING REQUIREMENTS

There are three requirements for an engine to run properly. These are correct air/fuel mixture, compression and properly timed spark (**Figure 1**). If one is not correct, the engine will not run or will run poorly. Four-stroke engine principles are described in **Figure 2**.

STARTING THE ENGINE

Before starting the engine, always perform a pre-ride check of the vehicle as described in Chapter Three.

Starting a Cold Engine

Use the following procedure for starting the engine when outdoor temperatures are 10°-35° C (50°-95° F). If temperatures are less than this, allow the choke to remain closed longer, if necessary, to keep the engine running.

1. Set the parking brake lever (**Figure 3**).

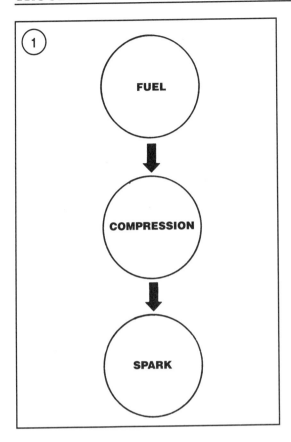

2. Shift the transmission into neutral. The neutral indicator (A, **Figure 4**) should align with the arrow on the engine case.
3. Turn the fuel valve (A, **Figure 5**) to the ON position.
4. Place the engine stop switch in the RUN position (**Figure 6**).
5. Fully turn the choke lever (B, **Figure 5**) *counterclockwise* to choke the engine.
6. Turn the ignition key to the ON position (**Figure 7**).
7. Press the throttle lever (**Figure 8**) so the throttle is a fourth open or fully open if the throttle limiter screw (**Figure 9**) is being used.
8. Grasp the starter handle (B, **Figure 4**) and slowly pull it until resistance is felt, then briskly and fully pull the starter rope to start the engine. After the engine is started, slowly allow the starter rope to return.
9. Operate the throttle lever to reduce the engine speed and allow the engine to warm up.
10. After the engine has run for about 30 seconds, fully turn the choke lever *clockwise* to open the choke.

NOTE
Do not allow the choke to remain closed. Excessive choking can cause the vehicle to run poorly, foul the spark plug and potentially cause engine damage.

Starting a Warm Engine

Use the following procedure for starting the engine when it is warm or when outdoor temperatures are above 35° C (95° F).
1. Set the parking brake lever (**Figure 3**).
2. Shift the transmission into neutral. The neutral indicator (A, **Figure 4**) should align with the arrow on the engine case.
3. Turn the fuel valve (A, **Figure 5**) to the ON position.
4. Place the engine stop switch in the RUN position (**Figure 6**).
5. Turn the ignition key to the ON position (**Figure 7**).
6. Press the throttle lever (**Figure 8**) so the throttle is a fourth open or fully open if the throttle limiter screw (**Figure 9**) is being used.
7. Grasp the starter handle (B, **Figure 4**) and slowly pull it until resistance is felt, then briskly and fully pull the starter rope to start the engine. After the engine is started, slowly allow the starter rope to return.
8. Operate the throttle lever to reduce the engine speed and allow the engine to warm up.
9. Allow the engine to run for approximately 30 seconds before riding.

Starting a Flooded Engine

If the engine cannot start after several attempts (particularly if the choke has been used), it may be flooded. This occurs when too much fuel is drawn into the engine and the spark plug fails to ignite it. The smell of gasoline is often evident when the engine is flooded. Troubleshoot a flooded engine as follows:
1. Look for gasoline overflowing from the carburetor or overflow hose. If gasoline is evident, the float in the carburetor bowl is stuck. Remove and repair the float assembly as described in Chapter Eight.
2. Place the engine stop switch in the RUN position.

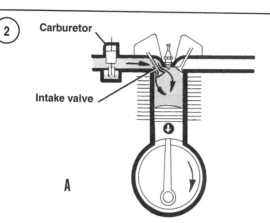

Carburetor

Intake valve

A

As the piston travels downward, the exhaust valve is closed and the intake valve opens, allowing the new air-fuel mixture from the carburetor to be drawn into the cylinder. When the piston reaches the bottom of its travel (BDC), the intake valve closes and remains closed for the next 1 1/2 revolutions of the crankshaft

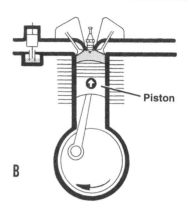

Piston

B

While the crankshaft continues to rotate, the piston moves upward, compressing air-fuel mixture.

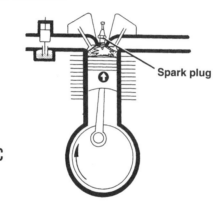

Spark plug

C

As the piston almost reaches the top of its travel, the spark plug fires, igniting the compressed air-fuel mixture. The piston continues to top dead center (TDC) and is pushed downward by the expanding gases.

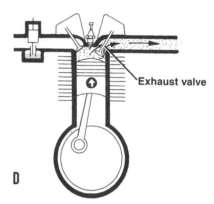

Exhaust valve

D

When the piston almost reaches BDC, the exhaust valve opens and remains open until the piston is near TDC. The upward travel of the piston forces the exhaust gases out of the cylinder. After the piston has reached TDC, the exhaust valve closes and the cycle starts all over again.

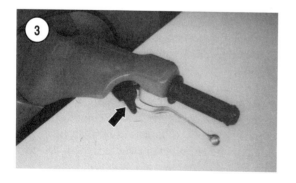

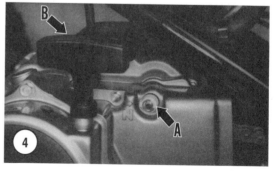

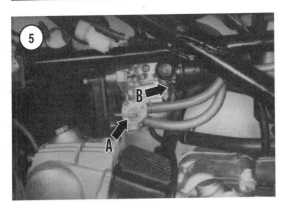

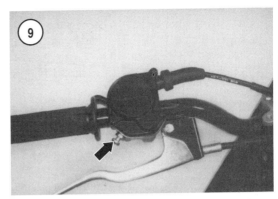

3. Check that the choke lever is fully open (turned *clockwise*).

4. Hold the throttle lever fully open and operate the recoil starter several times.

5. If the engine does not start, remove and inspect the spark plug. If the engine is severely flooded, the spark plug will be wet with fuel. Clean and dry the spark plug or replace the plug. Install the spark plug and repeat this starting procedure. If necessary, perform a spark test as described in this chapter. If the engine does not start or continues to be hard to start, refer to the troubleshooting sections for possible causes.

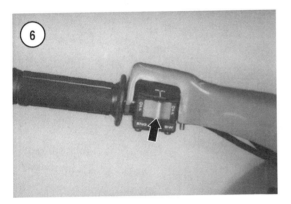

ENGINE SPARK TEST

An engine spark test will indicate whether the ignition system is providing power to the spark plug. It is a quick way to determine if a problem is in the electrical system or fuel system.

> *CAUTION*
> *When performing this test, ground the spark plug lead before cranking the engine. If the spark plug is not grounded, damage to the CDI circuitry could occur. A spark plug can be used for this test, but a spark tester (**Figure 10**) will clearly show if spark is occurring. Purchase this tester at a parts supply store or a supplier of ignition test equipment.*

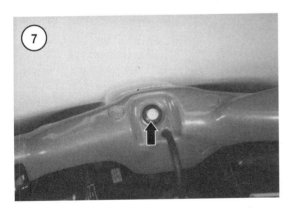

1. Remove the spark plug. Inspect the spark plug by comparing its condition to the plugs shown in Chapter Three.

2. Connect the spark plug lead to the spark plug or to a spark tester.

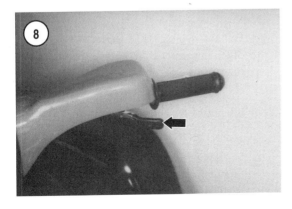

3. Ground the plug to bare metal on the engine (**Figure 11**). Position the plug so the firing end can be viewed.

4. Place the engine stop switch in the RUN position.

5. Turn the ignition switch to ON.

6. Using the recoil starter, crank the engine and observe the spark. A fat, blue spark should appear at the firing end. The spark should fire consistently as the engine is cranked.

7. If the spark appears weak or fires inconsistently, check the following areas for the cause:

    a. Fouled or improperly gapped spark plug.

    b. Defective spark plug lead and cap.

    c. Dirty/shorted engine stop switch or ignition switch.

    d. Loose connection in ignition system.

    e. Defective neutral or top gear switch.

    f. Defective ignition control module.

    g. Defective coil.

    h. Defective ignition pulse generator.

    i. Defective alternator.

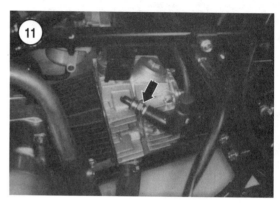

ENGINE PERFORMANCE

If the engine does not operate at peak performance, the following lists can help isolate the problem. The potential causes are grouped by areas to check and in general order of probability. Always perform the easiest checks throughout the list before proceeding to component disassembly.

Engine will not Start or Starts and Dies

1. *Fuel system:*

    a. Fuel tank empty.

    b. Contaminated fuel.

    c. Improper operation of choke knob.

    d. Engine flooded.

    e. Dirty air filter.

    f. Plugged carburetor fuel cup or shutoff valve.

    g. Plugged fuel line.

    h. Fuel tank vent tube plugged.

    i. Idle speed too low.

    j. Pilot air screw misadjusted.

    k. Air leaks at intake manifold.

    l. Wrong carburetor jet for altitude.

    m. Carburetor float valve sticking.

    n. Plugged carburetor jets.

2. *Ignition:*

    a. Fouled or improperly gapped spark plug.

    b. Defective spark plug lead and cap.

    c. Dirty/shorted engine stop switch or ignition switch.

    d. Loose connection in ignition system.

    e. Defective neutral or top gear switch.

    f. Defective ignition control module.

    g. Defective coil.

    h. Defective ignition pulse generator.

    i. Defective alternator.

3. *Engine:*

    a. Low compression.

    b. No valve clearance.

    c. Leaking cylinder head gasket.

    d. Stuck or seized valve.

    e. Incorrect valve timing.

Poor Idle and Low Speed Performance

1. *Fuel system:*

    a. Improper operation of choke knob.

    b. Engine flooded.

    c. Dirty air filter.

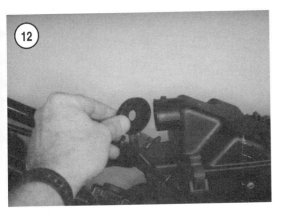

d. Idle speed too low.
e. Pilot air screw not adjusted.
f. Wrong carburetor jet for altitude.
g. Carburetor float valve sticking.
h. Plugged carburetor jets.
i. Loose carburetor mounting bolts.
j. Air leaks at intake manifold.

2. *Ignition:*
   a. Fouled or improperly gapped spark plug.
   b. Faulty/shorted spark plug lead and cap.
   c. Defective ignition control module.
   d. Defective coil.
   e. Defective ignition pulse generator.
   f. Defective alternator.

3. *Engine:*
   a. Improper valve clearance.
   b. Low compression.
   c. Incorrect valve timing.

Engine Lacks Power and Acceleration

1. *Fuel system:*
   a. Air intake restrictor on air filter housing (**Figure 12**).
   b. Throttle limiter screw in use (**Figure 9**).
   c. Choke lever in use.
   d. Dirty air filter.
   e. Restricted muffler.
   f. Wrong carburetor jet for altitude.
   g. Fuel tank vent tube plugged.
   h. Restricted fuel flow.
   i. Plugged carburetor jets.

2. *Ignition:*
   a. Fouled or improperly gapped spark plug.
   b. Faulty/shorted spark plug lead and cap.
   c. Defective ignition control module.
   d. Defective ignition pulse generator.

e. Improper flywheel installation.

3. *Engine:*
   a. Incorrect valve clearance.
   b. Worn/damaged valves.
   c. Worn cylinder and piston rings.
   d. Incorrect valve timing.
   e. Excessive oil level in crankcase.
   f. Inadequate oil level in crankcase.

4. *Wheels/axle:*
   a. Inadequate air pressure in tires.
   b. Drive chain too tight.
   c. Brake shoes dragging.
   d. Damaged/stuck brake cables.
   e. Damaged axle or wheel bearing.

5. *Clutch:*
   a. Improperly adjusted clutch.
   b. Worn/damaged clutch shoes.
   c. Worn/damaged clutch discs/plates.

Poor High Speed Performance

1. *Fuel system:*
   a. Air intake restrictor on air filter housing (**Figure 12**).
   b. Throttle limiter screw in use (**Figure 9**).
   c. Choke lever in use.
   d. Dirty air filter.
   e. Restricted muffler.
   f. Wrong carburetor jet for altitude.
   g. Fuel tank vent tube plugged.
   h. Restricted fuel flow.
   i. Plugged carburetor jets.

2. *Ignition:*
   a. Defective ignition control module.
   b. Defective ignition pulse generator.

3. *Engine:*
   a. Incorrect valve clearance.
   b. Worn/damaged valve springs.
   c. Worn cylinder and piston rings.
   d. Incorrect valve timing.

Engine Backfires

1. Lean fuel mixture.
2. Defective ignition control module.

ENGINE NOISE

Noise is often the first indicator that something is not correct with the engine. In many cases, damage can be avoided or minimized if the rider immediately stops the vehicle and diagnoses the source of the noise. Anytime engine noises are ignored, even when the vehicle seems to be running correctly, the rider risks causing more damage.

Pinging During Acceleration

1. Poor quality or contaminated fuel.
2. Lean fuel mixture.
3. Excessive carbon buildup in combustion chamber.
4. Faulty ignition control module.
5. Faulty ignition pulse generator.

Knocking, Ticking or Rattling

1. Loose exhaust system.
2. Loose/missing body fasteners.
3. Incorrect valve clearance.
4. Excessive connecting rod bearing clearance.

ENGINE LEAKDOWN TEST

The condition of the piston rings and valves can be accurately checked with a leakdown tester. With both valves in the closed position, screw this tester (**Figure 13**) into the spark plug hole and apply air pressure to the combustion chamber. Observe the gauge on the tester to determine the rate of leakage from the combustion chamber. An air compressor is required to use the leakdown tester.

1. Start the engine and allow it to warm up.
2. Shut off the engine and remove the air filter assembly.
3. Secure the throttle lever in the fully open position.
4. Remove the spark plug.
5. Set the piston to top dead center (TDC) on the compression stroke.
6. Install the leakdown tester following the manufacturer's instructions. The tester must not leak around the spark plug threads.
7. Make the test following the manufacturer's instructions for the tester. When pressure is applied to

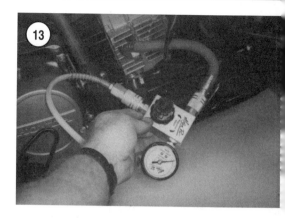

the cylinder, check that the engine remains at TDC. If necessary, put the transmission in gear and set the parking brake.

8. While the cylinder is under pressure, listen for air leakage.
   a. If leakage is detected at the exhaust pipe, the exhaust valve is leaking.
   b. If leakage is detected at the carburetor, the intake valve is leaking.
   c. If leakage is detected at the crankcase breather tube, the piston rings are leaking.
9. Cylinders with a leakdown of 10% or more should be serviced.

HANDLING

Poor handling should be corrected immediately after it is detected, since loss of control of the vehicle is possible. Check the following areas:

1. *Tires:*
   a. Incorrect/uneven air pressure.
   b. Punctured/damaged tire.
2. *Wheels:*
   a. Loose lug nuts.
   b. Improper toe-in.
   c. Damaged wheel bearings.
   d. Damaged wheel.
3. *Handlebars:*
   a. Loose handlebars.
   b. Steering shaft holder too tight.
   c. Damaged steering shaft bearing or bushing.
4. *Brakes:*
   a. Uneven adjustment of front brake cables.
   b. Brake shoes dragging.
   c. Damaged/stuck brake cables.
5. *Rear axle and swing arm:*
   a. Loose axle bearing holder.

b. Loose shock absorber.

c. Worn shock absorber bushings.

d. Worn swing arm pivot bushings.

e. Bent axle.

6. *Front axle:*

a. Worn/damaged tie rods.

b. Loose shock absorbers.

c. Worn shock absorber bushings.

d. Worn control arm bushings/kingpins.

7. *Frame:*

a. Bent/broken frame.

b. Broken weld on frame member.

ELECTRICAL TESTING

Refer to Chapter Nine for testing the switches and ignition system. When doing electrical tests, always refer to the diagram at the back of the manual.

Before testing a component, check the electrical connections related to that component. Check for corrosion and bent or loose connectors. Most of the connectors have a lock mechanism molded into the connector body. If these are not fully locked, a connection may not be made. If a connector is not locked, pull the connector apart and clean the fittings before reassembling.

2

CHAPTER THREE

LUBRICATION, MAINTENANCE AND TUNE-UP

This chapter provides procedures and information for properly lubricating, fueling and adjusting the vehicle. Refer to **Table 1** for the recommended service intervals and those components that require inspection, lubrication or adjustment. Refer to the sections in this chapter for performing the maintenance procedures described in **Table 1**. Additional tables at the end of the chapter are referenced as needed throughout the procedures.

SERVICE PRECAUTIONS AND PRACTICES

When performing maintenance procedures on the vehicle, observe the following shop and safety practices.

WARNING
Gasoline and most cleaning solvents are extremely flammable. Do not smoke or use electrical tools in the vicinity of the work area. Heating appliances and appliances with a pilot light should be shut off. If gasoline can be smelled in the work area, a potential hazard exists.

1. Turn off the fuel valve.
2. Never work on a hot engine.
3. Wipe up fuel and solvent spills immediately.
4. Work in a well-ventilated area.
5. When raising the vehicle, always support it with jackstands or other stable supports.
6. Wear eye protection when using compressed air and when spraying solvents or degreasers.
7. Keep a fire extinguisher in the shop, rated for class B (fuel) and class C (electrical) fires.

PRE-RIDE CHECKLIST

For a safe and enjoyable ride, perform the following checks before the first ride of the day. Refer to **Figure 1** for the location of each check. Refer to the procedures and tables in this chapter for information concerning fuel, lubricants, tire pressure and component adjustments. Start the vehicle as described in *Starting the Engine* in Chapter Two.
1. Check fuel lines and fittings for leakage.

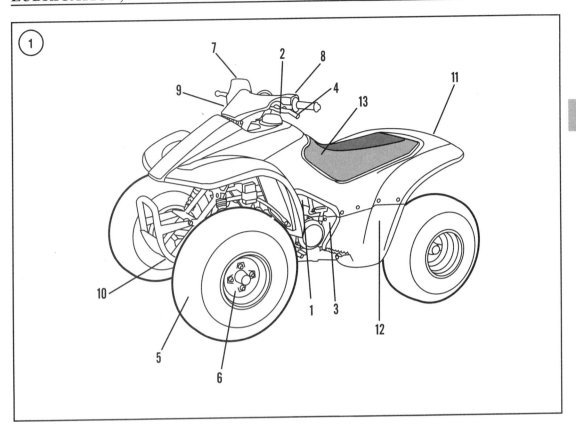

2. Check fuel level.
3. Check oil level. The dipstick is located on right side of engine.
4. Check brake operation and lever/pedal free play.
5. Check tire condition and air pressure.
6. Check axle nut and wheel lug nuts for tightness.
7. Check throttle operation and lever free play.
8. Check engine stop switch for proper operation.
9. Check steering for smooth operation.
10. Check for dirt/debris buildup under the frame and body.
11. Check exhaust system for tightness.
12. Check drive chain condition and adjustment.
13. Check air cleaner for dirt/debris buildup.

SERVICE INTERVALS

The service intervals in **Table 1** are recommended by the manufacturer. These intervals are based on typical use of the vehicle in average weather conditions. If the vehicle is regularly operated in extreme weather conditions, subjected to water or sand or used for competition, perform the service procedures more frequently.

Keep a record of when each service is performed. It will be easier to plan maintenance and have the necessary parts on hand.

TIRES AND WHEELS

Check the the tires prior to each daily use.

Tire Pressure

The tires for this vehicle are low-pressure tubeless tires and are sensitive to over- and under-inflation. Improper tire pressure is often the cause of poor steering and premature or uneven tire wear. Besides air leakage, tire pressure is affected by outdoor temperature and altitude changes.

Refer to **Table 2** for recommended pressures. Check tire pressure with a gauge (**Figure 2**), not visually. Check tires when they are *cold*, not after riding the vehicle.

WARNING
If using an air compressor to inflate the tires, quickly attach and remove

the air hose from the valve stem, then check the pressure. Over-inflation can occur quickly when using an air compressor.

Tire Inspection

Off-road riding subjects tires to many hazards and stresses. Check all tires for the following conditions.

1. Check the sidewalls and tread for cuts, tears and objects embedded in the tire. If damage is found, flood the area with soapy water and check for leakage. A leak will cause the water to bubble. Replace or repair the tire as described in Chapter Ten.

2. Check the tread for abnormal or uneven wear. Check the suspension components and the toe-in adjustment as described in Chapter Ten.

3. Check the sidewalls for cracks or swollen areas. This type of damage can indicate ply separation or torn cords.

4. Inspect the valve stem for damage. Keep the valve covered with a cap.

5. Measure the tread depth at the center of the tire. Tread depth should not be less than 4 mm (3/16 in.).

> *WARNING*
> *Replace worn tires. They are much more susceptible to failure and may cause loss of vehicle control.*

Rim Inspection

Inspect the rims for damage, particularly near the edge, where the tire seats. A bent rim can cause tire leakage, vibration and excessive tire wear. Replace damaged rims.

Check that lug nuts are in place and tight. Torque lug nuts to the specification listed in **Table 4**.

FUEL AND LUBRICANTS

Fuel Requirement

The engine is designed to operate on any gasoline that has an octane rating of 86 or higher. Use unleaded fuel, as it produces fewer engine emissions and spark plug deposits. It also extends the life of the exhaust system.

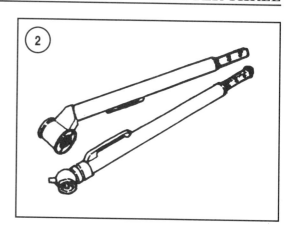

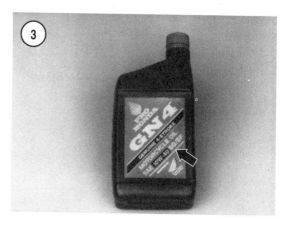

Oxygenated fuels (those blended with alcohol, ether or other compounds) can be used in the engine as long as the minimum octane rating is met. The following list includes the compounds and percentages that are approved by the EPA (Environmental Protection Agency) for oxygenated gasoline. Do not use fuels containing more than the approved percentages, or metal, plastic and rubber components in the fuel system may become damaged or corroded.

1. The fuel may contain up to 10% ethanol (ethyl or grain alcohol) by volume. Fuel containing ethanol is often marketed as *gasohol.*

2. The fuel may contain up to 15% MTBE (Methyl Tertiary Butyl Ether) by volume.

3. The fuel may contain up to 5% methanol (methyl or wood alcohol) by volume.

Engine Oil

For most operating conditions, operate the engine using a multigrade oil with an SAE 10W-40 viscos-

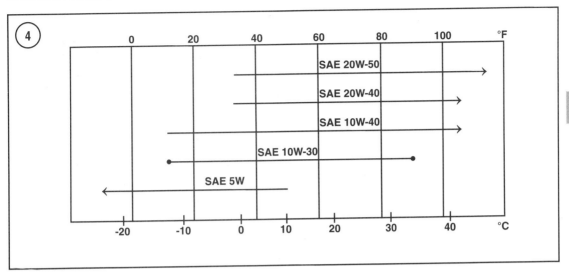

④

```
            0      20      40      60      80      100    °F
                                SAE 20W-50 ──────────→
                                SAE 20W-40 ──────────→
                                SAE 10W-40 ──────────→
                      SAE 10W-30 ●──────────●
              SAE 5W
          ←──────────────
           -20    -10     0      10      20      30      40    °C
```

⑤

ity rating. Use oil with a service classification of SF/SG. The oil viscosity rating and classification are indicated on the oil container (**Figure 3**).

The SAE viscosity rating indicates the *weight* of the oil. The higher the number, the thicker the oil and its resistance to flow. A multigrade oil has the ability to vary its viscosity and can be used over a wider range of temperatures. As shown in **Figure 4**, the recommended viscosity drops as the outdoor temperature lowers. In cold operating conditions, a light weight oil provides easier starting and quick flow through the oil circulation system. During hot operating conditions, a heavier oil provides the necessary lubrication and cooling qualities. Always use the appropriate oil for the temperature range in which the vehicle will be operated. If possible, use the same brand of oil at each oil change.

CAUTION
Do not use nondetergent, vegetable- or castor-based racing oils. Also, do not use oils or oil additives that contain graphite or molydenum. These additives can cause clutch slippage and erratic operation.

Grease

Use a good quality, lithium-based grease to lubricate components requiring grease. Some components require the extreme-pressure qualities of a grease containing molydenum disulfide. The procedures throughout this manual indicate when this grease is required. If the vehicle is routinely operated in wet or dusty conditions, grease the components frequently. This will purge water and grit from the components and extend life.

Chain Lubricant

Use a good quality chain lubricant that is compatible with O-ring chains. Chain lubricants that do not specifically indicate their use with O-ring chains can damage the chain O-rings. This will significantly shorten chain life and lubrication intervals. If chain lubricant is not available, use an SAE 80 or 90 weight gear oil.

PERIODIC LUBRICATION

Engine Oil Level Check

The oil is checked and replenished at the dipstick in the right engine cover (**Figure 5**).

1. Park the vehicle on level ground in a well-ventilated area.

2. Set the parking brake and check that the transmission is in neutral.

3. Start the engine and allow it to warm up.

4. Shut off the engine.

5. Unscrew the dipstick (**Figure 6**) and wipe it clean.

6. Reinsert and seat the dipstick, but do not screw it into the engine.

7. Remove the dipstick and check the oil level.

  a. The oil level should be between the lower and upper marks on the dipstick. The oil level should not exceed the upper mark (**Figure 7**).

  b. If necessary, add the appropriate weight of oil to bring the level to within the marks on the dipstick. Add oil in small quantities and check the level often. Overfilling the engine is not beneficial and can cause engine problems.

Engine Oil Change

> *WARNING*
> *Prolonged contact with used motor oil may cause skin cancer. Minimize contact with the motor oil.*

> *NOTE*
> *Never dispose of motor oil in the trash, on the ground or down a storm drain. Many service stations accept used motor oil and waste haulers provide curbside used motor oil collection. Do not combine other fluids with motor oil to be recycled. To locate a recycler, contact the American Petroleum Institute (API) at www.recycleoil.org.*

Change the oil at the intervals recommended in **Table 1**. If the vehicle is used in extreme conditions such as hot, cold, wet or dusty, change the oil more often and use the appropriate grade of oil as recommended in *Fuel and Lubricants*.

Always change the oil when the engine is warm. Contaminants will remain suspended in the oil and it will drain faster and more completely.

1. Park the vehicle on level ground in a well-ventilated area.

2. Set the parking brake and check that the transmission is in neutral.

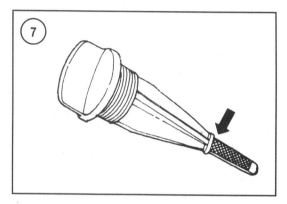

3. Start the engine and allow it to warm up.

4. Shut off the engine.

5. Remove the dipstick (**Figure 6**).

6. *Loosen* the engine drain plug (**Figure 8**), then place a drain pan below the plug. Remove the drain plug and allow the oil to drain from the engine.

7. Inspect the drain plug and sealing washer (**Figure 9**). Replace the sealing washer if it leaks or is severely worn. Replace the drain plug if the threads are damaged or severely worn.

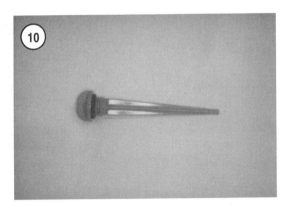

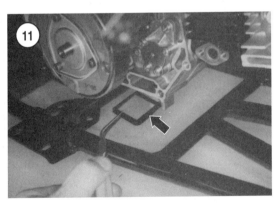

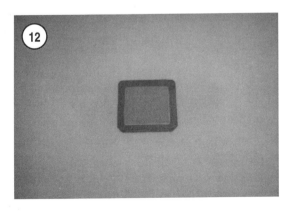

8.   ipe dirt and oil from around the drain plug hole.

9. Install and torque the drain plug to the value listed in **Table 4**.

10. Inspect the O-ring on the dipstick (**Figure 1**). Replace the O-ring if torn or missing. The O-ring must be in place to prevent the entry of water and dirt into the crankcase.

11. Fill the crankcase with the required quantity and weight of motor oil. Refer to **Table 3** for engine oil capacity.

12. Insert the dipstick and screw it into place.

13. Start the engine and allow it to idle for a few minutes.

14. Shut off the engine, then check the engine for
    a. Leaks around the drain plug.
    b. Proper oil level.

15. Dispose of the used motor oil in an environmentally-safe manner.

16. Dispose of oily rags and wash hands thoroughly.

Engine Oil Filter and cr een

Periodically, the centrifugal oil filter and oil strainer screen (**Figure 11**) must be cleaned. These filters are located behind the right crankcase cover.

1. Remove the right crankcase cover as described in Chapter Six.

2. Remove and clean the oil strainer screen (**Figure 12**) as follows
    a. Remove the screen from the lower right corner of the crankcase.
    b. Clean the screen in solvent and dry with compressed air.
    c. Reinstall the screen into the crankcase.

3. Clean the centrifugal oil filter as follows
    a. Remove the three screws from the oil filter rotor-cover (**Figure 13**). Remove the cover and gasket.
    b.   ipe the interior of the chamber (A, **Figure 14**) with a clean cloth.

CAUTION
Do not use compressed air to clean the chamber or other components in the crankcase. Doing so can blow dirt into the oil passages and throughout the crankcase.

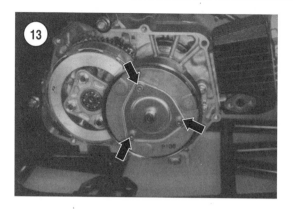

c. Check and clean the oil passage in the end of the crankshaft (B, **Figure 14**)

d. Place a new gasket on the oil filter rotor-cover (**Figure 15**).

e. Apply threadlocking compound to the threads of the cover screws.

f. Align the cover and finger-tighten the screws.

g. Torque the screws to the specification listed in **Table 4**.

4. Install the right crankcase cover as described in Chapter Six.

Cable Lubrication

If the brake pedal, brake levers or throttle lever binds or drags, this can indicate a lack of cable lubrication or damaged parts. Lubricate all cables internally to ensure long life, as well as smooth and safe operation. Although there is no recommended service interval, always lubricate cables at the beginning and end of each riding season. If the vehicle is operated in severe conditions, lubricate the cables frequently during the riding season.

The following procedure describes cable lubrication using a cable lubricator (**Figure 16**). This tool attaches to the cable end and allows pressurized cable lubricant to be forced into the cable housing. Some lubricators allow the cables to remain connected during the lubrication process.

1A. For brakes, refer to Chapter Twelve for removing and installing the brake cable ends, if necessary.

1B. For the throttle housing, remove the cover (**Figure 17**) and clean and lubricate the throttle assembly as described in Chapter Eight.

2. Attach the cable lubricator to the end of the cable, following the manufacturer's instructions.

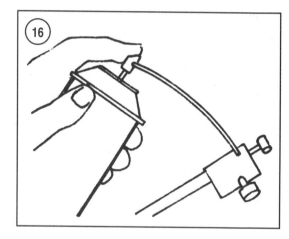

3. Fit the nozzle of the cable lubricant into the lubricator.

4. Hold the cable upright so the lubricant will run down into the housing. Place a shop cloth below the cable to catch excess lubricant.

5. Hold a shop cloth over the lubricator, then press and hold the button on the lubricant can.

6. Hold the button down until lubricant drips from the opposite end.

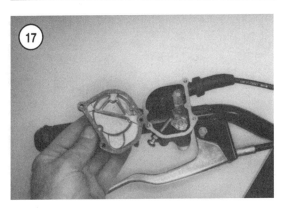

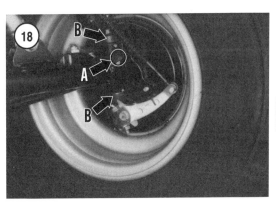

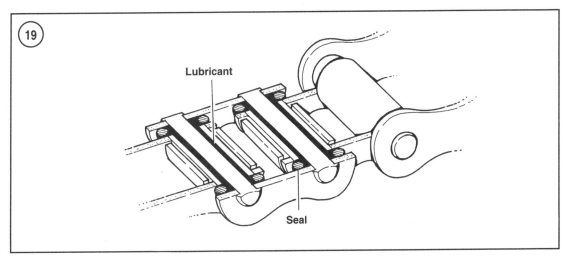

Lubricant

Seal

NOTE
If the lubricator backsprays, or does not allow lubricant into the cable end, try lubricating at the opposite end. If the cable will not accept lubricant or does not easily move in the housing after lubrication, replace the cable.

7. Disconnect the lubricator, then pull the cable back and forth in the housing to distribute the lubricant.

8. Apply grease to the cable ends and reinstall the cables. Adjust the cables as described in this chapter.

9. For brake levers, lubricate the lever pivot.

Control Arm Lubrication

The kingpin and bushings located in each control arm must be lubricated with molydisulfide grease. Use a grease gun and lubricate each control arm at

the fitting (A, **Figure 18**). Lubricate the fitting until fresh grease is visible at the dust seals (B).

Drive Chain Cleaning and Lubrication

Engine power is transferred to the rear sprocket by an endless, O-ring chain. This type of chain is internally lubricated and sealed by O-rings (**Figure 19**). The chain does require regular cleaning, lubrication and adjustment for long life. Perform the maintenance procedures more frequently than recommended if the vehicle is operated under severe conditions.

Never clean the chain with high-pressure water sprays or strong solvents. If water is forced past the O-rings, water will then be trapped inside the links. Strong solvents can soften the O-rings so they tear or damage easily.

Ideally, the chain should be removed from the vehicle for a thorough cleaning. However, this requires breaking the chain or partially disassembling the swing arm in order to remove the chain. These removal procedures are described in Chapter Eleven. If these chain removal procedures are not possible, the following procedure is an acceptable alternative.

   a. Loosen the chain as described in *Drive Chain Adjustment* so it has maximum slack.

   b. Remove the chain cover and guard (**Figure 20**) to access the chain.

   c. Lift the chain off the driven sprocket and allow it to hang on the axle.

   d. Place a pan of solvent under the chain so it can be rotated through the solvent.

Whichever method is chosen, clean the chain as follows:

1. Immerse the chain in kerosene and work the links so dirt is loosened.

2. Lightly scrub the chain with a soft-bristle brush.

> *CAUTION*
> *Brushes with coarse or wire bristles can damage the O-rings.*

3. Rinse the chain with clean kerosene and wipe dry.

4. Lubricate the chain with a lubricant specifically for O-ring chains. If chain lubricant is not available, use an SAE 80 or 90 weight gear oil.

> *CAUTION*
> *Since the links of an O-ring chain are permanently lubricated and sealed, O-ring chain lubricant is formulated to condition the O-rings and prevent exterior corrosion of the chain. It is not tacky and resists the adhesion of dirt. Avoid lubricants that are tacky and that are for conventional chains. These lubricants will attract dirt and subject the O-rings to unnecessary abrasion.*

5. Install the chain and adjust it as described in this chapter.

PERIODIC MAINTENANCE

Fastener Inspection

To maintain a safe and reliable vehicle, all fasteners on the vehicle should be inspected for tightness and security.

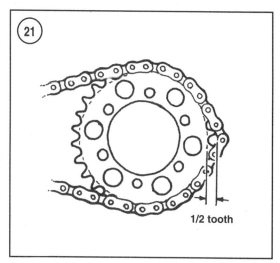

1/2 tooth

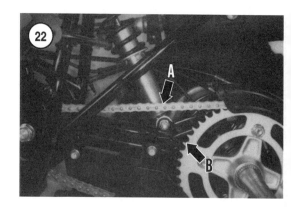

1. Retorque nuts, bolts and screws as recommended in the tables at the end of each chapter.

2. Check that all cotter pins are secure and undamaged.

3. Check that tie straps used to secure cables and electrical wiring are not broken or missing.

4. Check that all fasteners are in the body panels.

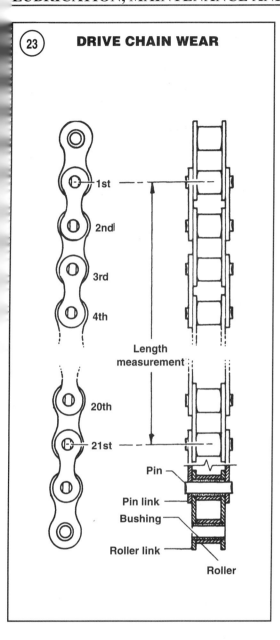

DRIVE CHAIN WEAR

(23)

1st
2nd
3rd
4th

Length measurement

20th
21st

Pin
Pin link
Bushing
Roller link
Roller

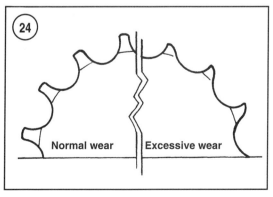

(24)

Normal wear   Excessive wear

3

Drive Chain and Sprocket Wear Inspection

A worn drive chain and sprockets are unreliable and potentially dangerous. Inspect the chain and rear sprocket for wear and replace them if necessary. If wear is detected, replace both sprockets and the chain. Mixing old and new parts will prematurely wear the new parts. Front sprocket inspection is described in Chapter Five.

To determine if the chain should be measured for wear, perform the following test:

    a. At the rear sprocket, pull one chain link away from the sprocket.

    b. If more than half the height of the sprocket tooth is visible (**Figure 21**), the chain should be accurately measured for wear. Refer to the following procedure to measure chain wear and inspect the rear sprocket.

1. Loosen the axle bearing holder and turn the chain adjuster nut until the chain is taut (A, **Figure 22**).

2. Measure the length of any 21-pin span along the top of the chain (**Figure 23**).

    a. The service limit for the chain is 268 mm (10.6 in.). If the measured distance meets or exceeds the service limit, replace the chain.

    b. If the chain is within the service limit, inspect the inside surfaces of the link plates. The plates should be shiny at both ends of the chain roller. If one side of the chain is worn, the chain has been running out of alignment. This also causes premature wear of the rollers and pins. Replace the chain if abnormal wear is detected.

3. Inspect the teeth on the rear sprocket (B, **Figure 22**). Compare the sprocket to **Figure 24**. The teeth should be symmetrical and uniform. If the sprocket is worn out, also replace the front sprocket.

4. Adjust the drive chain as described in this section.

Drive Chain Adjustment

The drive chain must have adequate free play so it can adjust to the movement of the swing arm when the vehicle is in use. Too little free play will cause the chain to become excessively tight when the rear suspension is compressed. Too much free play will cause the chain to become excessively loose when the rear suspension is extended. A tight chain will cause unnecessary wear to the drive line components, while a loose chain may come off the sprockets, possibly causing vehicle damage and personal injury.

1. Check the amount of free play by measuring midway between the two sprockets (**Figure 25**).

2. Hold a ruler in position (**Figure 25**), then measure the free play by pulling up on the chain. Free play may also be measured on the lower section of the chain (**Figure 26**). Since chains do not wear evenly, check several sections of the chain and find the tightest length (least amount of free play). The amount of play should be 20-30 mm (3/4-1 1/4 in.).

3. Adjust chain free play as follows:

   a. Loosen the two axle bearing holder bolts (**Figure 27**) on each side of the holder.

   b. If the chain is too loose, tighten the adjuster nut (**Figure 28**) in small increments and remeasure free play.

   c. If the chain is too tight, loosen the adjuster nut (**Figure 28**) in small increments and move the axle bearing holder forward. Remeasure free play.

   d. When free play is correct, tighten the axle bearing holder bolts to lock the setting. Torque the bolts to the value listed in **Table 4**.

4. If free play cannot be adjusted within the limits of the adjuster, the chain is excessively worn and should be replaced.

Drive Chain Slider Inspection

Refer to *Swing Arm Inspection* in Chapter Eleven.

Throttle Cable Adjustment

Before adjusting the throttle cable, check that it is lubricated and in good condition. To achieve accurate cable adjustment, the cable must not bind or drag.

1. Measure the amount of throttle lever free play (**Figure 29**). Measure the free play at the end of the lever. Correct free play is 3-8 mm (1/8-5/16 in.). If free play is more or less than this, adjust the throttle in the following steps.

2. Remove the handlebar cover as described in Chapter Thirteen.

3. Slide the rubber boot (A, **Figure 29**) off the cable adjuster.

4. Loosen the locknut (B, **Figure 29**) and turn the adjuster (C, **Figure 29**) in/out to increase/decrease the lever free play.

5. When adjustment is correct, tighten the locknut and reinstall the boot.

6. Install the handlebar cover.

Clutch Adjustment

The gear change clutch must be adjusted properly to ensure smooth shifting and minimal wear on the clutch plates. The clutch adjuster is located on the right crankcase cover (**Figure 30**). Perform the adjustment with the engine off.

1. Loosen the locknut with a wrench (A, **Figure 31**). Do not completely remove the locknut.

2. While holding the locknut with the wrench, turn the clutch adjuster *counterclockwise* using a screwdriver (B, **Figure 31**). Turn the adjuster until slight resistance is felt.

3. Turn the adjuster a fourth turn *clockwise* and hold the position.

4. Tighten the locknut.

5. Test ride the vehicle. If clutch operation is erratic or difficult, recheck the adjustment. If necessary, remove the right crankcase cover and make repairs as described in Chapter Six.

Air Filter Cleaning

The engine is equipped with a reusable, foam air filter. Clean the air filter frequently if the vehicle is regularly operated in dusty conditions.

1. Remove the seat.

3

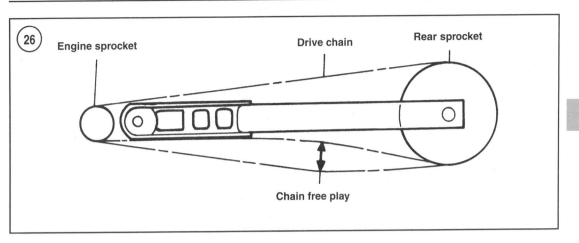

26

Engine sprocket

Drive chain

Rear sprocket

Chain free play

27

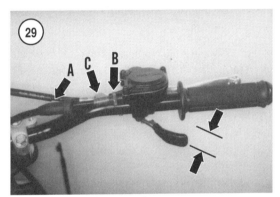

29

A C B

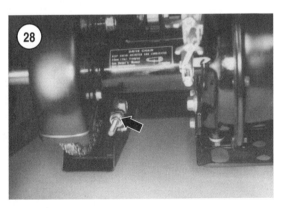

28

30

2. Unlatch the four retainer clips on the air cleaner housing (**Figure 32**).

3. Remove the housing cover.

4. Unhook the air filter retainer band (A, **Figure 33**) and remove the air filter (B).

5. Remove the filter sleeve from the air cleaner body (**Figure 34**).

6. Wash the filter sleeve in kerosene, a commercial filter wash or hot soapy water. *Squeeze* the cleaner

from the filter. Do not wring the filter, as tearing may occur.

7. Allow the filter to completely dry.

8. Apply filter oil to the filter, squeezing out the excess oil. Follow the manufacturer's instructions when oiling the filter.

NOTE
Use oil specifically formulated for
foam filters. This type of oil stays ad-

hered to the foam and traps dust effectively. Pro Honda Air Filter Oil is available at dealerships. Do not use motor oil.

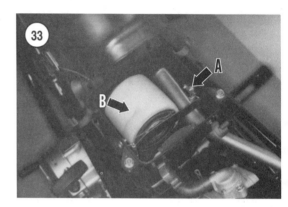

9. For 1999 and 2000 models, remove and wash the two foam filters (**Figure 35**) that are part of the Pulse Secondary Air Injection System (PAIR). It is not necessary to oil the filters.

10. Wipe clean the interior of the air filter housing and cover.

11. Wipe clean the air cleaner body, then reinstall the filter sleeve.

12. Fit the filter(s) back into the housing.

13. Secure the air filter band and housing cover.

14. Install the seat.

PAIR System Inspection

For 1999 and 2000 models, an exhaust emission control system is fitted to the engine (**Figure 36**). The system, known as PAIR, routes fresh air into the exhaust port so unburned gasses can be burned. The system also directs crankcase blowby gases back into the air filter housing. The gasses are then drawn into the intake manifold and burned in the cylinder. The system control valve is located behind the air filter housing (**Figure 37**). Perform the following checks of the system.

1. Clean the filters in the air filter housing as described in *Air Filter Cleaning* in this section.

2. Inspect all hoses and fittings. Replace cracked, damaged or missing hoses. Tighten or clamp loose fittings.

3. Remove the cover (**Figure 38**) from the control valve and inspect the check valve (**Figure 39**).

   a. Inspect the rubber seal around the check valve. It should not be cracked or damaged

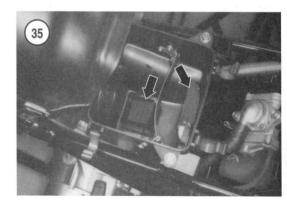

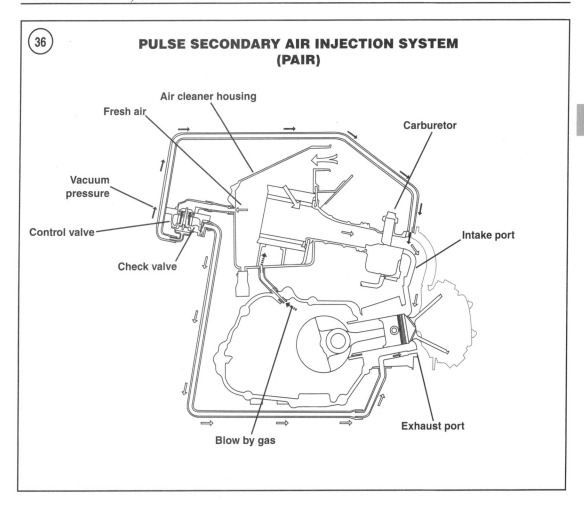

36

PULSE SECONDARY AIR INJECTION SYSTEM (PAIR)

Air cleaner housing

Fresh air

Carburetor

Vacuum pressure

Control valve

Intake port

Check valve

Exhaust port

Blow by gas

3

37

38

b. Inspect the check valve reed. It must lie flat. There should be no clearance between the reed and its seat.

c. Replace the check valve if it is damaged or fatigued. The valve is not repairable.

d. Install the check valve in the control valve, then screw the cover into place.

Fuel Line Inspection

Inspect the fuel and drain lines attached to the carburetor (**Figure 40**). Inspect the fuel lines and their routing to the fuel tank. Replace lines that are cracked or leaking. Check that all fuel lines are clamped at both ends.

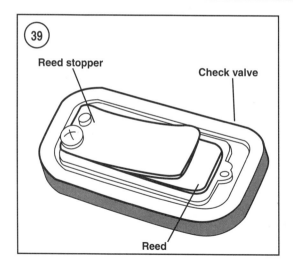

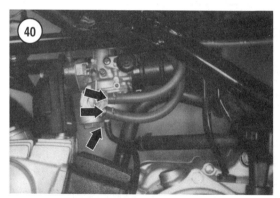

Brake Shoe Inspection

The brake shoes can be inspected for wear without disassembling the brake units. A wear indicator arrow (A, **Figures 41** and **42**) and reference mark (B, **Figures 41** and **42**) are located at each brake housing. For front brakes, refer to **Figure 41**. For rear brakes, refer to **Figure 42**. Check front or rear brake wear as follows:

1. Check that the brake cable(s) is properly adjusted so the brakes can be fully engaged.

2. Fully apply and hold the brake.

3. Observe the position of the wear indicator arrow to the reference mark.

    a. If the arrow does not align with the reference mark, the brake shoes are still usable.

    b. If the arrow aligns with the reference mark, the brake shoes are worn and must be replaced.

Front Brake Lever Adjustment

As the brake shoes and cables wear, they will require adjustment. The front brake lever is located on the right handlebar.

1. Measure the amount of brake lever free play (**Figure 43**), before the brakes begin to engage. Measure the free play at the end of the lever. Correct free play is 10-20 mm (3/8-3/4 in.). If free play is more or less than this, adjust the brakes according to the procedures in the following steps.

2. Remove the front cover from the front fender assembly as described in Chapter Thirteen.

3. Loosen/tighten the adjusting nut (A, **Figure 44**) to increase/decrease the lever free play. The adjusting nut controls the length of the primary cable (B).

4. When adjustment is correct, check that the adjusting nut seats against the joint piece (C, **Figure 44**).

5. Install the front cover and check that the brakes are engaging equally.

    a. At a *slow* vehicle speed, slowly apply the front brakes.

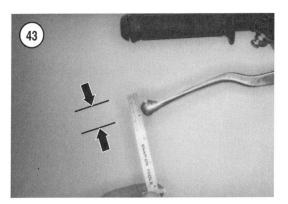

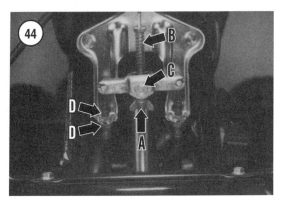

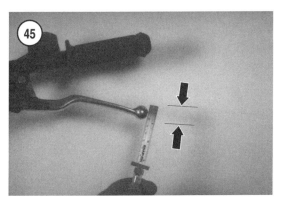

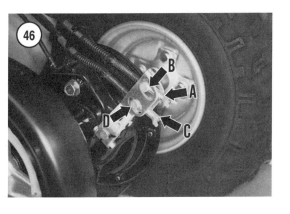

3

b. If the vehicle stops in a straight line, both brakes are engaging equally. Brake adjustment is completed.

c. If the vehicle pulled to one side, the brake on that side is engaging sooner than the other front brake. Adjustment of the secondary cable(s) is required.

6. Adjust the secondary cable(s) as follows:

a. Remove the front cover from the front fender assembly.

b. Loosen the locknuts (D, **Figure 44**) on the cable being adjusted.

c. Adjust the cable housing up/down to lengthen/shorten the cable.

d. Tighten the locknuts and recheck lever free play. Adjust if necessary.

e. Test ride the vehicle to check the adjustments. Repeat the adjustment procedure if necessary.

f. Install the front cover.

Rear Brake/Parking Brake
Lever Adjustment

As the brake shoes and cables wear, the rear brake lever and cable will require adjustment. The rear brake lever is located on the left handlebar.

1. Measure the amount of brake lever free play (**Figure 45**) before the brakes begin to engage. Measure the free play at the end of the lever. Correct free play is 10-20 mm (3/8-3/4 in.). If free play is more or less than this, adjust the brakes according to the procedures in the following steps.

2. Loosen/tighten the upper adjusting nut (A, **Figure 46**) to increase/decrease the lever free play.

3. When adjustment is correct, check that the adjusting nut seats against the joint piece (B, **Figure 46**).

Rear Brake Pedal Adjustment

As the brake shoes and cable wear, the rear brake pedal and cable will require adjustment. The rear brake pedal is located on the right side of the engine.

1. Measure the amount of brake pedal free play (**Figure 47**) before the brakes begin to engage. Measure the free play at the end of the pedal. Correct free play is 10-20 mm (3/8-3/4 in.). If free play is more or less than this, adjust the brakes in the following steps.

2. Loosen/tighten the lower adjusting nut (C, **Figure 46**) to increase/decrease the lever free play.
3. When adjustment is correct, check that the adjusting nut seats against the joint piece (D, **Figure 46**).

Rear Brake Housing Draining

Check the rear brake housing for water at the intervals indicated in **Table 1**. Anytime the vehicle is operated in water, check the brake housing for water.
1. Park the vehicle on level ground and set the parking brake.
2. Remove the drain plug (**Figure 48**) and allow any water to drain from the housing.
3. Install the plug and torque it to the value listed in **Table 4**.

> *WARNING*
> *If water is entering the brake housing, inspect and replace the damaged seals. Refer to Chapter Twelve for brake inspection and repair.*

Skid Plates

The skid plates (**Figures 49** and **50**) protect the frame, steering components, rear brakes, chain and sprocket. Check the guards for the following:
1. Check that all guards are secure and no mounting bolts are missing.
2. Check all guards for cracks or damage.
3. Check that the chain guard is not contacting the chain and sprocket.
4. Check that the brake guard is not contacting the brake housing.
5. Replace broken or damaged guards. Align and tighten loose guards.

Muffler Cleaning

Purge the muffler of carbon to ensure good engine performance.
1. Park the vehicle in a well-ventilated area.
2. Put the transmission in neutral and set the parking brake.
3. With the engine cold, remove the purge plug (A, **Figure 51**) from the muffler.
4. Start the engine.

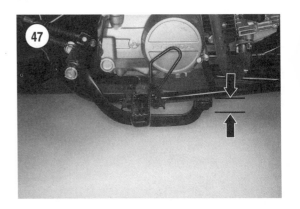

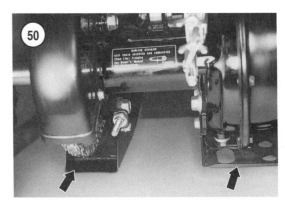

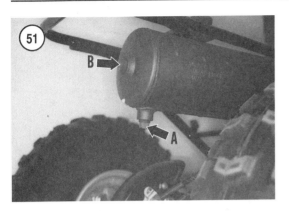

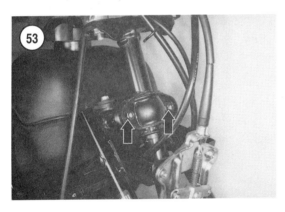

WARNING
Wear heavy gloves to prevent burns while holding the shop cloth over the muffler outlet.

5. While holding a folded shop cloth over the muffler outlet (B, **Figure 51**), momentarily raise the engine speed to blow carbon out of the purge hole. Continue raising and lowering the engine speed until no carbon is exiting the muffler.

6. Shut off the engine and allow it to cool.

7. Install the purge plug in the muffler and tighten securely.

Steering Shaft Inspection

Inspect the steering shaft for smooth operation and play.

1. Park the vehicle on level ground and set the parking brake.

2. Raise and support the front of the vehicle so the front tires are off the ground.

3. Turn the handlebar in both directions and check for roughness and binding.

4. Pull the handlebar up, down and side to side. Check for play in any direction.

5. If roughness, binding or play is detected in the steering shaft:

    a. Inspect the bearing at the end of the steering shaft (**Figure 52**).

    b. Inspect the tightness of the bolts securing the steering shaft holder (**Figure 53**) and the bushing below the holder.

    c. Refer to Chapter Ten for servicing worn or damaged parts.

Tie Rod Inspection

Keep the tie rods in good condition to ensure a safe vehicle. All handlebar and steering shaft movement is transferred through the tie rods and to the front wheels. The tie rod ends are an expendable part and must be replaced when they are worn. Anytime the tie rod ends are replaced or when tire wear is abnormal, check the toe-in adjustment as described in Chapter Ten.

1. Inspect both tie rod ends that connect to the steering shaft (**Figure 54**) and the tie rod end at each front wheel (**Figure 55**).

    a. Inspect the rubber boots for tears.

b. Grasp the tie rod and check for looseness, dryness or the entry of water into the ball joint.

c. Check that the cotter pins and nuts are in place.

d. Check the tie rods for straightness.

2. If damage is detected, refer to Chapter Ten for service procedures.

Shock Absorber Inspection

1. Check all shock absorbers for the following problems.

a. Tightness of mounting bolts.

b. Worn or damaged rubber bushings.

c. Leakage at the damper rod seal.

d. Broken springs or damaged shock body.

2. If damage is detected, refer to Chapter Eleven for service procedures.

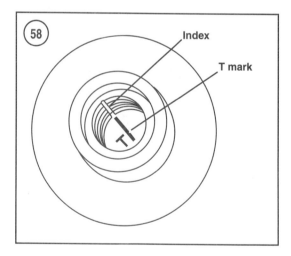

ENGINE TUNE-UP

Valve Clearance Adjustment

The engine is designed with one intake valve and one exhaust valve. Valves must be adjusted correctly so they will completely open and close during the combustion cycle. Valves that are out of adjustment can cause poor performance and engine damage. Valve clearance should be checked when the engine temperature is below 35° C (95° F).

1. Park the vehicle on a level surface and set the parking brake.

2. Remove the front fender assembly as described in Chapter Thirteen.

3. Remove the cap from the timing hole located on the left crankcase cover (**Figure 56**).

4. Remove the caps from the valve adjustment holes. The intake valve cap (**Figure 57**) is above the cylinder head. The exhaust valve cap is below the cylinder head.

5. Set the engine at top dead center (TDC) on the compression stroke as follows:

a. While looking into the timing hole, slowly pull the recoil starter rope until the T mark on

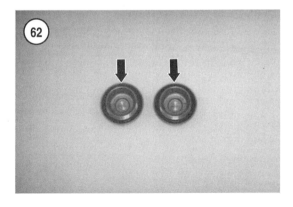

the flywheel is aligned with the index mark in the timing hole (**Figure 58**).

NOTE
Remove the spark plug if it is difficult to align the T mark.

b. Confirm that the T mark is set on the compression stroke and both valves are closed. Move both rocker arms (**Figure 59**) by hand. If the exhaust rocker arm is tight and will not move, the engine is on the exhaust stroke. Rotate the engine one revolution and realign the T mark. Both valves should now be closed. Recheck the rocker arms for play.

6. Refer to **Table 5** for the valve clearance specification.

7. Check both valves by inserting a flat feeler gauge between the adjusting screw and valve stem (**Figure 60**). Clearance is correct when a slight resistance is felt as the gauge is inserted and withdrawn.

8. To adjust clearance:

a. Loosen the locknut with a 9 mm wrench (A, **Figure 61**) (part No.07708-0030100). Do not remove the locknut.

b. Increase or decrease the valve clearance with a valve adjusting wrench fitted to the adjuster (B, **Figure 61**) (part No. 07708-0030400 or part No. 07908-KE90200).

c. When clearance is correct, hold the adjuster in place and tighten the locknut. Torque the locknut to the specification listed in **Table 4**.

d. Recheck valve clearance.

9. Inspect the O-rings in the valve caps (**Figure 62**). Replace O-rings that are deteriorated or missing. Lubricate the O-rings and screw the caps into the valve adjustment holes. Torque the caps to the specification listed in **Table 4**.

10. Install the timing hole cap. Torque the cap to the value listed in **Table 4**.

11. Install the spark plug, if removed.

12. Install the front fender assembly.

Carburetor Adjustment

The original equipment carburetor is jetted and preset for operation at altitudes up to 5000 ft. (1500 m). If the vehicle will be operated at higher altitudes, rejet as described under *High Altitude Jetting* in Chapter Eight.

The pilot air screw (A, **Figure 63**) is preset and does not need routine adjustment. If the screw has been replaced, the carburetor rebuilt, or the setting is unknown because of tampering, reset the screw as described under *Pilot Air Screw* in Chapter Eight.

The idle speed is adjusted with the throttle stop screw (B, **Figure 63**). To accurately set idle speed, a tachometer is required. Use the following procedure to set idle speed.

1. Check the air filter for cleanliness. Clean if necessary.

2. Attach a tachometer to the engine following the manufacturer's instructions.

3. Start the engine and allow it to warm up.

WARNING
Do not run the engine in an enclosed area. Carbon monoxide can build up and cause unconsciousness and death.

4. Adjust the throttle stop screw (B, **Figure 63**) to set the engine idle speed to the specification in **Table 6**.

5. Raise and lower the engine speed a few times to assure that it returns to the idle speed.

6. Turn off the engine and disconnect the tachometer.

Engine Timing

The ignition timing is electronically controlled by the ignition control module. No adjustment is possible to the ignition timing. Check the timing to verify the ignition control module is functioning properly. If the engine shows symptoms of ignition problems, refer to *Ignition Timing* in Chapter Nine to check the control module.

Compression Check

A cylinder compression check can quickly verify the condition of the piston, rings, valves and cylinder head gasket without disassembling the engine. By keeping a record of the compression reading at each tune-up, readings can be compared to determine if normal wear is occurring. If a current reading is extremely different from the previous

readings, this may indicate a developing problem. Operating the engine when compression readings are abnormal can lead to severe engine damage.

1. Warm the engine to operating temperature.

2. Remove the spark plug. Insert the spark plug into the cap, then ground the plug to the cylinder.

3. Attach a compression gauge to the spark plug hole (**Figure 64**). The gauge must fit airtight for an accurate reading.

4. Hold or secure the throttle fully open.

5. Rapidly pull on the recoil starter rope several times until the highest gauge reading is achieved.

6. Record the reading and compare it to the engine compression reading in **Table 5**. Compare the reading with previous readings, if available. Under normal operating conditions, compression will slowly lower from the original specification, due to wear of the piston rings and valves.

   a. A reading that is higher than normal can be caused by carbon buildup in the combustion chamber. This can cause high combustion chamber temperatures and potential engine damage.

   b. A reading that is lower than normal can be caused by worn piston rings, damaged piston,

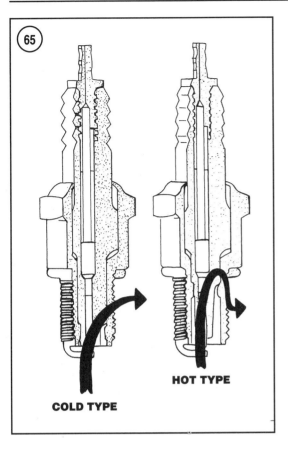

HOT TYPE

COLD TYPE

that operate well in a wide range of engine speeds. As long as engine speeds vary, these plugs will stay relatively clean and perform well.

If the engine is run in hot climates, at high speed or under heavy loads for prolonged periods, use a spark plug with a colder heat range. A colder plug quickly transfers heat away from its firing tip and to the cylinder head (**Figure 65**). This is accomplished by a short path up the ceramic insulator and into the body of the spark plug. By transferring heat quickly, the plug remains cool enough to avoid overheating and preignition problems. If the engine is run slowly for prolonged periods, this type of plug will foul and result in poor performance.

If the engine is run in cold climates or at slow speed for prolonged periods, use a spark plug with a hotter heat range. A hotter plug slowly transfers heat away from its firing tip and to the cylinder head. This is accomplished by a long path up the ceramic insulator and into the body of the spark plug (**Figure 65**). By transferring heat slowly, the plug remains hot enough to avoid fouling and buildup. If the engine is run in hot climates or fast for prolonged periods, this type of plug will overheat, cause preignition problems and possibly melt the electrode. Damage to the piston and cylinder assembly is possible.

In order to change the spark plugs to a different heat range, choose a spark plug one step hotter or colder from the plugs recommended in **Table 7**. Do not try to correct poor carburetor or ignition problems by using different spark plugs. This can only compound the existing problems and lead to unreliable service.

worn valves and seats, leaking head gasket, or a combination of these factors. To help pinpoint the source of leakage, pour 15 cc (1/2 oz.) of motor oil through the spark plug hole and into the cylinder. Turn the engine over to distribute the oil. Recheck compression. If compression increases significantly, the piston rings are worn or damaged. If compression is the same, the valves or head gasket is worn or damaged.

Spark Plug Selection

A resistor-type spark plug is recommended for this vehicle. Refer to **Table 7** for the recommended spark plugs, operating conditions and gap.

Heat range

Spark plugs are available in several heat ranges to accommodate the load and performance demands placed on the engine. The standard spark plugs recommended in **Table 7** are medium heat range plugs

Reach

Besides heat range, spark plugs can vary in their reach. Reach is the length of the threaded portion of the plug (**Figure 66**). Always use a spark plug that is the correct reach. Too short of a reach (**Figure 67**) can lead to deposits or burning of the exposed threads in the cylinder head. Misfiring can also occur since the tip of the plug is shrouded and not exposed to the fuel mixture. If the reach is too long (**Figure 67**), the exposed plug threads can burn, causing preignition. The piston may contact the plug on the upstroke, causing severe engine damage.

Spark Plug Cap

The spark plug cap should fit tight to the spark plug and be in good condition. A cap that does not seal and insulate the spark plug terminal can lead to flashover (shorting down the side of the plug), particularly when the vehicle is operated in wet conditions. To help prevent water from migrating under the cap, apply a small amount of dielectric grease around the interior of the cap before installing it on the plug.

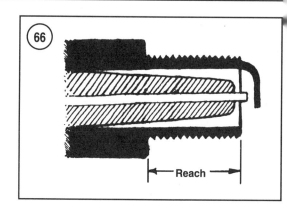

Spark Plug Removal

Careful removal of the spark plug is important in preventing debris from entering the combustion chamber. It is also important to know how to remove a plug that is seized or resistant to removal. Forcing a seized plug can destroy the threads in the cylinder head.

1. Grasp the spark plug cap and twist it from side to side to loosen it from the spark plug. There may be slight suction and resistance as the cap is pulled up for removal.

2. Blow and wipe away any dirt that has accumulated around the spark plug hole and cylinder head.

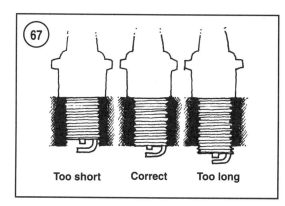

3. Fit a spark plug wrench over the spark plug, then remove it by turning the wrench counterclockwise. If the plug is seized or is difficult to remove, stop and try the following techniques:

   a. Apply a penetrating lubricant such as Liquid Wrench or WD-40 and allow it to soak in for about 15 minutes.

   b. If the plug is completely seized, apply moderate pressure in both directions with the wrench. Only attempt to break the seal so lubricant can penetrate under the spark plug and into the threads. If this fails, and the vehicle is still operable, replace the spark plug cap and start the engine. Allow it to completely warm up. The heat of the engine may be enough to expand the parts and allow the plug to be removed.

   c. When the spark plug has been loosened, but is still difficult to remove, apply penetrating lubricant around the spark plug threads. Turn the plug *clockwise* to help distribute the lubricant onto the threads. Slowly remove the plug, working it in and out of the cylinder

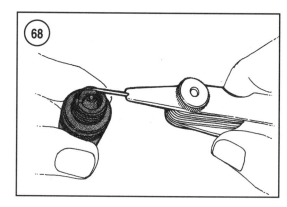

head while adding lubricant. Do not reuse the spark plug.

   d. Inspect the threads in the cylinder head for damage. Clean and true the threads with a spark plug thread-chaser.

4. Inspect the plug condition to determine if the engine is operating properly.

5. Clean spark plugs that will be reused after inspection with electrical contact cleaner and a shop rag. Do not use abrasives or wire brushes to clean the plugs.

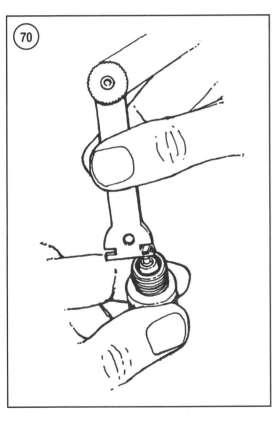

small, adjust the gap by bending the ground electrode (**Figure 69**) to achieve the required gap. Use an adjusting tool (**Figure 70**) to bend the electrode. Do not pry the electrode with a screwdriver or other tool. Damage to the center electrode and insulator is possible.

4. Make sure the spark plug is fitted with a crush washer.

5. Apply a *small* amount of antiseize compound onto the spark plug threads. Do not allow the compound to get on the electrodes.

6. Insert and finger-tighten the spark plug into the cylinder head. This will ensure the plug is not cross-threaded.

7. Torque the spark plug to the specification listed in **Table 4**. If a torque wrench is not available, turn a new spark plug a fourth to a half turn from the seated position. Turn a used spark plug an eighth to a fourth turn from the seated position.

8. Press and twist the cap onto the spark plug.

Reading Spark Plugs

The spark plug is an excellent indicator of how the engine is operating. By correctly evaluating the condition of the plug, you can diagnose and pinpoint problems, or potential problems. Compare the firing tip with the examples shown in **Figure 71**. The following paragraphs provide a description as well as common causes for each of the conditions.

> *CAUTION*
> *If the spark plug is not normal, find the cause of the problem before continuing engine operation. Severe engine damage is possible when abnormal plug readings are ignored.*

Spark Plug Gapping and Installation

Proper adjustment of the electrode gap is important for reliable and consistent spark. Also, the proper preparation of the spark plug threads will ensure that the plug can be removed easily in the future, without damage to the cylinder head threads.

1. Refer to **Table 7** for the required spark plug gap.
2. Insert a wire feeler gauge between the center electrode and the ground electrode (**Figure 68**).
3. Pull the gauge through the gap. If there is slight drag, the setting is correct. If the gap is too large or

Normal

The plug has light tan or gray deposits on the tip. No erosion of the electrodes or abnormal gap is evident. This indicates an engine that has properly adjusted carburetion, ignition timing and proper fuel. This heat range of plug is appropriate for the conditions in which the engine has been operated. The plug can be cleaned and reused.

⑦¹

SPARK PLUG CONDITIONS

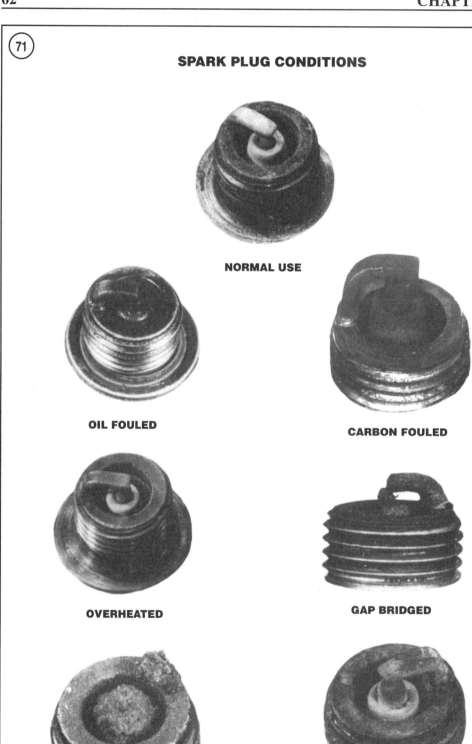

NORMAL USE

OIL FOULED

CARBON FOULED

OVERHEATED

GAP BRIDGED

SUSTAINED PREIGNITION

WORN OUT

Oil fouled

The plug is wet with black, oily deposits on the electrodes and insulator. The electrodes do not show wear.

1. Incorrect carburetor jetting.
2. Prolonged idling or low idle speed.
3. Ignition component failure.
4. Spark plug range too cold.
5. Worn valve guides.
6. Worn piston rings.

Carbon fouled

The plug is black with a dry, sooty deposit on the entire plug surface. This dry, sooty deposit is conductive and can create electrical paths that bypass the electrode gap. This often results in misfiring of the plugs.

1. Fuel mixture too rich.
2. Spark plug range too cold.
3. Defective ignition control module.
4. Prolonged idling.
5. Dirty air filter.
6. Low compression.

Overheated

The plug is dry and the insulator has a white or light gray cast. The insulator may also appear blistered. The electrodes may have a bluish-burnt appearance.

1. Fuel mixture too lean.
2. Advanced ignition timing.
3. Spark plug range too hot.
4. Air leak into intake system.
5. No crush washer on plug.
6. Plug improperly tightened.

Gap bridged

The plug has combustion deposits between the electrodes. The electrodes do not show wear.

1. Wrong oil type being used.
2. Improper fuel or fuel contamination.
3. Carbon deposits in combustion chamber.
4. High speed operation after excessive idling.

Preignition

The plug electrodes are severely eroded or melted. This condition can lead to severe engine damage.

1. Advanced ignition timing (faulty ignition control module).
2. Spark plug range too hot.
3. Air leak into intake system.
4. Carbon deposits in combustion chamber.

Worn out

The plug electrodes are rounded from normal combustion. There is no indication of abnormal combustion or engine conditions. Replace the plug.

STORAGE

Vehicles that are used seasonally should be prepared for storage at the end of the riding season. General vehicle deterioration and poor engine performance occur when vehicles are simply parked until the following season. Typical problems include fuel deterioration and obstruction of the fuel system, internal engine corrosion due to acids in used motor oil, drive chain corrosion, and fatigued/cracked tire sidewalls due to low air pressure and wheels not being elevated. This type of damage can be avoided by thorough preparation of the vehicle prior to storage. The vehicle will remain in good condition and be easier to return to service.

Preparation

If possible, prepare the vehicle near the area in which it will be stored. When preparation is completed, the vehicle will not be drivable and must be pushed to the storage area.

1. Wash the entire vehicle, removing all dirt from the underside of the body and frame. Apply wax to painted parts.
2. Warm up the engine and change the engine oil as described in this chapter.
3. Drain all fuel from the fuel tank, fuel lines and carburetor. Attempt to start the engine and allow it to run all fuel out of the carburetion system.
4. Clean and lubricate the drive chain as described in this chapter.

5. Remove the spark plug and pour 15 cc (1/2 oz.) of engine oil into the cylinder. Install the spark plug and turn the engine over several times to distribute the oil.

6. Wipe exposed metal parts with a lightly oiled rag.

7. Inflate the tires to the recommended pressure.

8. Park the vehicle in the storage area, preferably out of direct sunlight.

9. Raise and support the vehicle so all wheels are off the ground.

10. Loosely cover the vehicle. Covering the vehicle tightly with a plastic cover can trap condensation. Allow air to circulate under the cover.

NOTE
During the storage period, check the vehicle for deterioration and damage that may be caused by rodents or other pests. Turn the engine over sev- *eral times to keep the oil in the cylinder distributed.*

Returning to Service

1. Remove the vehicle from the storage area and wipe the vehicle clean.

2. Inflate the tires to the recommended pressure.

3. Remove the spark plug and turn the engine over several times to purge any motor oil that is in the cylinder. Install a new spark plug.

4. Refill the fuel tank with fresh fuel.

5. Check the engine oil level.

6. Check inside the air filter housing for possible damage caused by rodents or other pests.

7. Start the engine and allow it to warm up.

8. Check the engine stop switch, throttle and brakes for proper operation.

9. Test ride the vehicle.

10. Perform an engine tune-up if necessary.

Table 1 MAINTENANCE AND LUBRICATION SCHEDULE

	Initial 20 hours[1] (100 miles or 150 km)	Every 100 hours[1] (600 miles or 1000 km)	Every 200 hours[1] (1200 miles or 2000 km)
Adjust and lubricate drive chain[2]	x		
Change engine oil	x		
Check valve clearance	x	x	x
Check engine idle speed	x	x	x
Grease control arm kingpins	x	x	x
Inspect control levers/pedal adjustment	x	x	x
Inspect rear brake housing	x	x	x
Inspect/adjust clutch	x	x	x
Inspect wheels, tires and lug nuts	x	x	x
Inspect nuts, bolts and fasteners	x	x	x
Inspect drive chain and sprockets		x	x
Lubricate and inspect cables		x	x
Inspect shock absorbers		x	x
Clean air filter		x	x
Clear PAIR system filters		x	x
Inspect/replace spark plug		x	x
Inspect skid plates		x	x
Clean muffler		x	x
Inspect/replace fuel line			x
Clean engine oil strainer			x
Clean engine oil centrifugal filter			x
Inspect steering system			x

1. Perform the procedures at either the hours or mileage indicated; whichever occurs first.
2. After the initial adjustment and lubrication, adjust and lubricate the drive chain every 50 hours (300 miles or 500 km).

Table 2 TIRE INFLATION PRESSURES

	Front psi (kPa)	Rear psi (kPa)
Recommended operating pressure	2.9 (20)	2.9 (20)
Maximum pressure	3.3 (23)	3.3 (23)
Minimum pressure	2.5 (17)	2.5 (17)
Bead seating pressure	36 (250)	36 (250)

Table 3 FUEL, LUBRICANTS AND CAPACITIES

Engine fuel	Unleaded gasoline; 86 octane minimum
Fuel tank capacity	6.0 liters (1.58 U.S. gallons)
Fuel tank reserve	1.3 liters (0.34 U.S. gallon)
Engine oil[1]	SAE 10W-40; SF/SG rated or newer
Engine oil capacity	0.9 liter (1.0 U.S. quart)
Drive chain	O-ring type chain lubricant or SAE 80 or 90 weight gear oil
Control cables[2]	Cable lube
Air filter	Foam air filter oil
Steering kingpins	Molydisulfide grease

1. See text for oil recommendations for various riding conditions.
2. Do not use drive chain lubricant on control cables.

Table 4 TORQUE SPECIFICATIONS

	N•m	in.-lb.	ft.-lb.
Axle bearing holder bolts	90	–	66
Axle nut			
Front	70-90	–	52-66
Rear	60-80	–	44-59
Oil drain bolt	24	–	18
Oil filter rotor-cover screws	6	53	–
Parking brake lever pivot screw	9	80	–
Rear brake housing drain bolt	25	–	18
Shock absorber mounting bolts	25	–	18
Spark plug	12	106	–
Throttle housing cover screws	3.5	31	–
Timing hole cap	3	27	–
Valve adjusting hole cap	12	106	–
Valve adjuster locknut	9	80	–
Wheel lug nuts	55	–	40

Table 5 TUNE-UP SPECIFICATIONS

Compression ratio	9.2:1
Cylinder compression	178 psi (1226 kPa)
Ignition timing F mark	
1993-1998	7° @ 1600 rpm
1999-2000	7° @ 1500 rpm
Ignition timing full advance	30° BTDC @ 3050 rpm
Valve clearance	
Intake and exhaust	0.05 ± 0.02 mm (0.002 ± 0.0008 in.)

Table 6 CARBURETOR ADJUSTMENT SPECIFICATIONS

Pilot air screw initial opening	
1993-1998	1-3/8 turns out
1999-2000	2-1/2 turns out
Idle speed	1600 ± 100 rpm

Table 7 SPARK PLUG SPECIFICATIONS

Spark plugs	
Standard plug (mixed-speed riding)	NGK CR7HSA or Denso U22FSR-U
Hot plug (extended slow-speed riding)	NGK CR6HSA or Denso U20FSR-U
Cold plug (extended high-speed riding)	NGK CR8HSA or Denso U24FSR-U
Spark plug gap	0.6-0.7 mm (0.024-0.028 in.)

Table 8 DRIVE CHAIN MEASUREMENTS

Drive chain free play	20-30 mm (3/4-1 1/4 in.)
Drive chain length, 21-pin span	
Service limit	268 mm (10.6 in.)

Table 9 LEVER AND PEDAL CLEARANCES

Throttle lever free play	3-8 mm (1/8-5/16 in.)
Front brake lever free play	10-20 mm (3/8-3/4 in.)
Rear brake lever free play	10-20 mm (3/8-3/4 in.)
Rear brake pedal free play	10-20 mm (3/8-3/4 in.)

CHAPTER FOUR

ENGINE TOP END

This chapter provides information for the removal, inspection and replacement of the major assemblies that make up the engine top end. This includes the cylinder head, camshaft, valves, cylinder and piston. The parts can be removed with the engine mounted in the frame. This chapter shows the engine removed for clarity. Refer to the tables at the end of this chapter for specifications.

Read this chapter before attempting any repair to the engine top end. Become familiar with the procedures, photos and illustrations to understand the skill and equipment required. Refer to Chapter One for tool usage and techniques. When special tools are required or recommended, the part number is provided. The special tools can be ordered from a Honda dealership.

Procedures, photos and illustrations are representative of the model years covered in this manual. When necessary, information that is specific to a model year(s) is provided.

CLEANLINESS

Always clean the engine before starting repairs. If the engine will remain in the frame, clean the sur-rounding framework and under the fuel tank. Do not allow dirt to enter the engine.

Keep the work environment as clean as possible. Store parts and assemblies in well-marked plastic bags and containers. Keep reconditioned parts wrapped until reassembly.

CYLINDER HEAD

This section describes removal, inspection and installation of the cylinder head. When the cylinder head is removed, refer to the appropriate sections in this chapter for further disassembly, inspection and assembly procedures. If possible, perform a compression test as described in Chapter Three and leakdown test as described in Chapter Two prior to cylinder head removal.

Cylinder Head Removal

1. Remove the seat and front fender assemblies as described in Chapter Thirteen.
2. Remove the exhaust system as described in Chapter Eight.

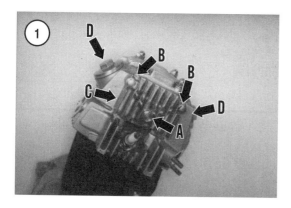

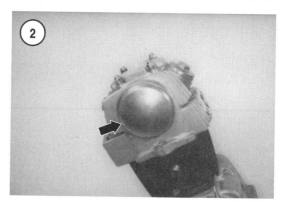

3. Remove the carburetor and intake manifold as described in Chapter Eight.

4. Remove the spark plug cap.

5. Remove the throughbolt and washer from the right cylinder head cover (A, **Figure 1**). This bolt secures the left cylinder head cover.

6. Remove the left cylinder head cover and gasket (**Figure 2**).

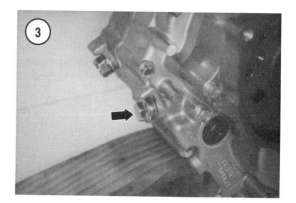

> *CAUTION*
> *Do not attempt to loosen the cover by prying the edge. If the cover is difficult to remove, loosely thread the throughbolt back into the cover and lightly tap the bolt head to loosen the cover.*

7. Remove the two bolts (B, **Figure 1**) that secure the right cylinder head cover.

8. Remove the right cylinder head cover (C, **Figure 1**) by lightly tapping it with a soft mallet. Remove the cover gasket if it did not come off with the head cover.

9. Remove the caps and O-rings (D, **Figure 1**) from the valve adjustment holes.

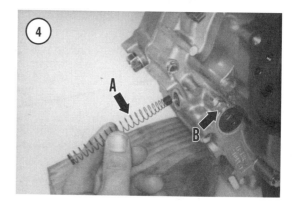

10. Remove the cam chain tensioner assembly as follows:

   a. Remove the chain tensioner bolt and washer (**Figure 3**).

   b. Remove the cam chain tensioner spring (A, **Figure 4**).

   c. Remove the cam chain tensioner push rod (**Figure 5**).

11. Prepare to remove the cam sprocket bolts (**Figure 6**). Before removing the bolts, align the crankshaft and camshaft timing marks as follows:

   a. Remove the cap from the timing hole (**Figure 7**) located on the left crankcase cover. Note

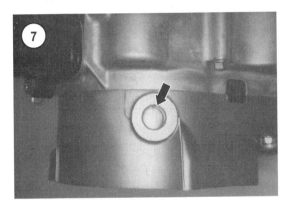

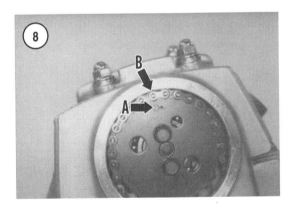

4

the index mark (**Figure 7**) down the side of the hole.

b. Remove the spark plug.

CAUTION
To prevent the possibility of jamming the cam chain on the crankshaft, pull the recoil starter slowly.

c. Slowly pull on the recoil starter rope and watch for the T mark to appear in the timing hole. Stop pulling on the rope when the T mark is aligned with the index mark.

d. Check that the O timing mark (A, **Figure 8**) on the cam sprocket is aligned with the index mark (B, **Figure 8**) on the cylinder head. If the O mark on the cam sprocket is not at the top of the cylinder head, repeat Steps 11c and 11d until both pairs of marks are aligned at the same time.

12. Remove the cam sprocket bolts (**Figure 6**).

CAUTION
As the second bolt is being removed, hold the cam sprocket to prevent it from moving.

13. Insert a screwdriver or drift (A, **Figure 9**) through one of the upper holes in the cam sprocket to prevent it from falling.

14. Remove the dowel pin (B, **Figure 9**) from the center of the cam sprocket.

15. Lower and tilt the cam sprocket away from the cylinder head so the cam chain is accessible (**Figure 10**).

16. Attach a length of wire to the cam chain so it cannot fall into the engine.

17. Remove the cam sprocket from the cam chain, then remove the sprocket from the engine (**Figure 11**).

18. Secure the cam chain as shown in A, **Figure 12**.

19. Remove the cylinder head bolt (B, **Figure 12**) from the left side of the cylinder head.

20. Remove the four cylinder head nuts and washers (A and B, **Figure 13**). Note the position of the copper washer on the cylinder head (B, **Figure 13**). This washer is a seal and must be installed on this crankcase stud.

21. Loosen the cylinder head cover (C, **Figure 13**) by lightly tapping it with a soft mallet. Remove the cover gasket if it did not come off with the head cover.

22. Loosen the cylinder head by lightly tapping around its base with a soft mallet. Lift the head from the engine while routing the cam chain out of the head. Remove the cylinder head gasket if it did not come off with the cylinder head.

23. If the cylinder will not be removed, check that the dowel pins (A, **Figure 14**) and O-ring (B) remain on the cylinder. The O-ring must be replaced during reassembly.

24. Secure the cam chain so it remains engaged with the crankshaft sprocket and will not fall into the engine (**Figure 14**). Cover the engine crankcase openings with clean shop rags to prevent debris from entering.

25. Inspect the cylinder head, cam sprocket chain and tensioner assembly as described in this chapter.

Cylinder Head Inspection

This inspection procedure does not require the removal of additional cylinder head parts. However, if parts are damaged or worn, refer to the appropriate sections in this chapter for additional procedures and inspections.

Anytime the cylinder head is removed, test the valves with a solvent test for leakage. This test is quick and easy to perform and will help identify problems in the valve train. Refer to *Valves and Valve Components* in this chapter for the solvent test. Also, check the cam chain tensioner assembly to ensure that it is within service limits. Refer to *Cam Chain Tensioner Inspection* in this chapter.

1. Remove all gasket residue from the cylinder head mating surfaces. Do not scratch or gouge the surfaces.

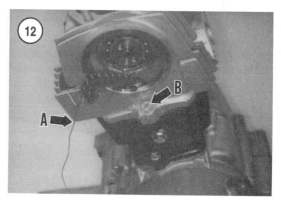

2. Remove all carbon deposits from the combustion chamber and valve ports (**Figure 15**). Use solvent and a fine wire brush or hardwood scraper. Do not use sharp-edged tools such as screwdrivers or putty knives.

> *CAUTION*
> *If the valves are removed from the head, the valve seats are exposed and can be damaged from careless cleaning. A scratched or gouged valve seat will not seal properly.*

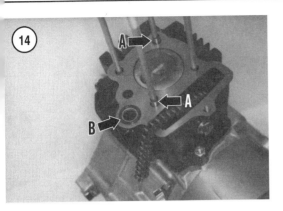

3. Inspect the spark plug hole threads. If the threads are dirty or mildly damaged, use a spark plug thread tap to clean and straighten the threads. Use kerosene or aluminum tap-cutting fluid to lubricate the threads.

NOTE
If the threads are galled, stripped or cross-threaded, fit the cylinder head with a steel thread insert, such as a HeliCoil.

NOTE
Thread damage can be minimized by applying antiseize compound to the

spark plug threads before installation. Do not overtighten the spark plug.

4. Clean the entire cylinder head assembly in fresh solvent.

CAUTION
If the head was bead-blasted, wash the entire assembly in hot soapy water to remove all blasting grit that is lodged in crevices and threads. Clean and chase all threads to assure no grit remains. Blasting grit that remains in the head will be circulated by the engine oil to other parts of the engine. This will damage the bearings, piston and rings.

5. Inspect the piston crown for signs of wear or damage. If the piston is pitted, overheating is likely occurring. This can be caused by a lean fuel mixture and/or preignition. If damage is evident, troubleshoot the problem as described in Chapter Two.

6. Inspect the cylinder head for cracks in the combustion chamber and exhaust port (**Figure 15**). If cracks are found, take the cylinder head to a dealership or machine shop to determine if the head can be repaired. If not, replace the head.

7. Inspect the cylinder head for warp as follows:
   a. Lay a machinist's straightedge across the cylinder head as shown in **Figure 16**.
   b. Try to insert a flat feeler gauge between the straightedge and the machined surface of the head. If clearance exists, record the measurement.
   c. Repeat substeps a and b at several locations on the head.
   d. Compare the measurements to the warp service limit listed in **Table 2**. If the clearance is not within the service limit, take the cylinder head to a dealership or machine shop to determine if the head can be resurfaced. If not, replace the head.

Cylinder Head Installation

1. Check that all gasket residue is removed from all mating surfaces. All cylinder head surfaces should be clean and dry.

2. Lubricate the following components of the cylinder head assembly with an oil and molydenum disulfide mixture in a ratio of 1:1.

   a. Camshaft lobes and bearings.

   b. Rocker arm faces and rocker shafts.

   c. Valve stems.

3. Check that the dowel pins (A, **Figure 14**) are on the cylinder, and are on the correct crankcase studs.

4. Install the collar, then place a new, lubricated O-ring (B, **Figure 14**) over the collar.

5. Install a new cylinder head gasket, checking that it lays flat on the cylinder (**Figure 17**).

6. Check that both valves are closed in the cylinder head. If they are not, rotate the cam so the valves are closed and can be timed with the crankshaft later in this procedure.

7. Lower the cylinder head over the crankcase studs, routing the cam chain through the head. Keep adequate tension on the cam chain so it does not fall off the crankshaft sprocket. Secure the cam chain when the cylinder head is seated (A, **Figure 12**).

8. Place a new cylinder head cover gasket on the cylinder head.

9. Install the cylinder head cover, checking that the arrow mark (A, **Figure 18**) on the cover is pointing down toward the exhaust valve.

10. Place a new copper sealing washer (B, **Figure 18**) on the lower right crankcase stud.

11. Place the three plain washers on the remaining crankcase studs.

12. Install the four cylinder head nuts and torque them to the specification listed in **Table 3**.

> *CAUTION*
> *Torque the head nuts in a crossing pattern as shown in* ***Figure 19***. *Torque the nuts in three stages, torquing the nuts equally at each stage.*

13. Install the cylinder head bolt at the left side of the cylinder head (**Figure 20**) and torque it to the specification listed in **Table 3**.

14. Install and time the cam sprocket to the crankshaft as follows:

   a. Check that the T mark in the timing hole is aligned with the index mark (**Figure 7**).

   b. Hold the cam sprocket so the O mark (A, **Figure 21**) is facing out, and is near the index mark (B) on the cylinder head.

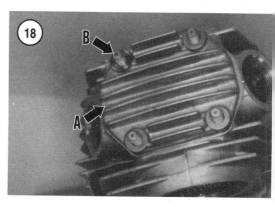

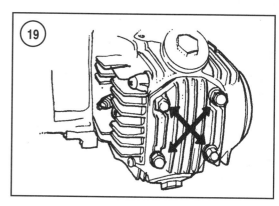

   c. Insert a screwdriver or drift (A, **Figure 9**) through one of the upper holes in the cam sprocket to prevent it from falling.

   d. Securely hold the cam sprocket and place the cam chain over the sprocket (**Figure 10**).

   e. Raise the cam sprocket and cam chain to the camshaft, then insert the dowel pin (B, **Figure 9**) through the sprocket to help hold it in place. Be careful to not drop the dowel pin or allow it to fall from the hole. A magnetic drift is being used in A, **Figure 9**.

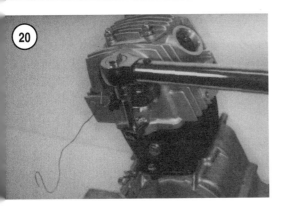

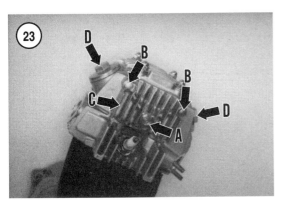

CAUTION
When raising the sprocket and chain, the crankshaft must not turn. If it does, the T mark will not be aligned properly and accurate timing will not be achieved. Severe engine damage could occur if the engine is not timed properly.

f. Align the sprocket holes with the camshaft holes, then insert and finger-tighten the cam sprocket bolts (**Figure 6**).

g. Check that the T mark in the timing hole and the O mark on the sprocket are aligned with their respective index marks. If either mark is not aligned, reposition the cam chain on the sprocket and recheck the alignments.

h. Torque the sprocket bolts to the specification listed in **Table 3**.

15. Install and lubricate the cam chain tensioner assembly as follows:

a. Install the cam chain tensioner push-rod, inserting the rubber-tipped end first (**Figure 5**).

b. Install the cam chain tensioner spring, inserting the tightly-wound coils first (A, **Figure 4**).

c. Install a new sealing washer on the chain tensioner bolt (**Figure 3**) and torque the bolt to the specification listed in **Table 3**.

d. Remove the bolt and sealing washer (B, **Figure 4**) from the cam chain tensioner oil-hole.

e. Squirt a minimum of 1 cc of engine oil into the oil hole.

f. Install a new sealing washer on the bolt, then install and tighten the bolt.

16. Adjust the valves as described in Chapter Three.

17. Check the timing by slowly pulling on the recoil starter rope and turning the engine over several times. Observe the alignment of the T mark in the timing hole when the cam sprocket O mark is aligned with its index mark. If the T mark is not exactly aligned, the cam chain is not on the correct teeth of the cam sprocket. Repeat Steps 14-17 if necessary.

18. Install new, lubricated O-rings on the valve hole caps (**Figure 22**). Install and torque the caps (D, **Figure 23**) to the specification listed in **Table 3**.

19. Install the left and right cylinder-head cover assembly (**Figure 24**) as follows:

a. Place a new gasket (A, **Figure 24**) on the right cylinder head cover.

b. Bolt the right cylinder head cover (C, **Figure 23**) to the cylinder head using the two small bolts (B, **Figure 23**). Finger-tighten the bolts.

c. Place a new gasket on the left cylinder head cover (B, **Figure 24**).

d. Align the lugs (**Figure 25**) on the cylinder head and cover. Hold it in place.

e. Insert the throughbolt with washer (A, **Figure 23**) through the right cylinder head cover, threading it into the left cylinder head cover. Finger-tighten the bolt.

f. Equally tighten the three bolts on the right cylinder head cover.

20. Install the carburetor and intake manifold as described in Chapter Eight.

21. Install the exhaust system as described in Chapter Eight.

22. Attach the spark plug cap.

23. Install the seat and front fender assemblies as described in Chapter Thirteen.

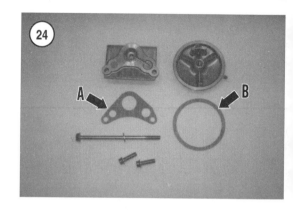

CAMSHAFT AND ROCKER ARM ASSEMBLIES

Refer to *Cylinder Head* in this chapter for removing and installing the cam chain tensioner. The cam chain tensioner can be removed from the engine without removing the cylinder head assembly.

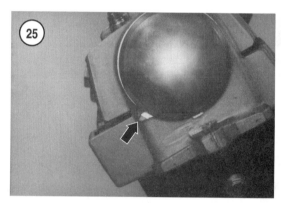

Camshaft and Rocker Arm Removal

1. Remove the cylinder head as described in this chapter.

2. Thread an 8 mm bolt (**Figure 26**) into the rocker arm shaft and pull out the shaft. Repeat for the other rocker arm shaft.

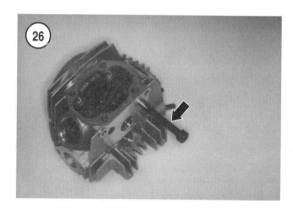

> *CAUTION*
> *When removing the rocker arm and rocker arm shaft for each valve, keep the intake and exhaust parts separated. Use plastic bags to mark and store the sets until they are inspected and ready for reassembly. The rocker arm and shaft sets have established wear patterns and should be reassembled in their original positions.*

3. Remove the rocker arms (**Figure 27**).

4. Remove the stopper plate (**Figure 28**).

5. Remove the camshaft (**Figure 29**).

Camshaft and Bearing Inspection

1. Clean the camshaft in solvent and dry thoroughly. Lubricate the bearings with engine oil.

2. Rotate the cam in the direction shown in **Figure 30**. The cam should only rotate in the direction shown. If the decompressor rotates in the opposite direction, replace the assembly.

3. Inspect the cam lobes for scoring or damage.

4. Measure the cam lobe height (**Figure 31**) with a micrometer, then check the measurements against the specifications in **Table 2**. Replace the camshaft if it is not within the service limit. A camshaft can be excessively worn even though it may not show visual signs of wear.

5. Inspect the oil holes in each cam lobe for debris. Clean if necessary.

6. Turn each camshaft bearing (**Figure 32**) and check for roughness and excessive play. Replace the bearing if either condition exists.

Cam Chain Tensioner Inspection

Measure the tensioner spring and push rod to determine if they are within their service limits.

1. Measure the outside diameter of the push rod at the two locations shown in **Figure 33**. Record the measurements.

2. Compare the measurements with the service limit in **Table 2**. If either measurement is less than the service limit, replace the push rod.

3. Inspect the rubber tip on the push rod. Replace the rod if it is broken or deteriorated.

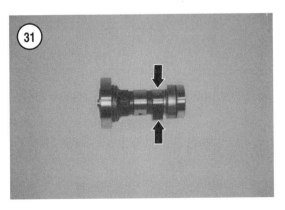

4. Measure the free length of the spring (**Figure 34**). Place the spring on a table and measure the overall length.

5. Compare the measurement with the service limit in **Table 2**. If the measurement is less than the service limit, replace the spring.

Camshaft Sprocket and Chain Inspection

1. Inspect the camshaft sprocket teeth (**Figure 35**) for wear or other damage. The profile of each tooth should be symmetrical. If the sprocket is worn, replace the cam chain and all sprockets, including crankshaft sprocket, as a set.

2. Inspect the cam chain as follows:
   a. Check the fit on the cam sprocket. The chain should completely seat between the sprocket teeth and not have a tendency to slide up the teeth.
   b. The chain should have no excessive play between the links. This indicates worn rollers and pins. If the chain is worn, replace the cam chain and both sprockets, including crankshaft sprocket, as a set.

Rocker Arm and Shaft Inspection

During the inspection of the rocker arms and rocker shafts, do not intermix the parts. Inspect one set of parts at a time, then return them to their plastic bag until reassembly.

1. Inspect the contact surfaces on each rocker arm (A, **Figure 36**) for wear, scratches or other damage. Replace the rocker arms if necessary.

2. Measure the rocker arm bore (B, **Figure 36**) with an inside micrometer. Record the measurement. Refer to **Table 2** to determine if the rocker arm bore is within the service limit. Replace the rocker arm if necessary.

3. Inspect the rocker arm shaft (C, **Figure 36**) for wear, scoring or other damage. Replace it if necessary.

4. Measure the outside diameter of the rocker arm shaft with a micrometer. Record the measurement. Refer to **Table 2** to determine if the rocker arm shaft is within the service limit. Replace the shaft if necessary.

5. Calculate the rocker arm-to-rocker arm shaft clearance as follows:

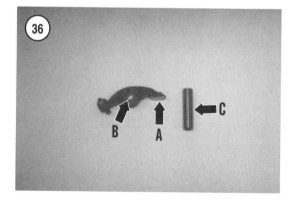

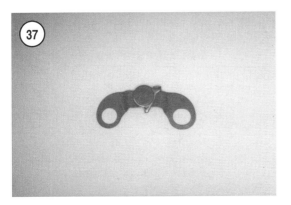

a. Subtract the rocker arm shaft diameter from the rocker arm bore diameter. Compare the result with the service limit in **Table 2**.

b. Replace the rocker arm and/or rocker arm shaft if the clearance meets or exceeds the service limit.

6. Inspect the stopper plate (**Figure 37**) for cracks, wear or other damage. Replace if necessary.

Camshaft and Rocker Arm Installation

1. Inspect the cylinder head and ensure that all bores and surfaces are clean (**Figure 38**).

2. Lubricate all bores and shafts (**Figure 39**) with engine oil.

3. Install the camshaft (**Figure 29**), positioning the cam so the cam lobes are facing down.

4. Position the stopper plate in the head, making sure the tab at the top of the plate points out (**Figure 28**).

5. Position the exhaust rocker arm in the head (**Figure 27**).

6. Install the exhaust rocker arm shaft (**Figure 40**), passing it through the stopper plate and rocker arm.

7. Repeat Steps 4 and 5 for the intake rocker and rocker shaft.

8. Install the cylinder head as described in this chapter.

VALVES AND VALVE COMPONENTS

Solvent Test

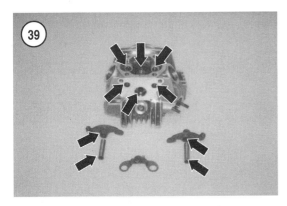

A solvent test is performed with the valve assembly in the cylinder head. The test can determine if valves are fully seating, and expose undetected cracks in the cylinder head.

1. Remove the cylinder head as described in this chapter.

2. Check that the combustion chamber is dry and the valves are seated.

3. Support the cylinder head so the exhaust port faces up.

4. Pour solvent or kerosene into the exhaust port as shown in **Figure 41**.

5. Inspect the combustion chamber for leakage around the valve.

6. Repeat Steps 3-5 for the intake port and valve.

7. Leakage can be caused by:

a. A worn or damaged valve face.

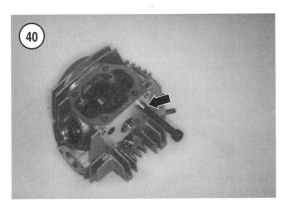

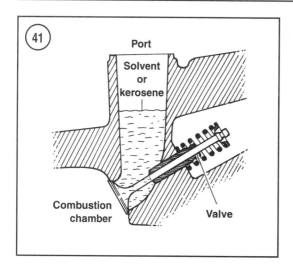

b. A worn or damaged valve seat in the cylinder head.

c. A bent valve stem.

d. A crack in the combustion chamber.

Valve Removal

Refer to **Figure 42**.

1. Remove the cylinder head as described in this chapter.

2. Perform the solvent test on the intake and exhaust valves as described in this section.

3. Remove the rocker assembly and camshaft as described in this chapter.

4. Install a valve spring compressor (part No. 07757-0010000 or equivalent) and attachment (part No. 07959-KM30101) over the valve assembly (**Figure 43**). Fit the tool squarely over the valve head and spring seat.

5. Tighten the compressor until the valve keepers are free. Lift the keepers from the valve stem.

CAUTION
Do not overtighten and compress the valve springs. This can result in loss of valve spring tension.

6. Slowly relieve the pressure on the valve spring and remove the compressor from the head.

7. Remove the spring collar.

8. Remove the inner and outer valve springs.

9. Inspect the valve stem for sharp and flared metal (**Figure 44**) around the groove for the keepers. Deburr the valve stem.

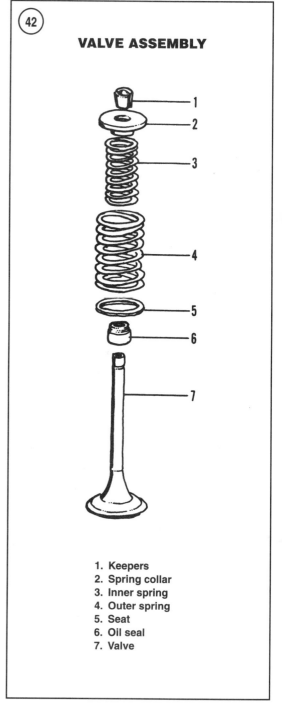

VALVE ASSEMBLY

1. Keepers
2. Spring collar
3. Inner spring
4. Outer spring
5. Seat
6. Oil seal
7. Valve

CAUTION
Failure to deburr the valve stem will result in damage to the valve guides.

10. Remove the valve from the cylinder head.

11. Remove the lower spring seat from the head.

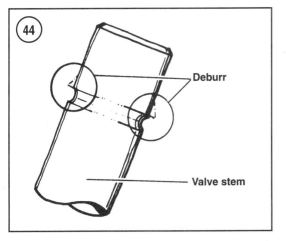

Deburr

Valve stem

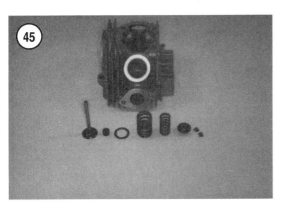

12. Remove the oil seal from the valve guide.

13. Place all valve components (**Figure 45**) removed in Steps 5-12 in a plastic bag.

CAUTION
When removing the valve assemblies, keep the intake and exhaust parts separated. Use separate plastic bags to mark and store the sets until they are inspected and ready for reassembly.

The valve assemblies should be reassembled in their original positions.

14. Repeat Steps 5-13 for the remaining valve assembly.

Valve Component Inspection

During the inspection of the valve assemblies, do not intermix the sets of parts (**Figure 45**). After each part is inspected, return it to its plastic bag until reassembly.

Refer to the troubleshooting chart (**Figure 46**) when inspecting the valve assemblies.

1. Clean each valve assembly in solvent.

CAUTION
The valve seating surface is critical and must not be damaged. Do not scrape on the seating surface or place the valve where it could roll off the work surface.

2. Inspect the perimeter of each valve (**Figure 47**). Check the edge and seating surface for burning or other damage. If the valve head appears uniform and other valve measurements are acceptable, the valve can be lapped as described in this chapter and reused. If the valve contact surface is uneven, replace the valve.

3. Inspect each valve stem for wear and roughness. Measure each valve stem diameter with a micrometer (**Figure 48**). Record the measurement. Refer to **Table 2** to determine if the diameter is within the service limit. Replace the valve if it is not within the service limit.

4. Clean the valve guides so they are free of all carbon and varnish. Use solvent and a stiff, narrow, spiral brush.

5. If using a small hole gauge and a micrometer, perform the following steps to measure each valve guide. If the proper measuring equipment is not available, go to Step 6.

    a. Measure each valve guide (A, **Figure 49**) at the top, center and bottom. Record the measurements.

    b. Refer to **Table 2** to determine if the diameters are within the service limit. Replace the guide if it is not within the service limit. See *Valve Guide Replacement* in this chapter.

(46)

VALVE TROUBLESHOOTING

Valve deposits

Check:
- Worn valve guide
- Carbon buildup from incorrect engine tuning
- Carbon buildup from incorrect carburetor adjustment
- Dirty or gummed fuel
- Dirty engine oil

Valve sticking

Check:
- Worn valve guide
- Bent valve stem
- Deposits collected on valve stem
- Valve burning or overheating

Valve burning

Check:
- Valve sticking
- Cylinder head warped
- Valve seat distorted
- Valve clearance incorrect
- Incorrect valve spring
- Valve spring worn
- Worn valve seat
- Carbon buildup in engine
- Engine ignition and/or carburetor adjustments incorrect

Valve seat/face wear

Check:
- Valve burning
- Incorrect valve clearance
- Abrasive material on valve face and seat

Valve damage

Check:
- Valve burning
- Incorrectly installed or serviced valve guides
- Incorrect valve clearance
- Incorrect valve, spring seat and retainer assembly
- Detonation caused by incorrect ignition and/or carburetor adjustments

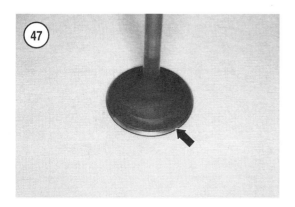

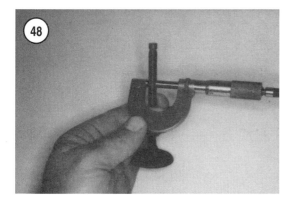

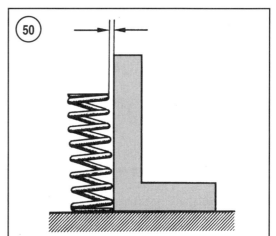

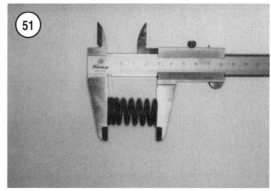

c. Subtract the valve stem measurement made in Step 3 from the largest valve guide measurement in Step 5a. Refer to **Table 2** to determine if the valve stem-to-valve guide clearance is within the service limit. If the parts are not within the service limit, replace the part(s).

6. If the proper gauges are not available to measure the valve guides, perform the following procedure.

a. Insert the valve into its guide.

b. With the valve head off the seat, rock the valve stem in the valve guide. Rock the valve in several directions, checking for any per-

ceptible play. If movement is detected, the valve guide and/or valve stem is worn.

c. Take the valves and cylinder head to a dealership or machine shop and have the parts accurately measured to determine which part(s) should be replaced.

7. Check the inner and outer valve springs as follows:

a. Visually check each spring for damage.

b. Stand each spring vertically, then place a square next to the spring to check for distortion or tilt (**Figure 50**).

c. Measure each valve spring length with a vernier caliper (**Figure 51**). Refer to **Table 2** to determine if the springs are within the service limit. If a spring requires replacement, replace both springs as a set.

8. Inspect the valve spring seat and keepers for wear or damage.

9. Inspect the valve seats (B, **Figure 49**) to determine if they must be reconditioned.

a. Clean and dry the valve seat and valve mating area with contact cleaner.

b. Lightly coat the valve seat with blue machinists' marking compound.

c. Install the appropriate valve into the guide, then *lightly* tap the valve against the seat so the marking compound transfers to the valve contact area.

d. Remove the valve from the guide and use a vernier caliper to measure the imprinted valve seat width (**Figures 52** and **53**) at several locations. Refer to **Table 2** to determine if the seat width is within the service limit. Regrind the valve seat as described under *Valve Seat Reconditioning* in this chapter if any width measurement exceeds the service limit, the width of the seat is not consistent, or if the valve contact-area is not centered. Always regrind or replace a valve seat that is burned or worn.

10. Clean all marking compound residue from the valves and seats.

Valve Guide Replacement

Read the entire procedure before attempting valve guide replacement. Steps requiring heat application must be performed quickly and with the correct tools. The following Honda tools, or equivalents, are required to remove and install the valve guides:

a. Valve guide remover (part No. 07942-MA60000).

b. Valve guide reamer, 5 mm (part No. 07984-MA60001 or 07984-MA6000C).

NOTE
Prior to the installation process, place the new valve guides in the freezer. This will slightly shrink the guides and ease installation.

NOTE
Install new O-rings on the new valve guides.

1. Place the cylinder head in a shop oven or on a hot plate set at 100-150° C (212-300° F). This will aid in removing the valve guides since they are an interference fit in the cylinder head.

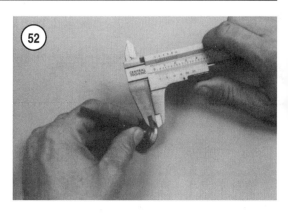

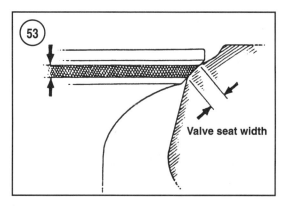

Valve seat width

CAUTION
Do not use any type of torch to heat the cylinder head. The uneven heating may warp the cylinder head.

2. After the head is heated, remove it from the oven or hot plate. Place the head on wooden blocks with the combustion chamber facing *up*.

WARNING
The head will be very hot. Wear welding gloves or similar insulated gloves in the following procedure.

3. While the head is still hot, insert the valve guide remover into the guide, then drive the guides out of the head (**Figure 54**).

4. Allow the head to cool.

5. Remove the valve guide O-rings from the head.

6. Inspect and clean the valve guide bores.

7. Reheat the cylinder head to 100-150° C (212-300° F).

8. After the head is heated, remove the head from the oven or hot plate. Place the head on wooden blocks with the combustion chamber facing *down*.

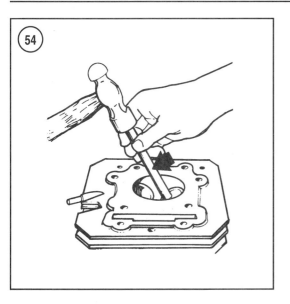

9. Remove the new valve guides from the freezer and install a new O-ring on each guide.

10. Align the valve guide in the bore. Insert the valve guide remover into the guide and drive the guide squarely into the head until it is seated.

NOTE
Check that the O-ring is seated and not pinched below the valve guide.

11. Allow the head to cool.

12. Ream the valve guides as follows:

  a. Place the head combustion-side *down*.

  b. Coat the valve guide and valve guide reamer with cutting oil.

  c. With a clockwise motion of the reamer, start the reamer into the guide.

CAUTION
*Always keep the reamer rotating in a **clockwise** direction while inserting and withdrawing the reamer from the guide. Rotating the reamer in a counterclockwise direction will damage the valve guide and it will no longer be usable. Keep the reamer square within the valve guide and apply even pressure. Keep rotating the reamer **clockwise** during the entire procedure.*

  d. Slowly work the reamer through the guide, periodically adding cutting oil.

  e. As the reamer passes into the combustion chamber, maintain the clockwise motion and work the reamer back out of the guide.

  f. Clean the reamed guide, then measure the inside diameter with a small hole gauge and micrometer. The measurement must be within the specifications listed in **Table 2**.

13. Repeat Step 12 for the other valve guide.

14. Clean the cylinder head and guides with solvent to remove all metal particles and residue. Dry the assembly with compressed air.

15. Apply engine oil to the valve guides to prevent corrosion.

16. Reface the valve seats with a 45° cutter after replacing valve guides. Reface the valve seats as described under *Valve Seat Reconditioning* in this chapter.

Valve Seat Reconditioning

Before reconditioning the valve seats, the seats should be inspected and measured as described under *Valve Component Inspection* in this chapter.

The following tools are required to cut the valve seats.

  a. Valve seat cutters (32°, 45° and 60°). See a Honda dealership for part numbers.

  b. A vernier caliper.

  c. Machinists' compound.

  d. A valve lapping tool.

NOTE
Follow the manufacturer's instructions when using the valve seat cutters.

CAUTION
Work slowly and make light cuts when reconditioning valve seats. Overcutting the valve seats will allow the valves to recede into the cylinder head, reducing valve adjustment tolerance. If overcutting is excessive, it will not be possible to adjust the valves and the cylinder head will have to be replaced.

1. Fit the 45° cutter onto the valve tool and lightly cut the seat to remove roughness.

2. Measure the valve seat width with a vernier caliper. Record the measurement and use as a reference point when making the remaining cuts.

3. Fit the 32° cutter onto the valve tool and lightly cut the seat to remove a fourth of the existing valve seat (**Figure 55**).

CAUTION
The 32° cutter removes material rapidly. Work carefully and check the progress often.

4. Fit the 60° cutter onto the valve tool and lightly cut the seat to remove the lower fourth of the existing valve seat (**Figure 56**).
5. Measure the valve seat width with a vernier caliper.
6. Fit the 45° cutter onto the valve tool and cut the seat to the width specified in **Table 2**.
7. Clean the valve seat and valve mating areas.
8. Lightly coat the valve seat with machinists' compound.
9. Install the appropriate valve into the guide, then use a lapping tool to rotate the valve against the seat.
10. Remove the valve and evaluate where the seat has contacted the valve (**Figure 57**).

   a. The seat contact area should be in the center of the valve face area.
   b. If the contact area is too high on the valve face, lower the seat using the 32° cutter.
   c. If the contact area is too low on the valve face, raise the seat using the 60° cutter.
   d. If substep b or c is performed, use the 45° cutter to reestablish the proper seat width.

11. When the seat width is correct, lap the valve as described in this chapter.

Valve Lapping

Valve lapping restores accurate sealing between the valve seat and valve contact area without machining. Perform lapping on valves and valve seats that have been inspected and are within specifications. Also perform lapping on valves and valve seats that have been reconditioned.
1. Lightly coat the valve face with fine-grade lapping compound.
2. Insert the valve into the head.
3. Wet the suction cup on the lapping tool and press it onto the head of the valve.
4. Lap the valve to the seat by rotating the stick back and forth between your hands. Every 5 to 10 seconds, rotate the valve 180° and continue to lap the valve into the seat.

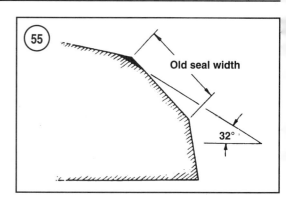

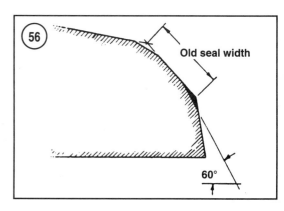

5. Frequently inspect the valve seat. Stop lapping the valve when the valve seat is smooth, even and highly polished.
6. Clean the valves and cylinder head in solvent and remove all lapping compound. Any abrasive remaining in the head will cause premature wear and damage to other engine parts.
7. After the valves are installed in the head, perform a *Solvent Test* as described in this chapter. If leakage is detected, remove that valve and repeat the lapping process.

Valve Installation

Perform the following procedure for each set of valve components. All components should be clean and dry.
1. Coat the valve stem with molydenum disulfide grease.
2. Insert the valves into the cylinder head (**Figure 58**). Hold the valve in place.
3. Install the lower spring seat into the head (**Figure 59**).
4. Install a new oil seal on the valve guide. Slide the seal down the valve stem and onto the guide.

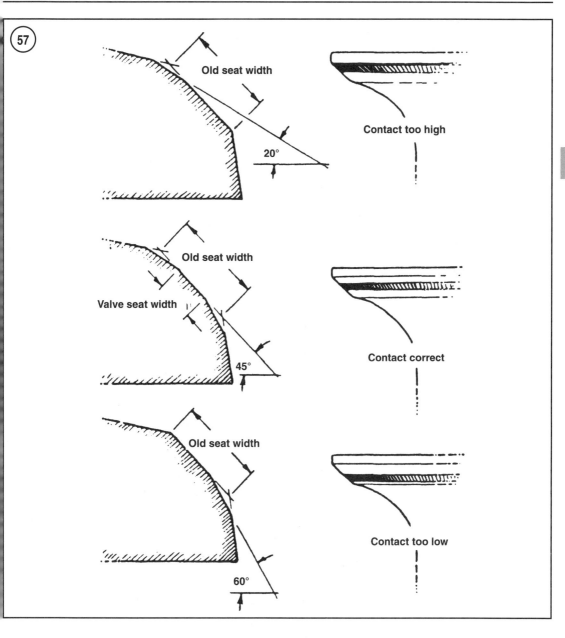

5. Install the inner and outer valve springs (**Figure 60**).

6. Install the upper spring collar (**Figure 61**).

7. Install a valve spring compressor (part No. 07757-0010000 or equivalent) and attachment (part No. 07959-KM30101) over the valve assembly (**Figure 43**). Fit the tool squarely over the valve head and spring seat.

8. Tighten the compressor until the upper spring collar is compressed enough to install the valve keepers (**Figure 62**).

CAUTION
Do not overtighten and compress the valve springs. This can result in loss of valve spring tension.

9. Insert the keepers around the groove in the valve stem (**Figure 63**).

10. Slowly relieve the pressure on the valve spring and remove the compressor from the head.

11. Tap the end of the valve stem with a soft mallet to ensure that the keepers are seated in the valve stem groove.

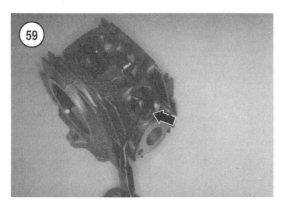

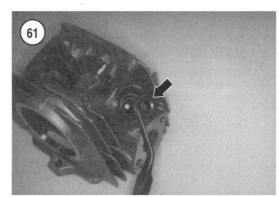

12. Perform the solvent test on the intake and exhaust valves as described in this chapter.

13. Install the cylinder head as described in this chapter.

CYLINDER

The cylinder head assembly, cylinder and piston can be removed with the engine mounted in the frame. This procedure shows the engine removed for clarity. Read all procedures completely before attempting a repair. Refer to **Table 3** for torque specifications. General torque specifications are listed for components not specifically called out.

Cylinder Removal

1. Remove the cylinder head as described in this chapter.

2. For 1999 and 2000 models, remove the bolts (A, **Figure 64**) from the air injection tube (B). Remove the tube and O-ring (C) from the cylinder.

3. Remove the dowel pins (A, **Figure 65**), O-ring (B) and the collar beneath the O-ring.

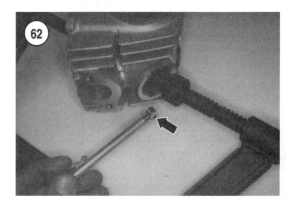

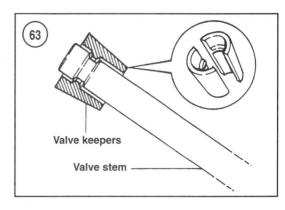

Valve keepers

Valve stem

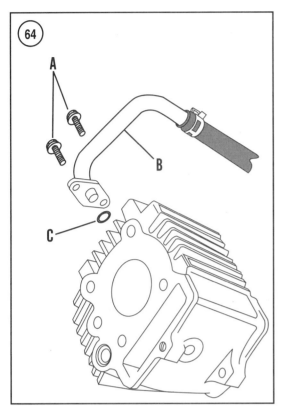

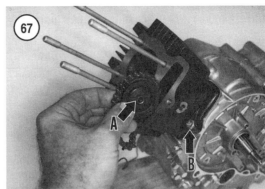

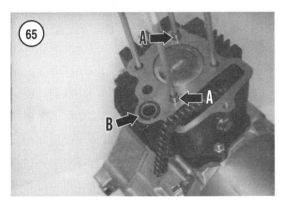

4. Loosen the guide roller pin bolt (**Figure 66**). Grasp the guide roller (A, **Figure 67**) and lift it from the cylinder while removing the bolt and washer.

5. Remove the cylinder mounting bolt (B, **Figure 67**).

6. Loosen the cylinder by tapping around the base.

7. Slowly remove the cylinder from the crankcase, routing the cam chain through the chain tunnel. Secure the cam chain after it passes through the cylinder.

8. Remove and discard the base gasket.

9. Remove the dowel pins (A, **Figure 68**) and O-ring (B).

Cylinder Inspection

1. Remove all gasket residue from the top and bottom cylinder block surfaces.

2. Wash the cylinder in solvent and dry with compressed air.

3. Inspect the cylinder bore for obvious scoring or gouges that indicate an overbore is required.

4. Measure the cylinder for wear, taper and out of round. Measure the inside diameter of the cylinder

with a bore gauge or inside micrometer (**Figure 69**) as follows:

a. Measure the cylinder at three points along the bore axis (**Figure 70**). At each point, measure in line (X measurement) with the piston pin, and 90° to the pin (Y measurement). Record and identify the six measurements so the cylinder checks can be made.

b. For *cylinder inside diameter,* use the largest measurement recorded (X or Y) and compare it to the specifications and service limit in **Table 2**. If the cylinder bore is not within the service limit, rebore the cylinder.

c. For *cylinder out of round,* determine the difference between the X and Y measurement for each of the three measurement points. Compare the results to the service limit in **Table 2**. If any of the cylinder bore measurements are not within the service limit, rebore the cylinder.

d. For *cylinder taper,* find the difference between the largest and smallest X measurements. Find the difference between the largest and smallest Y measurements. Compare the difference to the service limits in **Table 2**. If the cylinder bore is not within the service limit, rebore the cylinder.

5. Check the cylinder for warp as follows:

a. Lay a machinist's straightedge across the top of the cylinder as shown in **Figure 71**.

b. Try to insert a flat feeler gauge between the straightedge and the machined surface of the cylinder. If clearance exists, record the measurement.

c. Repeat substeps a and b at several locations, placing the straightedge parallel and diagonally across the cylinder.

d. Compare the measurements to the warp service limit listed in **Table 2**. If the clearance is not within the service limit, it may be serviceable by a dealership or machine shop. If not, replace the cylinder.

6. Take the cylinder to a dealership or machine shop to have the required machine work performed. If the cylinder is to be bored and fitted with the next size piston and rings, take the piston to the shop so the cylinder can be bored to match the piston size.

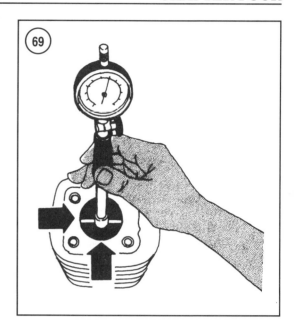

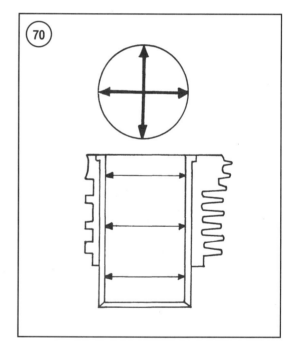

NOTE
If the cylinder is within all service limits, and the current piston and rings are reusable, do not deglaze or hone the cylinder. Do not remove the carbon ridge at the top of the cylinder bore. Removal of the buildup will promote oil consumption. The cylinder should only be washed as described in Step 7.

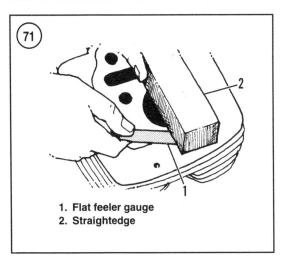

1. Flat feeler gauge
2. Straightedge

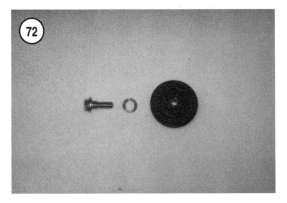

7. Wash the cylinder in hot, soapy water after inspection and service to remove all fine grit and material/residue left from machine operations. Check cleanliness by passing a clean, white cloth over the bore. No residue should be evident. When the cylinder is thoroughly clean and dry, lightly coat the cylinder bore with oil to prevent corrosion. Wrap the cylinder in plastic until engine reassembly.

CAUTION
Wash the cylinder in hot, soapy water. Solvents will not remove the fine grit left in the cylinder. This grit will cause premature wear of the rings and cylinder.

8. Inspect the cam chain guide roller and bolt (**Figure 72**). Replace the roller and bolt if the roller is worn/damaged, or if the bushing has excessive play when it is mounted on the bolt.

9. Perform any service to the piston assembly before installing the cylinder.

Cylinder Installation

1. Check that all gasket residue is removed from all mating surfaces. All cylinder and piston surfaces should be clean.

2. Install the dowel pins onto the crankcase (A, **Figure 73**).

3. Install a new, lubricated O-ring onto the crankcase (B, **Figure 73**).

4. Install a new base gasket onto the crankcase (C, **Figure 73**).

5. Lubricate the following components with engine oil.

   a. Piston and rings.
   b. Piston pin and small end of connecting rod.
   c. Cylinder bore.

6. Support the piston as shown in **Figure 74**.

NOTE
Fabricate a piston holding fixture. See Figure 75.

7. Check that the piston ring gaps are staggered on the piston as shown in **Figure 76**.

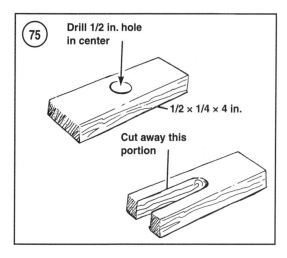

Drill 1/2 in. hole in center

1/2 × 1/4 × 4 in.

Cut away this portion

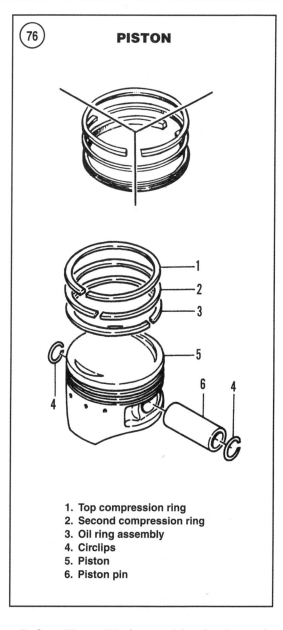

PISTON

1. Top compression ring
2. Second compression ring
3. Oil ring assembly
4. Circlips
5. Piston
6. Piston pin

8. Lower the cylinder over the crankcase studs, routing the cam chain through the chain tunnel. As the piston enters the cylinder, compress each ring so it can enter the cylinder. When the bottom ring is in the cylinder, remove the holding fixture and lower the cylinder onto the crankcase. Secure the cam chain so it cannot fall into the engine.

9. Install the cylinder mounting bolt (B, **Figure 67**) and torque to the specification listed in **Table 3**.

10. Hold the cam chain guide roller in the chain tunnel, then insert and torque the pin bolt (**Figure 66**). The guide roller must be between the lengths of cam chain.

11. For 1999 and 2000 models, place a new O-ring (C, **Figure 64**) on the air injection tube, then bolt into place.

12. Install the dowel pins (A, **Figure 65**), O-ring (B) and collar beneath the O-ring.

13. Install the cylinder head as described in this chapter.

PISTON AND PISTON RINGS

The piston is made of aluminum alloy and fitted with three rings. The piston is held on the small end of the connecting rod by a chrome-plated, steel piston pin. The pin is a precision fit in the piston and rod, and is held in place by circlips.

As each component of the piston assembly is cleaned and measured, record and identify all measurements. The measurements will be referred to when calculating clearances and checking wear limits.

Refer to **Figure 76** when servicing the piston, pin and rings in the following section.

Piston Removal

1. Remove the cylinder as described in this chapter.

2. Before removing the piston, hold the rod and try to rock the piston from side to side (**Figure 77**). If a rocking motion is detected, this indicates wear on either the piston pin, pin bore, rod bushing, or on any combination of the three parts. Carefully inspect them to determine which parts should be re-

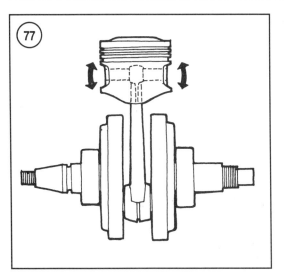

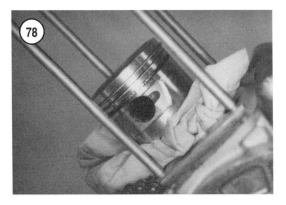

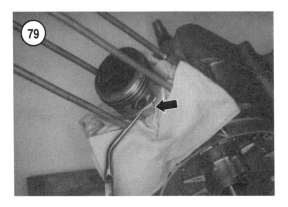

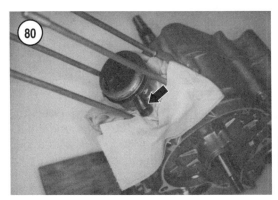

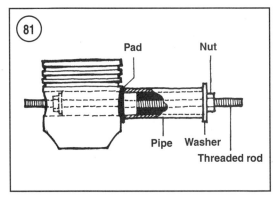

4. Remove the circlips from the piston pin bore (**Figure 79**). Discard the circlips.

NOTE
Install new circlips during assembly.

5. Press the piston pin out of the piston by hand (**Figure 80**). If the pin is tight, a simple removal tool can be made. See **Figure 81**.

CAUTION
Do not attempt to drive the pin out with a hammer and drift. The piston and connecting rod assembly will likely be damaged.

6. Lift the piston off the connecting rod.
7. Inspect the piston and piston pin as described in this chapter.

Piston Inspection

1. Remove the piston rings as described in this chapter.
2. Clean the carbon from the piston crown (**Figure 82**) using a soft scraper and solvent. Do not use

placed. Do not confuse the normal sliding motion of the piston with a rocking motion that indicates wear.

3. Place clean shop rags or paper towels around the connecting rod and in the cam chain tunnel (**Figure 78**). This will prevent the piston pin circlips from falling into the crankcase.

tools that can gouge or scratch the surface. This type of damage can cause hot spots on the piston when the engine is running.

3. Clean the piston pin bore, ring grooves and piston skirt. Clean the ring grooves with a soft brush, such as a toothbrush, or use a broken piston ring (**Figure 83**) to remove carbon and oil residue. Mild galling or discoloration can be polished off the piston skirt with fine emery cloth and oil. Use a piece of wire and compressed air to remove deposits from the oil control holes.

> *CAUTION*
> *Do not use a wire brush to clean the piston.*

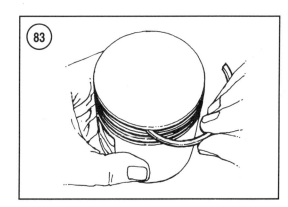

4. Inspect the piston crown for signs of wear or damage. If the piston is pitted, overheating is likely occurring. This can be caused by a lean fuel mixture and/or preignition. If damage is evident, determine the cause as described in Chapter Two.

5. Inspect the ring grooves for dents, nicks, cracks or other damage. The grooves should be square and uniform around the circumference of the piston. Inspect the top compression ring groove carefully. It receives less lubrication and is nearest the combustion temperatures. If the oil ring appears worn, or if the oil ring was difficult to remove, the piston has likely overheated and distorted. Replace the piston if any type of damage is detected.

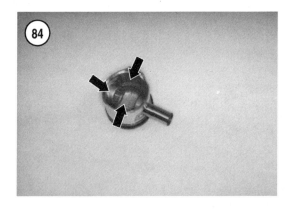

6. Inspect the piston skirt. If the skirt shows signs of severe galling or partial seizure (bits of metal imbedded in the skirt), replace the piston.

7. Inspect the interior of the piston (**Figure 84**). Check the crown, skirt, piston pin bores and bosses for cracks, wear and scoring. Check the grooves for cleanliness and damage. Replace the piston if necessary.

8. Measure the piston pin bores with a small hole gauge and micrometer. Measure each bore horizontally and vertically. Record the measurements. Compare the largest measurement to the specifications in **Table 2**.

9. Inspect the piston ring-to-ring groove clearance as described in *Piston Ring Inspection and Removal* in this chapter.

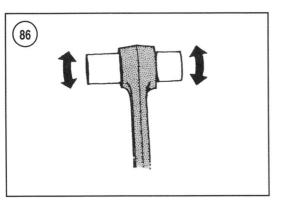

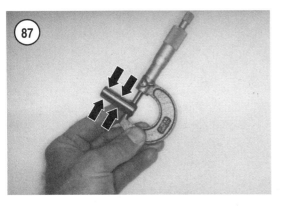

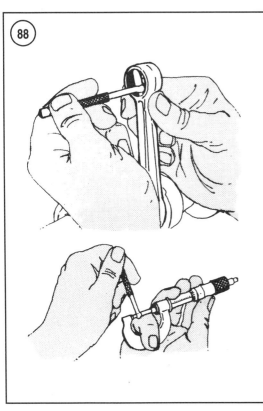

Piston Clearance Check

Determine the clearance between the piston and cylinder to determine if the parts can be reused. If parts do not fall within specification, bore the cylinder to match an oversize piston assembly. Clean and dry the piston and cylinder before measuring.

1. Measure the outside diameter of the piston. Measure 10 mm (3/8 in.) up from the bottom edge of the piston skirt and 90° to the direction of the piston pin (**Figure 85**). Record the measurement.

2. Determine clearance by subtracting the piston measurement from the largest cylinder measurement. If cylinder measurements have not been determined, refer to *Cylinder Inspection* in this chapter. If the clearance exceeds the specification in **Table 2**, the cylinder must be bored and fitted with an oversize piston assembly.

Piston Pin and Connecting Rod Inspection

1. Clean the piston pin in solvent, then dry.

2. Inspect the pin for chrome flaking, wear or discoloration from overheating.

3. Inspect the bore in the piston pin end of the connecting rod. Check for scoring, uneven wear, and discoloration from overheating.

4. Lubricate the piston and slide it into the connecting rod. Slowly rotate the pin and check for radial play (**Figure 86**). If play is detected, one or both of the parts are worn.

5. Determine the actual piston pin and connecting rod wear as follows:

    a. Measure the piston pin at both ends and the center (**Figure 87**) using a micrometer. Record the measurements. Replace the pin if any measurements exceed the service limit in **Table 2**.

    b. Measure the piston pin bore in the connecting rod with a small hole gauge and micrometer (**Figure 88**). Record the measurements. Replace the connecting rod if the measurement exceeds the service limit in **Table 2**.

    c. Determine the piston pin-to-connecting rod clearance. Subtract the *center* measurement made in substep a from the measurement made in substep b. Replace the part(s) that exceed the service limit in **Table 2**.

    d. Determine the piston pin-to-piston clearance. Subtract the smallest piston pin *end* measurement, made in substep b, from the largest piston pin bore measurement. This measurement is described in *Piston Inspection* in this chapter. Replace the part(s) that exceed the service limit listed in **Table 2**.

Piston Ring Inspection and Removal

Refer to **Figure 89** for ring identification.

1. Check the piston ring-to-ring groove clearance as follows:

   a. Clean the rings and grooves so accurate measurements can be made with a flat feeler gauge (**Figure 90**).

   b. Press the top ring into the groove, so the ring is nearly flush with the piston.

   c. Insert a flat feeler gauge between the ring and groove. Record the measurement. Repeat this step at other points around the piston. Replace the rings if any measurement exceeds the service limit in **Table 2**. If excessive clearance remains after new rings are installed, replace the piston.

   d. Repeat substeps b and c for the second compression ring.

2. Remove the top ring with a ring expander (**Figure 91**) or by hand (**Figure 92**). Spread the ring only enough to clear the piston. Repeat this step for the second compression ring.

> *WARNING*
> *Piston ring edges are sharp. Be careful when handling.*

> *CAUTION*
> *Piston rings are brittle. Do not overspread rings when removing.*

> *NOTE*
> *As each compression ring is removed, identify the ring and check that the **top** mark is visible. The top ring should be marked with the letter **R**. The second ring should be marked with **R** or **RN**.*

3. Remove the oil ring assembly by first removing the top rail (**Figure 93**), followed by the bottom rail. Remove the expander spacer last.

4. Clean and inspect the piston as described under *Piston Inspection* in this chapter.

5. Inspect the end gap of each ring as follows:

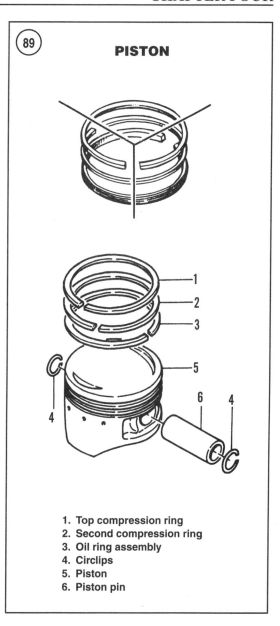

PISTON

1. Top compression ring
2. Second compression ring
3. Oil ring assembly
4. Circlips
5. Piston
6. Piston pin

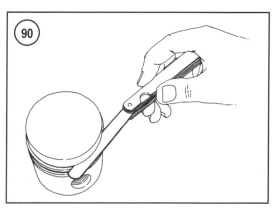

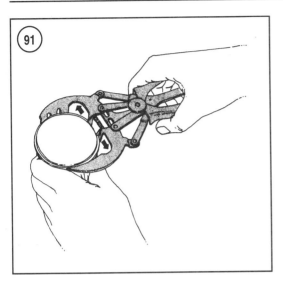

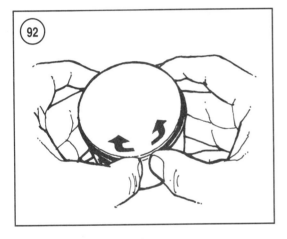

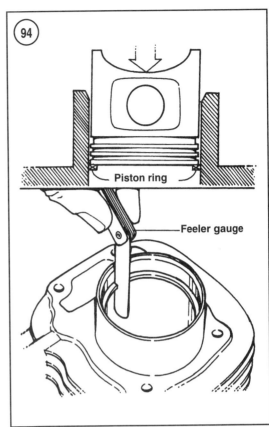

Piston ring

Feeler gauge

surement exceeds the service limit in **Table 2**. Always replace rings as a set. If installing new rings, gap the new rings after the cylinder has been serviced. If the new ring gap is too small, carefully widen the gap using a fine-cut file as shown in **Figure 95**. Work slow and measure the gap frequently.

NOTE
Measure only the ring rails of the oil control ring. It is not necessary to measure the expander spacer.

6. Rotate each ring around its piston groove and check for binding (**Figure 96**). Repair minor damage with a fine-cut file.

Piston Ring Installation

If installing new piston rings, hone or deglaze the cylinder to roughen and crosshatch the cylinder surface. The newly honed surface is important in controlling wear and lubrication of the new rings and will help them seat and seal properly. A dealership

a. Insert a ring into the bottom of the cylinder. Square the ring to the cylinder wall, using the piston as shown in **Figure 94**.

b. Measure the end gap with a feeler gauge (**Figure 94**). Replace all the rings if any gap mea-

or machine shop can hone the cylinder for a minimal cost. Refer to *Cylinder Inspection* in this chapter to determine if the cylinder should be honed.

1. Check that the piston and rings are clean and dry.

2. Install the rings into their respective grooves as follows:

> *NOTE*
> *Install the oil control ring assembly first, followed by the middle and top rings.*

> *WARNING*
> *Piston ring edges are sharp. Be careful when handling.*

> *CAUTION*
> *Piston rings are brittle. Do not over spread rings when installing. Install rings with a ring expander (**Figure 91**) or by hand (**Figure 92**). Spread rings only enough to clear the piston.*

    a. Install the oil ring expander spacer into the bottom groove.

    b. Install the two oil ring rails into the bottom groove; one above and one below the expander spacer.

    c. Install the black middle ring, checking that the top mark **R** or **RN** is facing up.

    d. Install the chrome top ring, checking that the top mark **R** is facing up.

3. Check that all rings rotate freely in their grooves.

Piston Installation

1. Install the piston rings onto the piston as described in this chapter.

2. Check that all parts are clean and ready to be installed (**Figure 97**). Use new circlips when installing the piston.

> *CAUTION*
> *Never install used circlips. Severe engine damage could occur. Circlips fatigue and distort when they are removed, even though they appear reusable.*

3. Install a new circlip into the end of the pin boss. Rotate the circlip in the groove until the end gap (A, **Figure 98**) is away from the piston cutout (B).

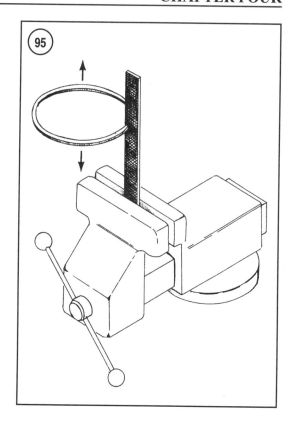

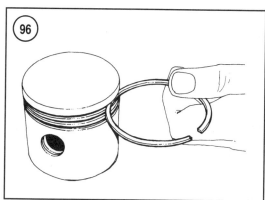

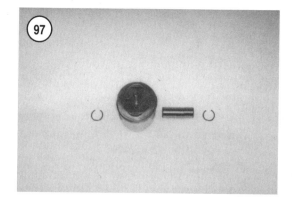

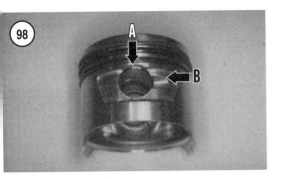

4. Lubricate the following components with an oil and molydenum disulfide mixture in a ratio of 1:1.
  a. Piston pin.
  b. Piston bores.
  c. Connecting rod bore.
5. Start the piston pin into the open pin bore. Place the piston over the connecting rod so the **IN** mark on the piston crown (**Figure 99**) faces the intake, or rear, side of the engine.

> *CAUTION*
> *The piston must be installed correctly to accommodate piston pin offset. Installing the piston backwards will cause rapid wear or seizure.*

6. Align the piston with the rod, then slide the pin through the rod and into the other piston bore.
7. Install the other new circlip into the end of the pin boss. Rotate the circlip in the groove until the end gap (A, **Figure 98**) is away from the piston cutout (B).
8. Install the cylinder as described in this chapter.

Table 1 ENGINE SPECIFICATIONS

Engine type	4-stroke, chain-driven SOHC
Engine displacement	85.8 cc (5.23 cu. in.)
Bore and stroke	47.0 × 49.5 mm (1.85 × 1.95 in.)
Compression ratio	9.2:1
Valve timing (at 1 mm lift)	
(1993-1998)	
Intake valve open	7.5° BTDC
Intake valve closes	12.5° ABDC
Exhaust valve opens	22.5° BBDC
Exhaust valve closes	2.5° ATDC
Valve timing (at 1 mm lift)	
(1999-2000)	
Intake valve opens	5° BTDC
Intake valve closes	15° ABDC
Exhaust valve opens	35° BBDC
Exhaust valve closes	7.5° ATDC

Table 2 ENGINE SERVICE SPECIFICATIONS

	New mm (in.)	Service limit mm (in.)
Cylinder compression	1226 kPa (178 psi)	–
Cylinder head warpage limit	–	0.05 (0.002)
Camshaft lobe height (1993-1998)		
Intake	27.865-28.025 (1.0970-1.1033)	27.55 (1.085)
Exhaust	25.996-26.156 (1.0237-1.0297)	25.69 (1.011)
Camshaft lobe height (1999-2000)		
Intake	26.581-26.701 (1.0464-1.0512)	27.55 (1.085)
Exhaust	26.348-26.468 (1.0373-1.0420)	25.69 (1.011)
Valve clearance		
Intake and exhaust	0.05 (0.002)	–
Valve stem diameter		
Intake	4.975-4.990 (0.1959-0.1965)	4.92 (0.194)
Exhaust	4.955-4.970 (0.1951-0.1956)	4.92 (0.194)
Valve guide inner diameter		
Intake and exhaust	5.000-5.012 (0.1968-0.1973)	5.03 (0.198)
Valve stem-to-guide clearance		
Intake	0.010-0.037 (0.0004-0.0014)	0.08 (0.003)
Exhaust	0.030-0.057 (0.0011-0.0022)	0.10 (0.004)
Valve seat width	1.0 (0.04)	1.6 (0.06)
Valve spring free length		
Inner intake and exhaust	32.41 (1.276)	31.2 (1.23)
Outer intake and exhaust	35.25 (1.388)	34.0 (1.34)
Rocker arm bore		
Intake and exhaust	10.000-10.015 (0.3937-0.3943)	10.10 (0.398)
Rocker arm shaft outer diameter		
Intake and exhaust	9.978-9.987 (0.3928-0.3931)	9.91 (0.39)
Rocker arm-to-rocker arm shaft clearance	0.013-0.037 (0.0005-0.0014)	0.08 (0.031)
Cam chain tensioner		
Spring free length	111.7 (4.40)	100.0 (3.94)
Push rod outer diameter	11.985-12.0 (0.4718-0.4724)	11.94 (0.470)
Cylinder		
Inside diameter	47.005-47.015 (1.8505-1.8509)	47.050 (1.852)
Out of round	–	0.10 (0.004)
Taper	–	0.10 (0.004)
Warpage limit	–	0.05 (0.002)
Connecting rod		
Small end ID	13.016-13.034 (0.5124-0.5131)	13.05 (0.514)

(continued)

Table 2 ENGINE SERVICE SPECIFICATIONS (continued)

	New mm (in.)	Service limit mm (in.)
Piston		
Mark direction	IN facing intake side	
Outside diameter	46.980-46.995	46.90
	(1.8496-1.8501)	(1.846)
Outside diameter measurement point	10 (0.4) from bottom	–
Piston to cylinder clearance	0.010-0.035	0.15
	(0.0004-0.0014)	(0.006)
Piston pin bore	13.002-13.008	13.055
	(0.5118-0.5121)	(0.514)
Piston pin		
Pin diameter	12.994-13.0	12.98
	(0.5115-0.5118)	(0.511)
Piston pin-to-piston clearance	0.002-0.014	0.075
	(0.0001-0.0006)	(0.003)
Piston pin-to-connecting rod clearance	0.016-0.040	0.07
	(0.0006-0.0015)	(0.002)
Piston ring-to-ring groove clearance		
Top ring and second ring	0.015-0.050	0.12
	(0.0005-0.0020)	(0.005)
Piston ring end gap		
Top ring and second ring	0.10-0.30	0.50
	(0.004-0.012)	(0.02)
Oil ring (side rails)	0.20-0.70	1.0
	(0.008-0.028)	(0.04)
Piston ring top mark identification		
Top ring (chrome)	R	–
Second ring (black)	R or RN	–

Table 3 ENGINE TORQUE SPECIFICATIONS

	N•m	in.-lb.	ft.-lb.
Cylinder head cover cap nut	14	–	10
Cylinder head nuts	10	88	–
Cylinder bolt	10	88	–
Cam sprocket bolt	9	80	–
Cam chain tensioner bolt	24	–	18
Cam chain guide roller pin bolt	10	88	–
Spark plug	12	106	–
Timing hole cap	3	27	–
Valve adjusting hole cap	12	106	–
Valve adjusting nut	9	80	–
5 mm bolt and nut	5	44	–
6 mm bolt and nut	10	88	–
8 mm bolt and nut	22	–	16

CHAPTER FIVE

ENGINE LOWER END

This chapter describes service procedures for the following lower end components:

1. Recoil starter.
2. Drive sprocket.
3. Oil pump.
4. Crankcase.
5. Crankshaft and connecting rod.

Read this chapter before attempting repairs to the engine bottom end. Become familiar with the procedures, photos and illustrations to understand the skill and equipment required. Refer to Chapter One for tool usage and techniques.

CLEANLINESS

Prior to removing and disassembling the engine, clean the engine and frame with degreaser. The disassembly job will be easier and there will be less chance of dirt entering the assemblies. Keep the work environment as clean as possible. Store parts and assemblies in well-marked plastic bags and containers. Keep reconditioned parts wrapped until reassembly.

SERVICING ENGINE IN FRAME

The only time the engine must be removed from the frame is when the transmission or crankshaft needs service. In order to service these two assemblies, all components attached to the crankcase must be removed so the crankcase halves can be separated. The following components can be removed or serviced while the engine is mounted in the frame. Refer to the listed chapters for removal, inspection and installation procedures.

1. For the cylinder head, refer to Chapter Four.
2. For the cylinder block and piston, refer to Chapter Four.
3. For the external gearshift mechanism, refer to Chapter Six.
4. For the clutch assembly, refer to Chapter Six.
5. For the recoil starter, refer to this chapter.
6. For the oil pump, refer to this chapter.

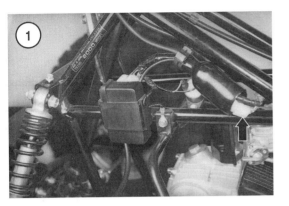

7. For the ignition stator and flywheel, refer to Chapter Nine.

8. For the drive sprocket, refer to this chapter.

SERVICING ENGINE OUT OF FRAME

The following removal and installation procedures outline the steps necessary to completely remove the engine from the frame to perform transmission or crankshaft service. Since the frame keeps the engine stabilized, it may be easier to remove many of the assemblies listed in *Servicing Engine In Frame* with the engine in the frame.

Throughout the procedure, refer to the appropriate chapter for removal, inspection and installation of specific assemblies.

Engine Removal/Installation

To remove the complete engine with a minimum number of steps and remove all subassemblies at the workbench, do not perform Steps 11,12, and 15-18 at this time.

1. Park the vehicle on a clean, flat surface. Set the parking brake and place the transmission in neutral.

2. If possible, perform a compression test described in Chapter Three and leakdown test described in Chapter Two before dismantling the engine.

3. Drain the engine oil. See Chapter Three.

4. Remove the front fenders and rear fender mudguards. See Chapter Thirteen.

5. Remove the exhaust system. See Chapter Eight.

6. Remove the spark plug cap from the plug.

7. Disconnect the alternator and gear indicator wires (**Figure 1**).

8. Disconnect the crankcase breather tube from the top of the crankcase.

9. Remove the carburetor, fuel tank, intake manifold and air injection pipe (Chapter Eight).

10. Remove the footpegs.

11. Loosen the pinch bolt on the shifter (**Figure 2**), then remove the shifter.

12. Remove the recoil starter assembly as described in this chapter.

13. Remove the left crankcase cover (**Figure 3**) as follows:

    a. Remove the circlip and the neutral indicator from the shaft (**Figure 4**).

    b. Remove the bolts from the locations shown in **Figure 5**, then remove the cover.

14. Remove the drive sprocket assembly. See Chapter Five.

15. Remove the alternator assembly. See Chapter Nine.

16. Remove the right crankcase cover (**Figure 6**) as follows:

    a. Remove the eight bolts from the perimeter of the cover.

    b. Remove the cover and account for the dowel pins that fit in the crankcase (**Figure 7**).

17. Remove the clutch and gearshift linkage. See Chapter Six.

18. Remove the oil pump, as described in this chapter.

19. Remove the engine mounting bolt and collar (A, **Figure 8**).

20. Remove the engine mounting bolt (B, **Figure 8**).

21. Remove the engine mounting bolt located below the engine (**Figure 9**).

WARNING
The following step may require the assistance of another person to remove the engine from the frame.

22. Carefully remove the engine from the frame.

23. Clean and inspect the engine mounting points in the frame. Check for cracks and damage.

24. Refer to *Crankcase* in this chapter for removal of the remaining components on the left side of the crankcase and crankcase separation.

25. Reverse the above steps to install the engine. Note the following:

    a. Install new gaskets and O-rings.

    b. Replace damaged or worn fasteners.

    c. Torque all nuts and bolts to the specifications in **Table 2**.

    d. Carefully route electrical wires so they are not pinched or in contact with surfaces that get hot.

    e. Apply dielectric grease to electrical connections before reconnecting.

    f. Check that the dowel pins in the right crankcase cover are in place before installing the cover.

    g. Fill the engine with fresh oil. See Chapter Three.

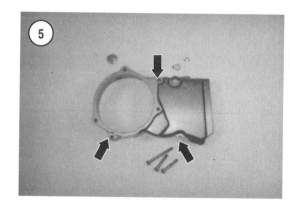

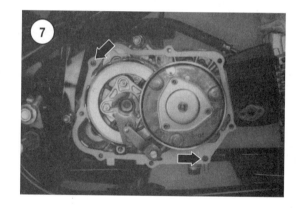

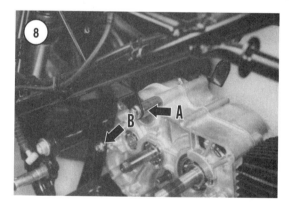

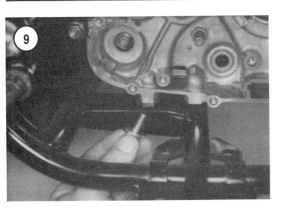

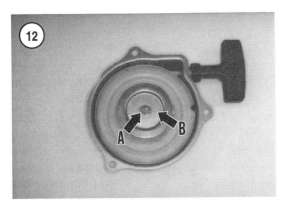

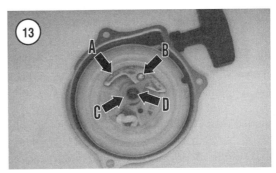

h. Adjust the clutch free play. See Chapter Three.

i. Check throttle cable adjustment. See Chapter Three.

j. Check chain adjustment. See Chapter Three.

k. Start the engine and check for leaks.

l. Check throttle operation.

m. Check gear engagement and check the alignment of the neutral indicator.

n. If the engine top-end has been rebuilt, perform a compression check. Record the results for future reference.

o. Review the *Engine Break-In* procedure in this chapter.

RECOIL STARTER

Removal/Installation

1. Remove the three bolts (**Figure 10**) securing the recoil starter.

2. Remove the starter from the engine.

3. If necessary, remove the four bolts from the starter driven pulley (**Figure 11**). Grip the pulley as shown so the bolts can be removed.

4. Reverse these steps to install the pulley and recoil starter.

Disassembly/Repair/Assembly

> *WARNING*
> *Wear eye protection when working on the recoil starter. The starter spring can quickly uncoil if it is not handled carefully.*

1. Remove the bolt (A, **Figure 12**) and ratchet cover (B).

2. Remove the ratchet (A, **Figure 13**), ratchet pin (B), ratchet guide (C) and spring cover (D).

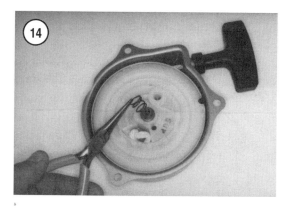

3. Remove the friction spring (**Figure 14**).

4. Pull the starter grip out so a short length of rope
is visible. Clamp the rope so it cannot retract (**Figure 15**).

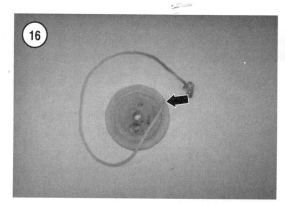

5. Slide the grip cover down the rope, then untie the
rope from the grip. Remove the clamp.

6. Carefully remove the starter reel from the housing. If a new rope is required, proceed as follows:

   a. Remove the old rope from the starter reel.

   b. Knot one end of the new rope and thread it
through the starter reel.

   c. Place the reel, ratchet side out, on a flat surface. Wind the new rope *clockwise* three and
one-half turns, then rest the remainder of the
rope in the starter reel notch (**Figure 16**).

7. Do not remove the recoil spring from the housing unless it is broken or unwound,. If the spring
must be rewound, proceed as follows:

   a. Screw the housing to a board (**Figure 17**).
This will leave both hands free to work with
the spring.

   b. Hook the outer end (A, **Figure 18**) of the
spring to the housing hook (B). Coil the
spring so it lies flat in the housing.

   c. If desired, leave the housing attached to the
board until the recoil starter is reassembled.

8. Assemble the starter reel to the recoil spring as
follows:

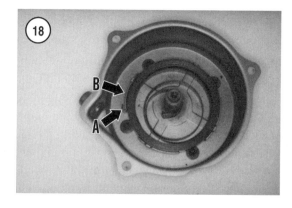

   a. Apply grease to the starter reel shaft in the
housing.

   b. Insert the starter reel over the recoil spring,
engaging the hook on the reel with the hook
(**Figure 19**) on the spring.

   c. With the rope extending from the notch in the
reel (**Figure 20**), preload the recoil spring by
turning the reel *clockwise* four turns. Align

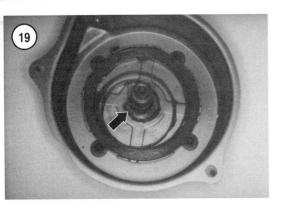

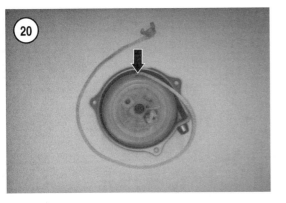

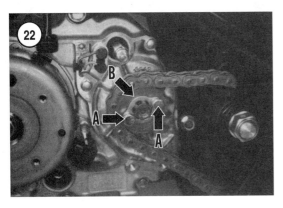

the notch in the reel so the rope can pass out of the housing. Hold the reel in this position.

d. Route the rope through the hole in the housing, then clamp the rope so the grip and cover can be attached (**Figure 21**).

e. Route the rope through the cover, then tie it to the grip.

f. Install the friction spring, spring cover, ratchet guide, ratchet pin, ratchet, ratchet cover and bolt. During assembly, apply grease to the friction points of the ratchet and ratchet guide.

DRIVE SPROCKET

Removal/Inspection/Installation

1. Remove the left crankcase cover as described in *Engine Removal/Installation* in this chapter.

2. Remove the two bolts (A, **Figure 22**) that secure the drive sprocket retaining plate (B) to the drive sprocket.

3. Remove the retaining plate, and sprocket and chain from the shaft.

4. Clean the sprocket. Inspect for damaged teeth and wear. Compare the sprocket to **Figure 23**. The teeth should be symmetrical and uniform. If the sprocket is worn, also replace the rear sprocket and chain. See Chapter Eleven for removal. Always replace the drive line components as a set. Mixing worn parts with new will prematurely wear the new parts.

5. Install the sprocket and chain on the shaft.

6. Install and align the retaining plate with the sprocket holes.

7. Install and torque the bolts to the value listed in **Table 2**.

8. Install the left crankcase cover.

OIL PUMP

Removal/Installation

1. Drain the engine oil.

2. Remove the right foot peg.

3. Remove the right crankcase cover as described in *Engine Removal/Installation* in this chapter.

4. Remove the clutch as describe in Chapter Six.

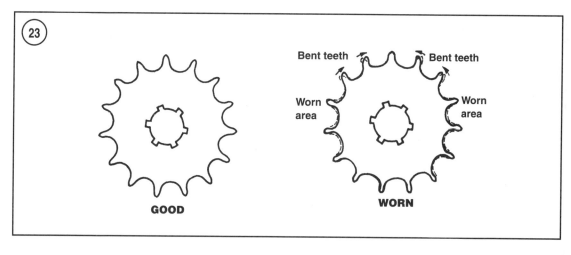

GOOD

Bent teeth

Bent teeth

Worn area

Worn area

WORN

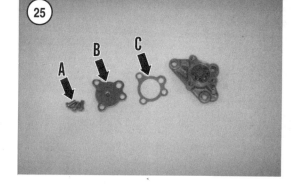

5. Remove the three mounting screws from the oil pump (**Figure 24**), then remove the pump and gasket.

6. Remove the cover screws (A, **Figure 25**), cover (B) and gasket (C).

7. Remove the inner rotor (A, **Figure 26**), oil pump shaft (B) and outer rotor (C) from the pump body. Account for the bushing (D) that fits in the recess around the cam guide spindle. It may come out with the pump.

8. Refer to the procedures in the following section to clean and inspect the pump.

9. Reverse these steps to assemble and install the oil pump. Note the following:

   a. Insert the bushing (A, **Figure 27**) tapered end first into the recess.

   b. Clean the oil passages (B, **Figure 27**) before installing the pump.

   c. Install new gaskets.

   d. Lubricate the inner rotor and outer rotor with engine oil.

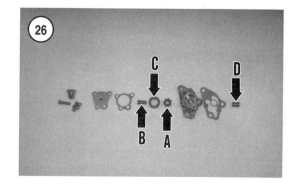

   e. Ensure that the slot on the oil pump shaft engages with the cam chain guide spindle located in the recess.

   f. Torque all screws to the specification in **Table 2**. Note that the mounting screw in the bottom right hole of the oil pump cover is longer and also secures the pump to the crankcase.

   g. Whenever the right crankcase cover is removed, clean the engine oil strainer screen

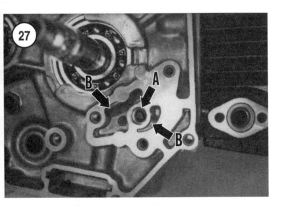

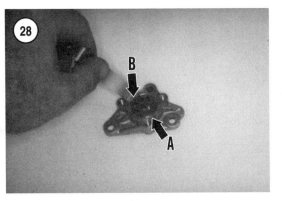

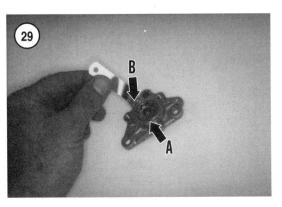

and the centrifugal oil filter in the clutch. See Chapter Three.

10. Fill the engine with oil.

Inspection

Inspect the oil pump rotors and pump body for wear and correct clearances. Make three measurements using a flat feeler gauge. Lay the pump components on a clean, flat surface to make the measurements.

1. Clean the pump assembly in solvent, then wipe dry.

2. Visually inspect all components for obvious wear or damage. Check the rotors for scoring.

3. Measure the inner rotor tip clearance as follows:

   a. Seat the inner rotor into the outer rotor (A, **Figure 28**).

   b. Opposite of where the two rotors are meshed (B, **Figure 28**), measure the clearance between the tip of the rotor and the outer rotor. The inner rotor should be positioned between the two depressions of the outer rotor.

   c. Refer to **Table 1** to determine if the measurement is within the service limit.

4. Measure the outer rotor-to-body clearance as follows:

   a. Seat the outer rotor against one side of the pump body (A, **Figure 29**).

   b. Opposite of where the parts are in contact (B, **Figure 29**), measure the clearance between the outer rotor and pump body.

   c. Refer to **Table 1** to determine if the measurement is within the service limit.

5. Measure the rotor end-clearance as follows:

   a. Place a machinist's straightedge across the top of the pump body.

   b. Measure the clearance between the straightedge and ends of the rotors.

   c. Refer to **Table 1** to determine if the measurement is within the service limit.

CRANKCASE

The following procedures detail the disassembly and reassembly of the crankcase. When the two halves of the crankcase are disassembled or split, the crankshaft and transmission assemblies can be removed for inspection and repair. Before servicing the crankcase, remove the engine as described in *Engine Removal/Installation* in this chapter.

The crankcase halves are cast aluminum alloy. The cases are manufactured as a matched set. The cases are aligned and sealed at the joint by dowel pins and a gasket. Do not hammer or pry on the cases. The cases will fracture or break and both case halves will need to be replaced.

The crankshaft is comprised of two full circle flywheels which are press-fit on the crankpin. The assembly is supported at each end by a ball bearing.

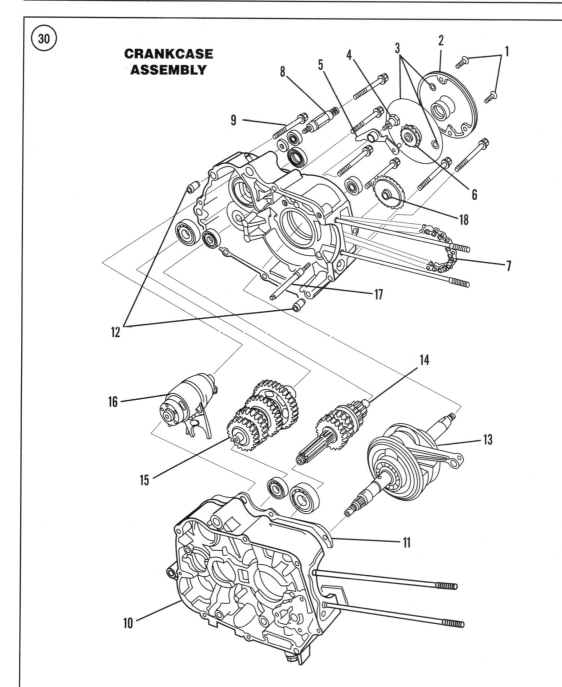

CRANKCASE ASSEMBLY

1. Screws
2. Stator base
3. O-rings
4. Pivot bolt
5. Cam chain tensioner arm
6. Cam chain tensioner roller
7. Cam chain
8. Neutral indicator shaft
9. Crankcase bolt
10. Right crankcase
11. Gasket
12. Dowel pins
13. Crankshaft
14. Mainshaft
15. Countershaft
16. Shift drum
17. Cam chain guide-spindle
18. Cam chain guide-sprocket

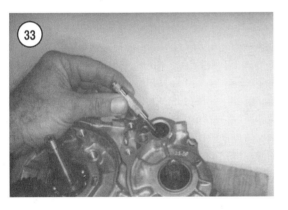

Removal of the connecting rod requires the use of a press.

Disassembly

No special tools are required to disassemble the crankcase. Any reference to the *left* or *right* side of the engine, refers to the engine as it is mounted in the frame (not as it sits on the workbench). As components are removed, keep each part/assembly separated from the other components. Keep seals and O-rings oriented with their respective parts. Refer to **Figure 30**.

1. Place the engine on wooden blocks with the left side facing up.

2. Use a hand impact-driver fitted with a No. 3 Phillips bit to remove the screws from the stator base (**Figure 31**).

3. Remove the stator base, screws, and the two O-rings seated in the screw holes.

4. Remove the pivot bolt (A, **Figure 32**), cam chain tensioner arm (B), roller (C) and chain (D).

5. Unscrew the neutral indicator shaft (**Figure 33**).

6. Working in a crisscross pattern, loosen each crankcase bolt a fourth turn. Continue to loosen the bolts until they can be removed by hand.

NOTE
Anytime the bolt lengths vary, make a drawing of the crankcase shape on a piece of cardboard. Punch holes in the cardboard at the same locations as the bolts. As each bolt is removed from the crankcase, place the bolt in its respective hole in the template.

7. Turn the engine over and support it so the right side is facing up (**Figure 34**).

CAUTION
Grip both halves of the crankcase tightly when turning over the engine. Use an assistant if necessary.

8. Loosen the crankcase halves by tapping around the perimeter with a soft-faced mallet.

CAUTION
Do not hammer or pry on the engine cases.

9. Slowly raise and remove the right crankcase.

10. Account for the thrust washer (**Figure 35**) installed on the transmission countershaft. Check the right crankcase and the end of the countershaft. Keep the washer with the countershaft.

11. Remove the gasket from the case.

12. Remove the two dowel pins from the case (A, **Figure 36**).

13. Remove the crankshaft assembly from the case (B, **Figure 36**).

> *CAUTION*
> *Be careful when removing, handling and storing the crankshaft. Wrap and store the crankshaft until it will be inspected. Do not expose the assembly to dirt or place it in an area where it could roll and fall. If the crankshaft is dropped, the crank pin will likely be knocked out of alignment. The crankshaft will have to be disassembled, aligned and pressed together.*

14. Lift the entire the transmission assembly out of the case (**Figure 37**).

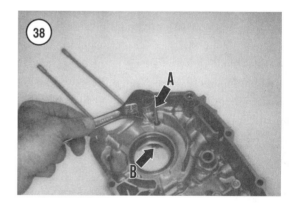

> *CAUTION*
> *Be careful when removing, handling and storing the transmission. Wrap and store the assembly until it will be inspected. Do not expose the assembly to dirt or place it in an area where it could roll and fall.*

15. In the left crankcase, remove the cam chain guide spindle (A, **Figure 38**) from the cam chain guide sprocket (B). Use an adjustable wrench to grip the flat end of the spindle. Hold the sprocket and remove the spindle from the sprocket.

16. Disassemble and inspect the transmission as described in Chapter Seven.

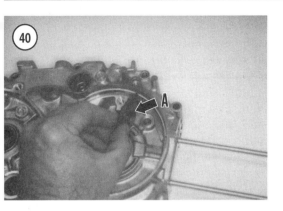

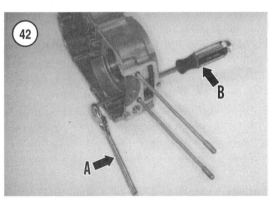

17. Inspect the crankcases and crankshaft assembly as described in this chapter.

Assembly

Refer to **Figure 30** as needed.

1. Perform the following prior to beginning assembly:

  a. Have new gaskets and O-rings on hand. Do not reuse gaskets and O-rings. Lubricate all O-rings as they are installed.

  b. Lightly oil the lip of each seal so the shafts can pass through smoothly. Wrap the drive sprocket end of the transmission countershaft with tape to prevent it from damaging the seal.

  c. Lubricate all surfaces of the transmission assembly and the crankshaft assembly with engine oil. Apply engine oil to the bearings.

2. In the left crankcase, install the cam chain guide sprocket and cam chain guide spindle (**Figure 39**) as follows:

  a. Insert the sprocket (**Figure 40**) with the largest sprocket shoulder facing in.

  b. Insert the spindle (**Figure 41**) from the opposite side of the case and thread it into the sprocket.

  c. Tighten the spindle by fitting an adjustable wrench (A, **Figure 42**) to the flat end of the spindle. Hold the sprocket by placing a screwdriver (B) between the sprocket teeth and the case.

3. Place the left case on blocks as shown in **Figure 43**.

4. Install the transmission assembly as follows:

  a. Align the mainshaft and countershaft as shown in **Figure 44**.

b. Place the shift drum over the transmission shafts, engaging the shift forks with the shaft grooves (**Figures 45** and **46**). Check that the shift drum is oriented properly.

c. Insert the transmission assembly into the left case (**Figure 37**), carefully guiding the countershaft end through the seal.

5. Install the crankshaft in the left case, aligning the connecting rod with the cylinder studs (**Figure 47**).

6. Insert the dowel pins (A, **Figure 36**) into the left case.

NOTE
*Insert the **flat end** of the dowel pins into the left case.*

7. Install a new gasket on the left case. Trim off the excess gasket material that bridges the cylinder opening (**Figure 48**). The trimmed gasket should resemble the one shown in **Figure 49**.

8. Install the thrust washer (**Figure 35**) on the end of the transmission countershaft.

9. Install the right crankcase, seating it over the dowels and gasket (**Figure 50**).

NOTE
Do not force the crankcase into position. If seating is a problem, remove the case and check the transmission assembly. Check for parts that are improperly installed.

10. Turn the engine over and support it so the left side is facing up.

CAUTION
Grip both halves of the crankcase tightly when turning over the engine. Use an assistant if necessary.

11. Insert the crankcase bolts and finger-tighten.

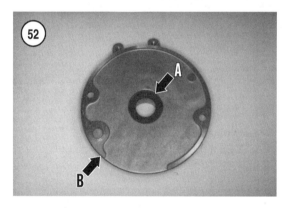

12. Turn all shafts and check for smoothness of operation. If binding or roughness is detected, remove the right case and inspect the assemblies.

13. Working in a crisscross pattern, tighten the bolts in three stages. Torque to the general torque specification in **Table 2**.

14. Install the neutral indicator shaft (**Figure 33**). Torque to the specification in **Table 2**.

15. Route the cam chain through the cylinder opening and onto the crankshaft sprocket (**Figure 51**).

16. Install the cam chain tensioner arm (B, **Figure 32**), roller (C) and pivot bolt (A).

17. Install a new seal into the stator base (A, **Figure 52**). Install the seal with the flat side facing the outside of the engine.

18. Install a new O-ring around the perimeter of the stator base (B, **Figure 52**).

19. Seat new O-rings into the screw holes for the stator base.

20. Align the holes in the stator base with the screw holes. The tabs on the stator base should be positioned as shown in **Figure 53**. Screw the base into position.

21. Follow the *Engine Removal/Installation* procedure described in this chapter to complete engine assembly.

Crankcase Inspection

1. Remove the seals as described in this chapter.

2. Remove all sealer and residue from the gasket surfaces.

3. Clean the crankcase halves with solvent. Flush all bearings last, using clean solvent.

4. Dry the cases with compressed air.

> *WARNING*
> *When drying a bearing with compressed air, do not spin the inner bearing race. The air can spin the bearing at excessive speed, possibly causing damage to the bearing.*

5. Blow through all oil passages with compressed air.

6. Lightly oil the engine bearings before inspecting their condition.

7. Inspect the bearings for roughness, pitting, galling and play. Replace any bearing that is not in good condition. Refer to Chapter One for bearing replacement procedures.

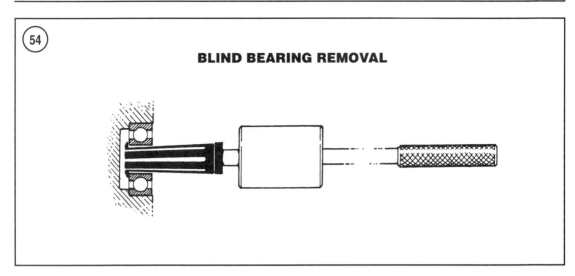

BLIND BEARING REMOVAL

NOTE
Always replace the opposing bearing
at the same time.

8. Inspect the cases for fractures around all bearing bosses, stiffening ribs and threaded holes. If repair is required, take the case to a dealership or machine shop that repairs precision aluminum castings.

9. Check all threaded holes for damage or debris buildup. Clean threads with the correct size metric tap. Lubricate the tap with kerosene or aluminum tap fluid.

Crankcase Bearings

When replacing crankcase bearings, note the following:

1. Refer to *Bearing Replacement* in Chapter One for bearing removal and installation techniques.

2. Identify and record the size code of each bearing before it is removed from the case. This will aid in installing the bearings in their correct bores.

3. Record the orientation of each bearing in its bore. Note if the size code faces toward the inside or outside of the case.

4. Use a press or a set of bearing drivers to remove and install bearings. Use a blind bearing tool (**Figure 54**) to remove bearings installed in blind holes.

Seal Replacement

When performing a complete engine rebuild, replace the seals in the crankcase halves. Replace seals as follows:

1. Pry out the old seal with a seal puller or wide-blade screwdriver (**Figure 55**). Place a folded shop rag under the screwdriver to prevent damage to the case.

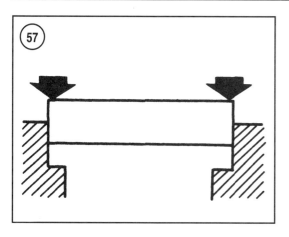

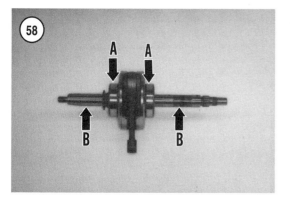

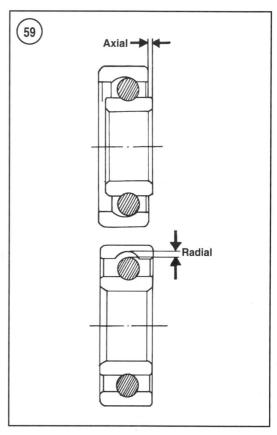

5

2. If a new bearing will be installed, replace the bearing before installing the new seal.

3. Clean the seal bore.

4. Pack waterproof grease in the lip of the new seal.

5. Place the seal in the bore with the closed side of the seal facing out. The seal must be square to the bore (**Figure 56**).

6. Use a seal driver to seat the seal in the bore.

CAUTION
*When driving seals, the driver must fit at the perimeter of the seal (**Figure 57**). If the driver presses toward the center of the seal, the seal can distort and the garter spring can become dislodged and cause the seal to leak.*

CRANKSHAFT

Inspection

Handle the crankshaft assembly carefully during inspection. Do not place the crankshaft where it could roll off the workbench. The crankshaft is an assembly-type with two halves joined by a crankpin. The crankpin is pressed into the flywheels and aligned, both vertically and horizontally, with calibrated equipment. If the crankshaft assembly shows signs of wear, have a dealership assess the wear. Overhaul or replace the crankshaft. Inspect the crankshaft assembly as follows:

1. Clean the crankshaft with solvent. Flush all bearings last, using clean solvent.

2. Dry the crankshaft with compressed air.

3. Blow through all oil passages with compressed air.

4. Lightly oil the bearings before inspecting their condition.

5. Inspect the bearings (A, **Figure 58**) for roughness, pitting and galling. Check the bearings for axial and radial play (**Figure 59**). Replace any bearing that is not in good condition.

6. Inspect the crankshaft journals (B, **Figure 58**) for scoring, heat discoloration or other damage.

7. Inspect the connecting rod as follows:

   a. Inspect the rod for scoring, galling or heat damage.

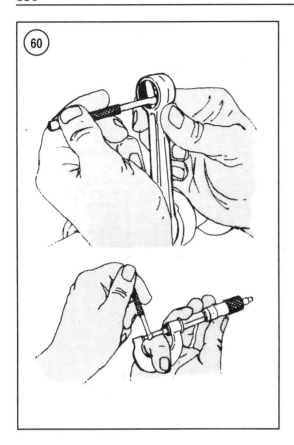

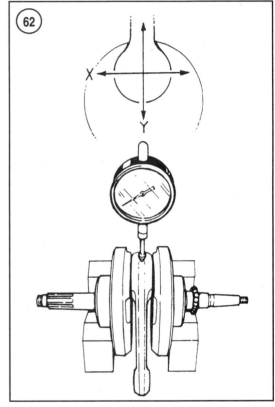

b. Measure the piston pin bore in the connecting rod with a small hole gauge and micrometer (**Figure 60**). Replace the connecting rod if the measurement exceeds the service limit in **Table 1**.

c. Slide the connecting rod to one side and check the side clearance with a flat feeler gauge (**Figure 61**). Replace the rod and/or crankshaft if the measurement exceeds the service limit listed in **Table 1**.

d. Place the crankshaft on a set of V-blocks and measure the crankpin-to-connecting rod radial clearance with a dial indicator. Measure in both directions as shown in **Figure 62**. Replace the rod and/or crankshaft if the measurement exceeds the service limit listed in **Table 1**.

8. Place the crankshaft on a set of V-blocks or lathe centers, and measure crankshaft runout with a dial indicator (**Figure 63**). Measure at the points shown in **Figure 64**. If the runout exceeds the service limit listed in **Table 1**, take the crankshaft to a dealership for service.

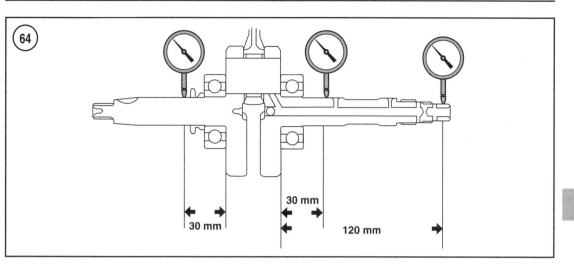

Cam Sprocket Inspection

Refer to Chapter Four for inspecting the cam chain and sprocket fitted to the camshaft and the cam chain tensioner push-rod and spring assembly.

1. Inspect the cam sprocket on the crankshaft (A, **Figure 65**). The profile of each tooth should be symmetrical. If the sprocket is worn, have it removed by a dealership.

2. If the chain or any sprocket is worn, replace all the parts as a set (B, **Figure 65**).

ENGINE BREAK-IN

Observe a proper break-in period after performing major service on the engine. The performance and service life of the engine depends greatly on a careful and sensible break-in.

a. Fill the engine with the correct amount and weight of engine oil.

b. Install a new spark plug.

c. Check that the air filter is clean.

d. For the first ten hours of operation, use no more than half throttle. Vary the speed as much as possible within this throttle range. Do not operate the machine at a steady speed, no matter how moderate. Avoid hard acceleration.

e. For the next five hours of operation, use no more than three-fourths throttle. Vary the speed as much as possible within this throttle range.

f. At the end of the break-in period, change the engine oil and clean the oil filter. This oil change removes the metallic particles left when the parts seat to one another.

Tables 1 and 2 are on the following page.

Table 1 ENGINE SERVICE SPECIFICATIONS

	New mm (in.)	Service limit mm (in.)
Oil pump		
Inner rotor tip clearance	0.15 (0.006)	0.20 (0.008)
Outer rotor to body clearance	0.02-0.07 (0.001-0.003)	0.12 (0.005)
Rotor end clearance	0.10-0.15 (0.004-0.006)	0.20 (0.008)
Connecting rod		
Piston pin bore	13.016-13.034 (0.5124-0.5131)	13.05 (0.514)
Side clearance	0.10-0.35 (0.004-0.014)	0.60 (0.024)
Crank pin radial clearance	0.0-0.008 (0.0-0.003)	0.05 (0.002)
Crankshaft		
Runout	– –	0.10 (0.004)
OD at clutch primary drive gear	18.967-18.980 (0.7467-0.7472)	18.92 (0.745)

Table 2 ENGINE TORQUE SPECIFICATIONS

	N•m	in.-lb.	ft.-lb.
Drive sprocket bolts	12	106	–
Engine mounting bolts			
Upper	29	–	21
Rear	49	–	36
Bottom	29	–	21
Footpegs	32	–	24
Neutral indicator shaft	12	–	9
Oil drain bolt	24	–	17
Oil pump mounting screws	8	106	–
5 mm bolt and nut	5	–	3.5
6 mm bolt and nut	10	88	–
8 mm bolt and nut	22	–	16
10 mm bolt and nut	35	–	26
12 mm bolt and nut	55	–	41
5 mm screw	4	35	–
6 mm screw	9	80	–
6 mm flange bolt (8 mm head)	9	80	–
6 mm flange bolt (10 mm head) and nut	12	106	–
8 mm flange bolt and nut	27	–	20
10 mm flange bolt and nut	40	–	29

CHAPTER SIX

CLUTCH AND GEARSHIFT LINKAGE

This chapter describes service procedures for the following components on the right side of the engine crankcase:

1. Right crankcase cover.
2. Centrifugal clutch.
3. One-way clutch.
4. Change clutch.
5. Gearshift linkage.

Read this chapter before attempting repairs to the clutches and linkage. Become familiar with the procedures, photos and illustrations to understand the skill and equipment required. Refer to Chapter One for tool usage and techniques.

RIGHT CRANKCASE COVER

Removal/Inspection/Installation

The components covered in this section include the right crankcase cover and clutch lifter. Refer to **Figure 1**.

1. Drain the engine oil as described in Chapter Three.
2. Remove the mudguard from the rear fender as described in Chapter Thirteen.
3. Remove the right footpeg.
4. Remove the eight bolts from the cover (**Figure 2**).
5. Remove the cover and account for the dowel pins that fit in the crankcase (**Figure 3**).
6. Remove the cover gasket.
7. Remove the locknut, washer and O-ring from the clutch adjusting bolt (**Figure 4**).
8. Remove the clutch lifter and adjusting bolt from the cover (**Figure 5**). Unscrew the adjusting bolt from the lifter.
9. Inspect the parts for wear and play, particularly the rollers on the clutch lifter (**Figure 6**). Replace any parts that are worn.
10. Reverse these steps to install the right crankcase cover assembly. Note the following:
    a. Remove and clean the centrifugal oil filter and oil strainer screen (**Figure 7**) anytime the crankcase cover is removed. Refer to Chapter Three for cleaning procedures.
    b. Install the boss on the clutch lifter in the hole in the cover (**Figure 8**).
    c. Install a new cover gasket.
    d. Install a new, lubricated O-ring on the clutch adjusting bolt.

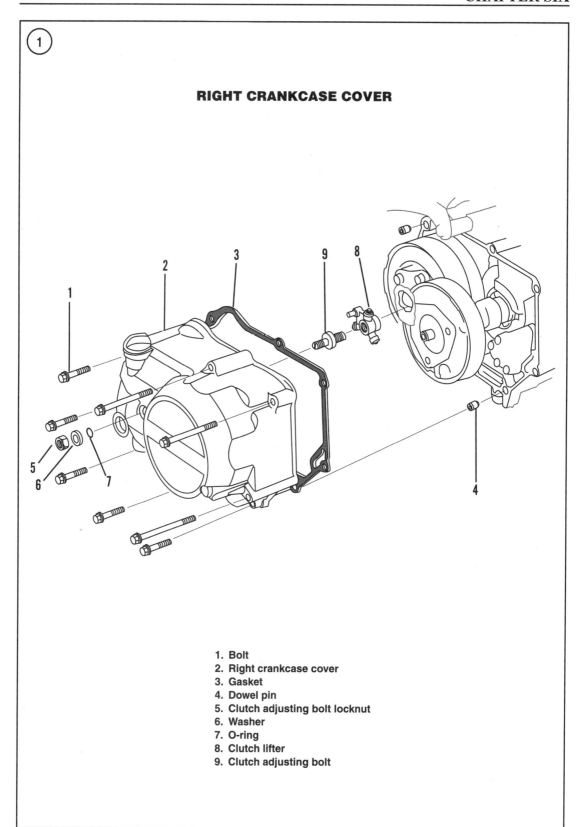

RIGHT CRANKCASE COVER

1. Bolt
2. Right crankcase cover
3. Gasket
4. Dowel pin
5. Clutch adjusting bolt locknut
6. Washer
7. O-ring
8. Clutch lifter
9. Clutch adjusting bolt

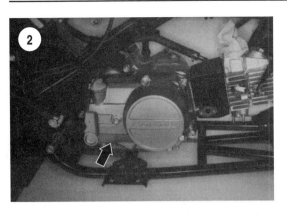

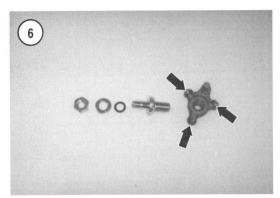

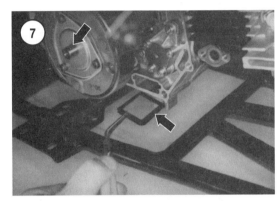

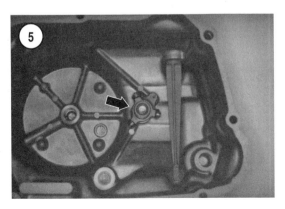

e. Torque all bolts to the specifications in **Table 2**.

f. Fill the engine with the correct quantity and weight of engine oil.

g. Adjust the clutch as described in Chapter Three.

CLUTCHES

The vehicle is equipped with two clutches to transmit power to the rear wheels. The clutches op-

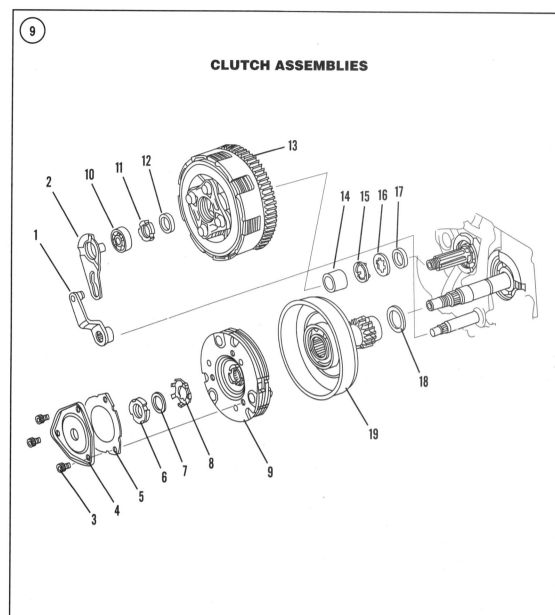

CLUTCH ASSEMBLIES

1. Clutch lifter lever
2. Clutch lifter cam
3. Allen bolt
4. Oil filter rotor cover
5. Gasket
6. Locknut
7. Lockwasher
8. Lockwasher
9. Clutch shoe assembly
10. Lifter bearing

11. Locknut
12. Lockwasher
13. Change clutch
14. Clutch outer guide
15. Stopper plate
16. Spline washer
17. Collar
18. Thrust washer
19. Centrifugal clutch drum

erate immersed in the engine oil supply. A three-shoe, centrifugal clutch is installed on the end of the crankshaft. This clutch transmits power to a multiplate gear change clutch, which interrupts the power flow whenever the transmission is being shifted. The centrifugal clutch is also equipped with a one-way clutch. This clutch will lock up the centrifugal clutch if the vehicle is rolled backward while in gear. The locked clutch will then utilize engine compression to help brake the vehicle. This helps control the vehicle if it is stalled on an incline.

Removal

Refer to **Figure 9**.

1. Remove the right crankcase cover as described in this chapter.

2. Remove the clutch lifter lever from the gearshift spindle (**Figure 10**). Note the alignment mark on the spindle. Reinstall the lifter lever in this position.

3. Remove the clutch lifter cam (**Figure 11**) from the lifter bearing.

4. Remove the three screws from the oil filter rotor cover (**Figure 12**). Remove the cover and gasket.

5. Remove the centrifugal clutch locknut as follows:

    a. Straighten the tabs on the lockwasher (**Figure 13**).

    b. Attach a holding tool (A, **Figure 14**) to the drive plate (B) to prevent the drive plate from moving. The tool shown (A, **Figure 15**) is a *Yamaha* rotor holding tool (part No. YU-01235). Several Honda clutch holders (part Nos. 07HMB-HB70100, 07GMB-HB30100 or 07923-HB3000B) can be obtained from a dealership. The Honda clutch holder can be attached to the drive plate using the oil filter rotor cover screws.

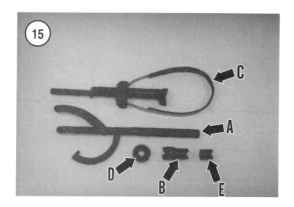

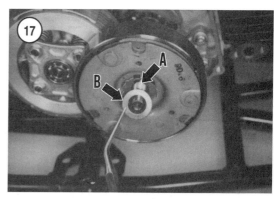

c. Remove the locknut (**Figure 16**) using a locknut wrench (20 × 24 mm, part No. 07716-0020100) and extension bar (part No. 07716-0020500). The wrench is shown in B, **Figure 15**.

d. Remove the lockwashers (A and B, **Figure 17**). The tabbed lockwasher (A) must be replaced during reassembly.

6. Remove the clutch shoe assembly from the clutch drum (**Figure 18**).

7. Remove the lifter bearing from the gear change clutch (**Figure 19**).

8. Remove the gear change clutch locknut as follows:

a. Remove the four bolts from the clutch lifter plate (**Figure 20**). Work in a crisscross pattern and loosen the bolts in several stages.

b. Place large washers on the four bolts (**Figure 21**), then reinstall the bolts and compress the clutch springs.

c. Install a strap wrench on the centrifugal clutch housing (A, **Figure 22**). The tool shown in C, **Figure 15** is a *Kawasaki* strap wrench (part No. 57001-1313). A similar

strap wrench can be obtained from an auto supply dealer. An alternative to using a strap wrench is to hold the gears with the discarded primary gear (D, **Figure 15**). The gear fits into the teeth of both clutches and prevents either clutch from turning (**Figure 23**).

CAUTION
Do not attempt to hold the gears with screwdrivers or other tools. This could result in gear damage.

d. Remove the locknut using an 18 mm locknut wrench (B, **Figure 22**) (part No. 07HMA-GN80100) and extension bar (part No. 07716-0020500). The wrench is shown in E, **Figure 15**.

e. Remove the clutch locknut (A, **Figure 24**) and lockwasher (B).

f. Remove the strap wrench from the centrifugal clutch.

9. Remove both clutches from their shafts (**Figure 25**).

10. Remove the clutch outer guide (A, **Figure 26**), stopper plate and plastic spline washer from the mainshaft.

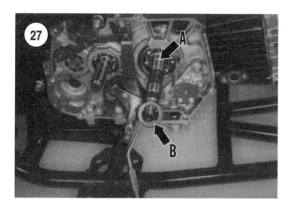

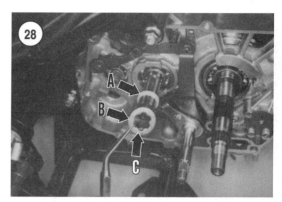

11. Remove the thrust washer (B, **Figure 26**) from the crankshaft.

12. Inspect the clutch assemblies as described in this section.

13. Remove the gearshift linkage as described in this chapter.

Installation

Refer to **Figure 9**.

1. Install the gearshift linkage as described in this chapter.

2. Lubricate the crankshaft (A, **Figure 27**) with a mixture of engine oil and molydisulfide grease at a ratio of 1:1. Slide the thrust washer (B) onto the crankshaft.

3. Slide the plastic collar (A, **Figure 28**) and spline washer (B) onto the mainshaft.

> *NOTE*
> *The word **OUT** (C, **Figure 28**) is printed on one side of the washer. Install the washer so **OUT** faces to the outside.*

4. Slide the stopper plate onto the mainshaft (**Figure 29**). The tabs on the stopper plate must engage with the spline washer. Adjust the two parts until the stopper plate tabs seat under the spline washer.

5. Lubricate the clutch outer guide with oil containing molydisulfied grease, then insert the guide into the back of the change clutch (**Figure 30**).

6. Check that the gear change clutch springs are compressed with the washers and bolts used during removal (**Figure 31**).

7. Mesh the gear teeth of the gear change clutch and centrifugal clutch drum (**Figure 32**). In order for the teeth to mesh properly, the spring-loaded

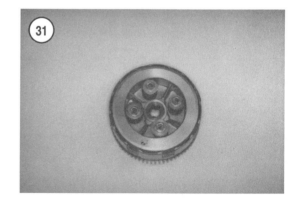

subgear (**Figure 33**) must be turned (preloaded) to align with the primary drive gear. Hold the clutches in this position and slide them onto their respective shafts.

8. Lubricate the threads of the gear change clutch locknut (A, **Figure 24**). Install the lockwasher (B) and locknut on the mainshaft. Finger-tighten the locknut.

NOTE
The word OUT SIDE is printed on one side of the lockwasher. Install the washer so OUT SIDE faces out.

9. Tighten the gear change clutch locknut as follows:

a. Install a strap wrench on the centrifugal clutch housing. If a discarded primary gear was used to hold the clutches, as described in the removal procedure, place the gear on top of the clutches as shown in **Figure 34**.

CAUTION
Do not attempt to hold the gears with screwdrivers or other tools. This could result in gear damage.

b. Tighten the locknut (**Figure 35**) with the 18 mm locknut wrench, used for removing the nut. Torque the locknut to the specification in **Table 2**.

c. Remove the four bolts and washers that are compressing the clutch springs (**Figure 36**).

10. Align the clutch lifter plate over the springs and bolt holes (**Figure 37**), then bolt the plate into position. Work in a crisscross pattern and tighten the bolts in several stages.

11. Install the lifter bearing into the gear change clutch (**Figure 38**).

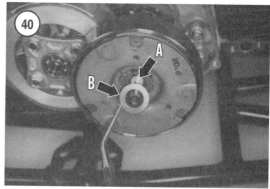

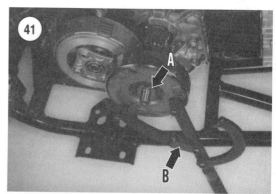

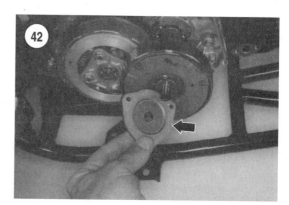

12. Insert the clutch shoe assembly into the clutch drum (**Figure 39**).

13. Install the centrifugal clutch locknut as follows:

    a. Place a new tabbed lockwasher (A, **Figure 40**) onto the crankshaft. The tabs must face out.

    b. Place the lockwasher (B, **Figure 40**) onto the crankshaft.

NOTE
*The word **OUT SIDE** is printed on one side of the lockwasher. Install the washer so **OUT SIDE** faces out.*

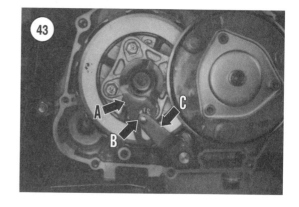

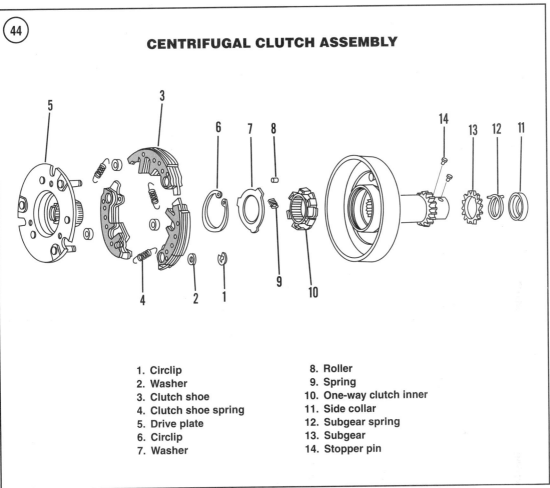

CENTRIFUGAL CLUTCH ASSEMBLY

1. Circlip
2. Washer
3. Clutch shoe
4. Clutch shoe spring
5. Drive plate
6. Circlip
7. Washer
8. Roller
9. Spring
10. One-way clutch inner
11. Side collar
12. Subgear spring
13. Subgear
14. Stopper pin

c. Install the locknut on the crankshaft and finger-tighten (A, **Figure 41**).

d. Attach a holding tool (B, **Figure 41**) to the drive plate to prevent the drive plate from moving.

e. Torque the locknut to the specification in **Table 2**. After the torque is achieved, continue to turn the nut until the notches in the nut are aligned with the tab(s) of the lockwasher.

f. Bend the aligned tabs into the locknut.

14. Install the oil filter rotor cover as follows:

a. Place a new gasket on the oil filter rotor cover (**Figure 42**).

b. Apply threadlocking compound to the threads of the cover screws.

c. Align the cover on the clutch drive plate, then insert and finger-tighten the screws.

d. Torque the screws to the specification in **Table 2**.

15. Install the clutch lifter cam (A, **Figure 43**) into the lifter bearing.

16. Lubricate the actuator (B, **Figure 43**) of the clutch lifter lever (C), then slide the lever onto the gearshift spindle. Check that the actuator is engaged with the lifter cam, and the lever is aligned on the spindle as noted in the removal procedure (**Figure 10**).

17. Install the right crankcase cover as described in this chapter.

Centrifugal Clutch Disassembly/Inspection/Assembly

Clutch shoe and drive plate

Remove the clutch from the engine as described in this section. Refer to **Figure 44**.

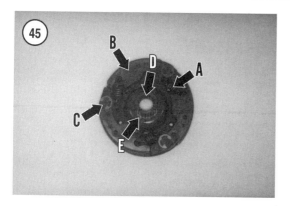

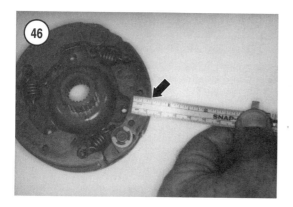

1. Clean the assembly in solvent and dry with compressed air.

2. Visually inspect the springs (A, **Figure 45**) shoes (B) and pivot points (C) for wear and broken parts. Check the inner splines (D) and outer splines (E) of the drive plate for cracks and wear.

3. If wear or broken parts are evident, replace the parts or the clutch assembly.

4. Measure the thickness of the shoe linings (**Figure 46**). If any measurement exceeds the specification in **Table 1**, or if the linings are worn unevenly, replace the clutch shoes.

Clutch drum and one-way clutch

1. Disassemble the clutch drum as follows:

   a. Remove the circlip retaining the one-way clutch in the drum (**Figure 47**).

   b. Remove the washer (**Figure 48**).

   c. Lift the springs from the one-way clutch (**Figure 49**).

   d. Lift the rollers from the one-way clutch (**Figure 50**).

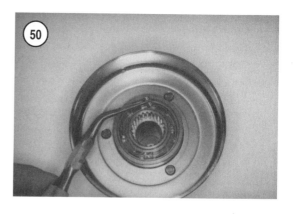

e. Remove the one-way clutch inner (**Figure 51**).

f. Remove the side collar (**Figure 52**). Remove and install the collar using a press.

g. Remove the spring, subgear and stopper pins.

> *NOTE*
> *Before disassembling, note how the subgear is spring-loaded and does not align with the other primary drive gear. This minimizes backlash noise during deceleration.*

2. Clean all parts in solvent and dry with compressed air.

3. Visually inspect the parts, particularly the gears, for excessive wear.

4. Measure the centrifugal clutch drum inside diameter (**Figure 53**). If the measurement exceeds the specification in **Table 1**, replace the drum.

5. Measure the one-way drum inside diameter (**Figure 54**). If the measurement exceeds the specification in **Table 1**, replace the drum.

6. Measure the one-way clutch roller outside diameter (**Figure 55**). If the measurement exceeds the specification in **Table 1**, replace all rollers and springs.

7. Measure the primary drive-gear inside diameter (**Figure 56**). If the measurement exceeds the specification in **Table 1**, replace the drum.

8. Measure the crankshaft diameter, at the primary drive-gear location (**Figure 57**). If the measurement exceeds the specification in **Table 1**, replace the crankshaft.

9. Reverse these steps to assemble the one-way clutch and clutch drum. Note the following:

a. Use engine oil to lubricate the one-way clutch assembly and the clutch shoe pivot points.

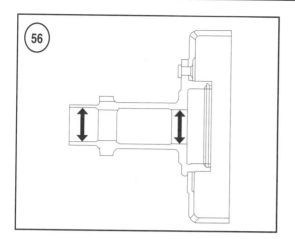

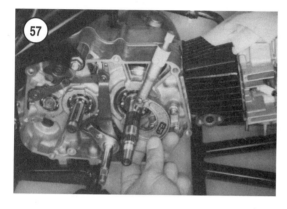

b. Install the circlip so the *sharp* edge is facing out.

c. Check the one-way clutch operation. The clutch should only turn in one direction. If it does not, disassemble and inspect the parts.

10. Install the clutch as described in this section.

Gear Change Clutch
Disassembly/Inspection/Assembly

Remove the clutch from the engine as described in this section. Refer to **Figure 58**.

1. Slowly remove the bolts that are compressing the clutch springs if they are not already removed.

2. Remove the clutch center, plates and pressure plate from the clutch outer.

3. Clean the assembly in solvent and dry with compressed air.

4. Measure the thickness of the four friction plates (plates bonded with friction material) (A, **Figure 59**). Measure at several locations around the perim-

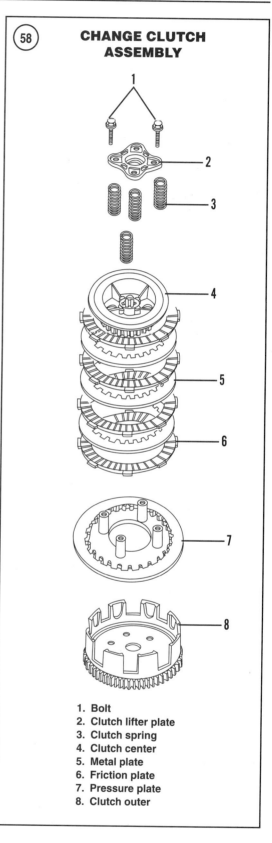

CHANGE CLUTCH ASSEMBLY

1. Bolt
2. Clutch lifter plate
3. Clutch spring
4. Clutch center
5. Metal plate
6. Friction plate
7. Pressure plate
8. Clutch outer

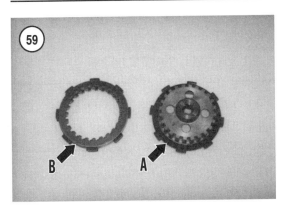

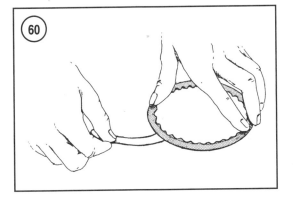

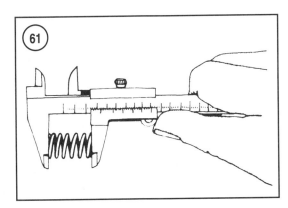

eter. If any measurement does not meet the specifications in **Table 1**, replace all the plates as a set.

5. Inspect the tabs on the friction plates. The tabs should not be damaged and should slide smoothly in the clutch outer.

6. Measure the three discs (metal plates) (B, **Figure 59**) for warpage. Lay each disc on a surface plate, or thick piece of glass, and measure any gap around the perimeter of the disc (**Figure 60**). If any measurement exceeds the specification in **Table 1**, replace all the plates as a set.

7. Inspect the inner teeth on the plates. The teeth should not be damaged and should slide smoothly on the clutch center.

8. Measure the free length of each clutch spring (**Figure 61**). If any measurement exceeds the specification in **Table 1**, replace all the springs as a set.

9. Inspect the outer guide (**Figure 62**) for wear and damage. Measure the outside diameter of the outer guide. If the measurement exceeds the specifications in **Table 1**, replace the guide.

10. Measure the inside diameter of the clutch outer (**Figure 63**). If the measurement exceeds the specifications in **Table 1**, replace the guide.

11. Inspect the clutch outer as follows:

   a. Check the gear teeth for wear or damage (A, **Figure 64**).

b. Check the slots for nicks, wear and damage
(B, **Figure 64**). Repair light damage using a
fine-cut file or oilstone.

c. If excessive wear or damage is detected, replace the clutch outer.

12. Inspect the clutch center for nicks, wear and
damage (C, **Figure 64**). If any wear or damage is
detected, replace the clutch center.

13. Inspect the lifter bearing. The bearing should
turn smoothly and have no play (**Figure 65**). Replace the bearing if necessary.

14. Reverse the disassembly procedure to assemble
the clutch. Refer to **Figure 58** to ensure that the
plates are installed in the proper order. Refer to the
Installation procedure in this section for compressing the clutch springs and installing the clutch.

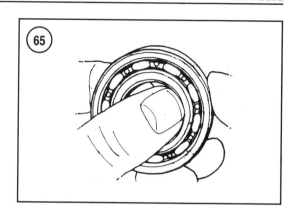

GEARSHIFT LINKAGE

Removal

Refer to **Figure 66**.

1. Remove the clutch assemblies as described in
this chapter.

2. Remove the pinch bolt from the gearshift pedal
(**Figure 67**) located on the left side of the vehicle.
Remove the pedal from the shaft.

3. Loosen the Allen bolt (A, **Figure 68**) and remove the drum stopper arm (B). Hold the arm to
slowly relieve the spring (C) pressure.

4. Remove the bolt securing the drum stopper plate
(A, **Figure 69**) and shift drum side plate (B).

5. Remove the four large dowel pins (A, **Figure
70**) and two small dowel pins (B) from the end of
the shift drum.

6. Pull the gearshift spindle assembly from the engine (**Figure 71**).

7. Inspect the parts as described in this section.

Inspection

Inspect all components of the gearshift linkage as
follows:

1. Inspect the gearshift spindle assembly for wear
(**Figure 72**).

a. Inspect the ends of the notched area (A, **Figure 72**). The ends must be slightly hooked in
order to maintain engagement with the dowel
pins as the vehicle is upshifted or downshifted. If the ends are worn, the dowels will

slide out of the notch and not engage the
transmission properly.

b. Inspect the springs (B, **Figure 72**) for wear at
their ends.

c. Inspect the pivot points for play or wear.

d. Inspect the splines at both ends of the shaft
(**Figure 73**). The teeth should be uniform and
show no signs of wear.

e. Replace any parts, or the entire shaft assembly, if wear is detected.

2. Inspect the dowel pins (A, **Figure 74**).

a. Inspect the fit of the dowels in the shift drum.
They should be tight with no play.

b. Inspect the side of each pin for wear or flat
spots.

c. Replace the dowel pins if wear is detected.

3. Inspect the shift drum side plate (B, **Figure 74**).
Inspect the fit of the dowels in the plate. The dowels
should fit firmly. Replace the plate and dowels if
wear is detected.

4. Inspect the drum stopper plate (C, **Figure 74**).

a. Inspect the *stop* area of the plate (D, **Figure
74**). The stop should be slightly hooked on
each side to maintain engagement with the
roller on the drum stopper arm.

b. Inspect the fit of the dowels in the plate. The
dowels should fit firmly.

c. Replace the stopper plate if wear is detected.

5. Inspect the drum stopper arm (**Figure 75**). The
roller should turn freely and have no play in its
pivot. Replace the arm if wear is detected.

Installation

Refer to **Figure 66**.

1. Insert the gearshift spindle assembly into the engine (**Figure 76**).

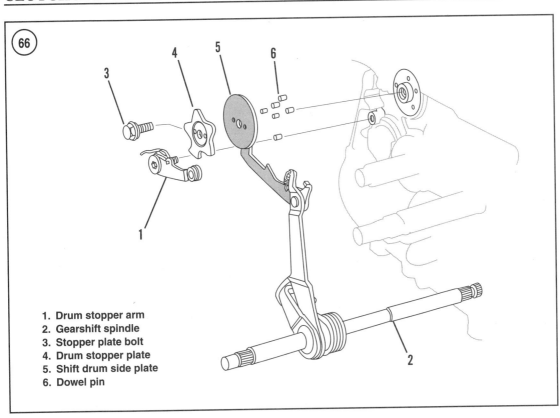

1. Drum stopper arm
2. Gearshift spindle
3. Stopper plate bolt
4. Drum stopper plate
5. Shift drum side plate
6. Dowel pin

6

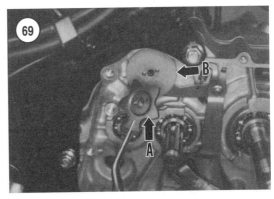

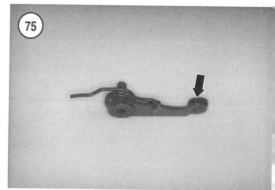

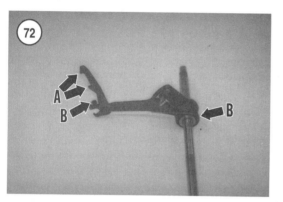

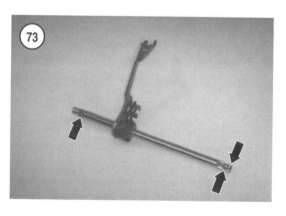

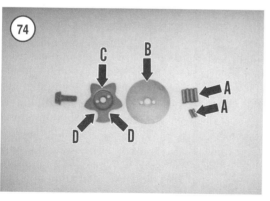

2. Insert the dowel pins into the shift drum, then engage the shift linkage with the dowel pins (**Figure 77**).

3. Mount the shift drum side plate and drum stopper plate on the two small dowels (**Figure 78**).

NOTE
The recessed side of the drum stopper plate should face out.

4. Insert and torque the stopper plate bolt (**Figure 79**) to the specification in **Table 2**.

5. Align the drum stopper arm (B, **Figure 68**) with its mounting hole and engage it with the drum stopper plate. Torque the Allen bolt (A) to the specification in **Table 2**.

NOTE
*Mount the drum stopper arm so the spring (C, **Figure 68**) is preloaded against the case.*

6. Before mounting the gearshift pedal and checking the action of the gearshift linkage, temporarily bolt a plate lightly against the gearshift spindle (**Figure 80**). This will hold the linkage in place while the pedal is installed, and the shifting is checked.

7. Mount the gearshift pedal on the right side of the vehicle. Torque the bolt to the specification in **Table 2**.

8. Check the shifting action of the linkage as follows:

    a. Check that there is clearance between the gearshift linkage and the temporary plate installed in Step 6.

    b. Operate the gearshift pedal and observe the action of the linkage. If necessary, turn the transmission mainshaft to help the linkage shift up and down through the gears.

    c. Correct any problems that are observed.

9. Remove the temporary plate from the engine (**Figure 80**).

10. Install the clutches as described in this chapter.

Tables 1 and 2 are on the following page.

Table 1 CLUTCH SERVICE SPECIFICATIONS

	New mm (in.)	Service limit mm (in.)
Shoe lining thickness	1.5 (0.06)	1.0 (0.04)
Centrifugal clutch		
Inside diameter	104.0-104.02 (4.094-4.095)	104.3 (4.11)
One-way clutch drum inner diameter	42.0-42.02 (1.6535-1.6543)	42.04 (1.655)
One-way clutch roller diameter	5.0 (0.197)	4.97 (0.196)
Primary drive gear inner diameter	19.030-19.059 (0.7492-0.7503)	19.11 (0.752)
Crankshaft diameter		
Location at clutch primary drive gear	18.967-18.980 (0.7467-0.7472)	18.92 (0.745)
Change clutch		
Disk thickness	2.92-3.08 (0.115-0.121)	2.6 (0.10)
Plate warpage	– –	0.2 (0.008)
Spring free length	25.2 (0.99)	25.5 (1.0)
Outer guide outer diameter	20.959-20.980 (0.8251-0.8259)	20.91 (0.823)
Clutch outer inner diameter	21.020-21.041 (0.8275-0.8283)	21.09 (0.830)

Table 2 TORQUE SPECIFICATIONS

	N•m	in.-lb.	ft.-lb.
Centrifugal clutch locknut	40	–	29
Gear change clutch locknut	40	–	29
Gearshift drum stopper arm bolt	10	88	–
Gearshift drum stopper plate bolt	17	–	13
Gearshift pedal bolt	16	–	12
Gearshift spindle return spring pin	30	–	22
Oil filter rotor cover screws	6	53	–
5 mm screw	4	35	–
6 mm screw	9	88	–
6 mm flange bolt (8 mm head)	9	88	–
6 mm flange bolt (10 mm head) and nut	12	106	9
8 mm flange bolt and nut	27	–	20

TRANSMISSION AND INTERNAL SHIFT MECHANISM

7

The vehicle is equipped with a four-speed transmission. The shift pedal is located on the left side of the engine. Clutch engagement and disengagement during shifting is automatic.

Read this chapter before attempting repairs to the transmission and shift mechanism. Become familiar with the procedures, photos and illustrations in order to understand the skill and equipment required. Refer to Chapter One for tool usage and techniques.

SERVICE NOTES

Separate the engine crankcase to remove the transmission (**Figure 1**) and shift drum (**Figure 2**). Remove and install the transmission assembly as described in Chapter Five, *Crankcase Disassembly and Assembly.*

Once the transmission is removed from the crankcase, dissassembly, inspection and assembly can be performed. Carefully measure the parts and keep them oriented. The gears, washers and circlips *must* be installed in the same direction. Since some of these parts are identical on both faces, remove and store the parts on each shaft in the order they are disassembled and in their direction prior to disassembly. Use a piece of wire threaded through the parts or an identification mark on each part.

Always install new circlips. The circlips will fatigue and distort when they are removed. Do not reuse them, even if they appear to be in good condition.

MAINSHAFT

Disassembly

Refer to **Figure 3**.
1. Clean the assembled mainshaft (**Figure 4**) in solvent and dry with compressed air.
2. Remove fourth gear from the mainshaft.
3. Remove the spline washer from the shaft.
4. Remove the circlip from the shaft.
5. Remove third gear from the shaft.
6. Remove the spline washer from the shaft.
7. Remove second gear from the shaft.
8. Keep the parts oriented and in the order of removal as shown in **Figure 5**. Inspect each part as

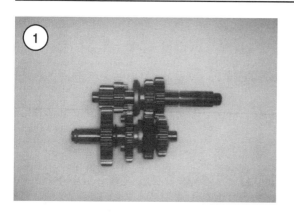

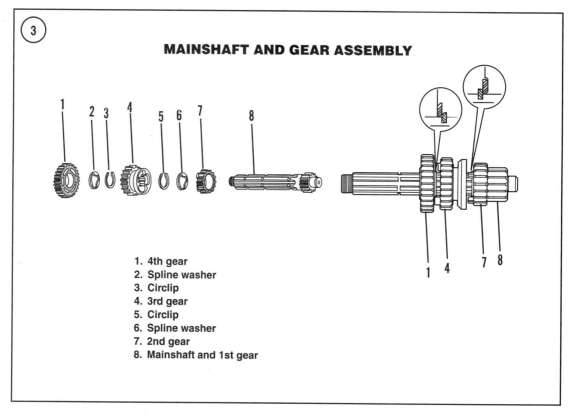

MAINSHAFT AND GEAR ASSEMBLY

1. 4th gear
2. Spline washer
3. Circlip
4. 3rd gear
5. Circlip
6. Spline washer
7. 2nd gear
8. Mainshaft and 1st gear

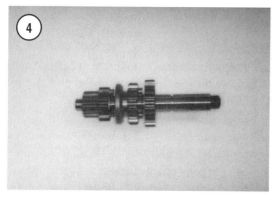

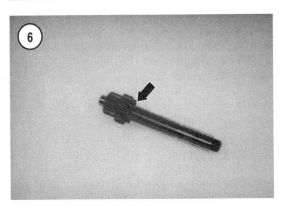

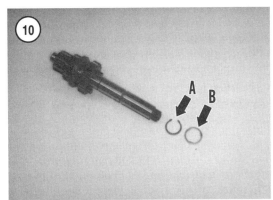

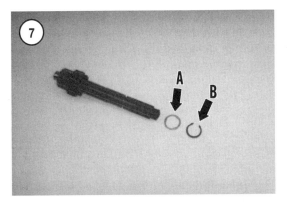

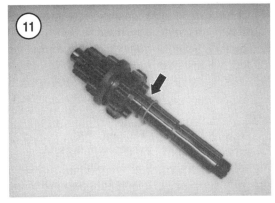

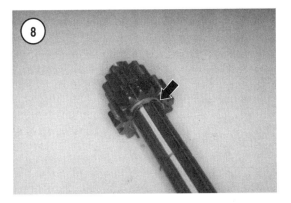

described in this chapter, then return it to its place until assembly.

Assembly

Before beginning assembly, have two new circlips (part No. 90601-001-000) on hand. Refer to **Figure 3**.

1. Lubricate all sliding surfaces with engine oil.

2. Install second gear on the mainshaft (**Figure 6**). The gear dogs must face *out*, away from first gear.

3. Install the spline washer (A, **Figure 7**) and a new circlip (B) on the shaft. The flat side of both parts must face *out*, away from first gear. Seat the circlip in the groove in the shaft (**Figure 8**).

4. Install third gear on the shaft (**Figure 9**). The gear dogs must face *out*, away from first gear.

5. Install a new circlip (A, **Figure 10**) and the spline washer (B) on the shaft. The flat side of both parts must face *in* toward first gear. Seat the circlip in the groove in the shaft (**Figure 11**).

6. Install fourth gear on the shaft. Orient the gear in the same position as it was prior to removal. See **Figure 12** for a correctly assembled mainshaft.

7. Wrap and store the assembly until it is ready for installation into the crankcase. Install the complete transmission assembly as described in Chapter Five, *Crankcase Assembly*.

COUNTERSHAFT

Disassembly

Refer to **Figure 13**.

1. Clean the assembled countershaft (**Figure 14**) in solvent and dry with compressed air.
2. Remove the thrust washer from the shaft.
3. Remove first gear from the shaft.
4. Remove the first gear bushing from the shaft.
5. At the opposite end of the shaft, remove the thrust washer.
6. Remove fourth gear from the shaft.
7. Remove the spline washer from the shaft.
8. Remove third gear from the shaft.
9. Remove the spline washer from the shaft.
10. Remove the circlip from the shaft.
11. Remove second gear from the shaft.
12. Remove the circlip from the shaft.
13. Remove the spline washer from the shaft.
14. Keep the parts oriented and in the order of removal as shown in **Figure 15**. Inspect each part as described in this section, then return it to its place until assembly.

Assembly

Before beginning assembly, have two new circlips (part No. 90601-459-000) on hand. Refer to **Figure 13**.

1. Lubricate all sliding surfaces with engine oil.
2. Install the spline washer (A, **Figure 16**) and a new circlip (B) on the countershaft. The flat side of both parts must face *out*, towards the end on which they were installed. Seat the circlip in the groove in the shaft (**Figure 17**).
3. Install second gear on the shaft (**Figure 18**). The gear *must* face as shown in **Figure 18**.
4. Install a new circlip (A, **Figure 19**) and the spline washer (B) on the shaft. The flat side of both parts must face *in*, away from the end on which they

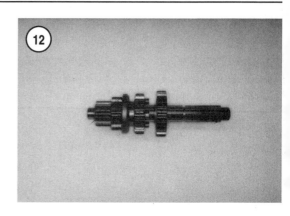

were installed. Seat the circlip in the groove in the shaft (**Figure 20**).

5. Install third gear on the shaft. The gear dogs must face *in* (**Figure 21**).
6. Install the spline washer (**Figure 22**) on the shaft. The flat side must face *in*, away from the end on which it was installed.
7. Install fourth gear on the shaft (**Figure 23**). The dot mark on one side of the gear must face *out*, towards the end on which it was installed.
8. Install the thrust washer on the end of the shaft (**Figure 24**). The flat side must face *in*, away from end on which it was installed.
9. At the opposite end of the countershaft, install the first gear bushing (A, **Figure 25**).
10. Install first gear (B, **Figure 25**) on the shaft. The recessed side of the gear (A, **Figure 26**) must face *out*.
11. Install the thrust washer on the end of the shaft (B, **Figure 26**). The flat side must face *out*, towards the end on which it was installed). See **Figure 27** for a correctly assembled countershaft.
12. Wrap and store the assembly until it is ready for installation into the crankcase. Install the complete transmission assembly as described in Chapter Five, *Crankcase Assembly*.

TRANSMISSION INSPECTION

Mainshaft Inspection

Record all measurements while performing the following procedure. Refer to **Table 1** for the specifications when measuring and inspecting the parts.

1. Inspect the mainshaft for:
   a. Worn or damaged splines (A, **Figure 28**).
   b. Broken or damaged teeth (B, **Figure 28**).

COUNTERSHAFT AND GEAR ASSEMBLY

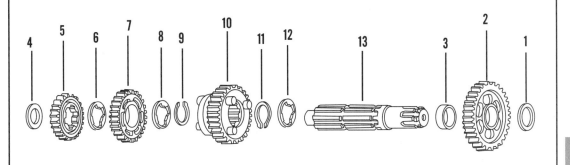

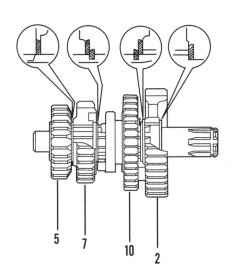

1. Thrust washer
2. 1st gear
3. 1st gear bushing
4. Thrust washer
5. 4th gear
6. Spline washer
7. 3rd gear

8. Spline washer
9. Circlip
10. 2nd gear
11. Circlip
12. Spline washer
13. Countershaft

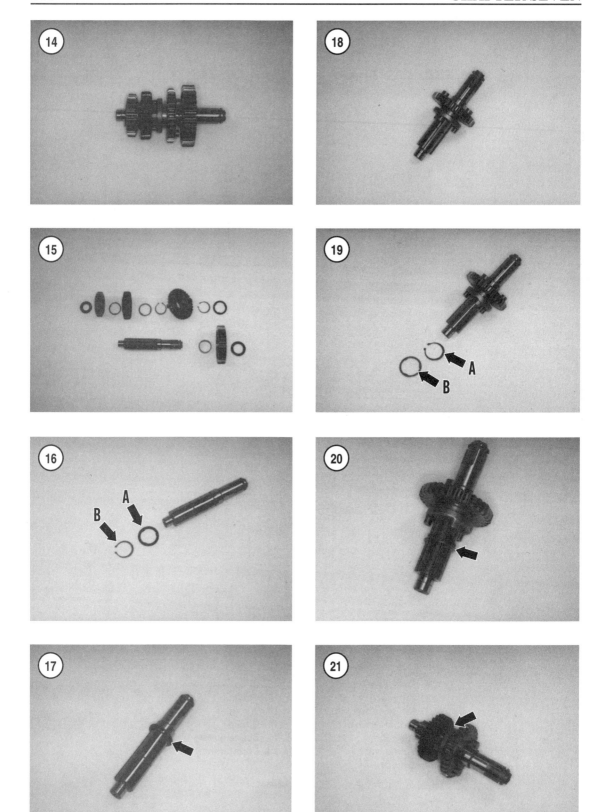

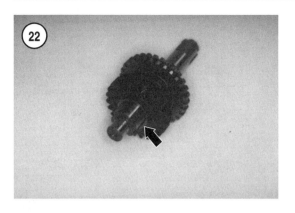

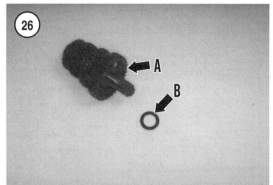

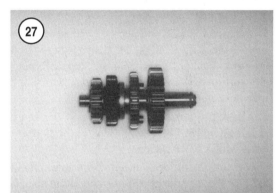

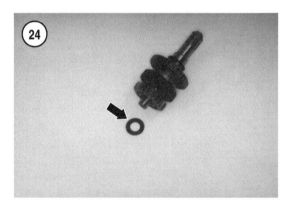

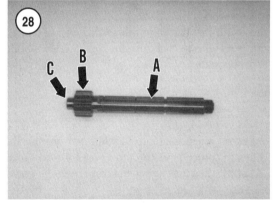

c. Wear or damage on the bearing end (C, **Figure 28**).

2. Check each mainshaft gear for:

   a. Broken or damaged teeth.

   b. Worn or damaged splines.

   c. Scored or fractured bore.

   d. Smooth operation on the mainshaft. If a gear is worn or damaged, also replace the gear it mates to on the countershaft.

   e. Worn, damaged or rounded gear dogs.

NOTE
The side of the gear dogs carrying the engine load wears and will become rounded. The unloaded side of the dogs remains unworn. Rounded gear dogs cause the transmission to jump out of gear.

3. Measure the mainshaft diameter at the second gear location (A, **Figure 29**). Replace the shaft if it is not within specifications.

4. Measure the inside diameter of second gear (**Figure 30**). Replace the gear if it is not within specifications.

5. Determine the second gear–to–mainshaft clearance. Subtract the main shaft diameter (Step 3) from the inside diameter of second gear (Step 5). Replace the worn part(s) to bring the clearance to within specifications.

6. Measure the mainshaft diameter at the fourth gear location (B, **Figure 29**). Replace the shaft if it is not within specifications.

7. Measure the inside diameter of fourth gear (**Figure 30**). Replace the gear if it is not within specifications.

8. Determine the fourth gear–to–mainshaft clearance. Subtract the main shaft diameter (Step 4) from the inside diameter of fourth gear (Step 7). Replace the worn part(s) to bring the clearance to within specifications.

Countershaft Inspection

Record all measurements while performing the following procedure. Refer to **Table 1** for the specifications when measuring and inspecting the parts.

1. Inspect the countershaft for:
   a. Worn or damaged splines (A, **Figure 31**).
   b. Wear or damage on the bearing end (B, **Figure 31**).
2. Check each countershaft gear for:
   a. Broken or damaged teeth.
   b. Worn or damaged splines.
   c. Scored or fractured bore.
   d. Smooth operation on the countershaft. If a gear is worn or damaged, also replace the gear it mates to on the mainshaft.
   e. Worn, damaged or rounded gear dogs.

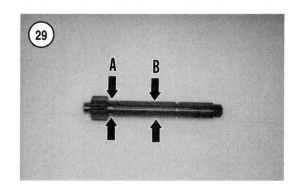

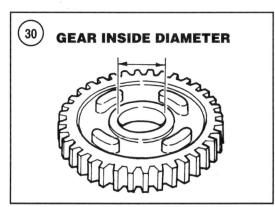

GEAR INSIDE DIAMETER

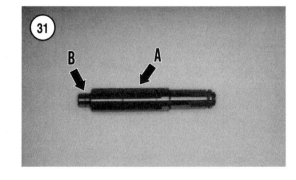

NOTE
The side of the gear dogs carrying the engine load wears and will become rounded. The unloaded side of the gear dogs remains unworn. Rounded gear dogs cause the transmission to jump out of gear.

3. Measure the countershaft diameter at the first gear bushing location (A, **Figure 32**). Replace the shaft if it is not within specifications.

4. Measure the inside diameter of the first gear bushing (**Figure 33**). Replace the bushing if it is not within specifications.

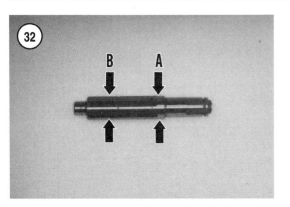

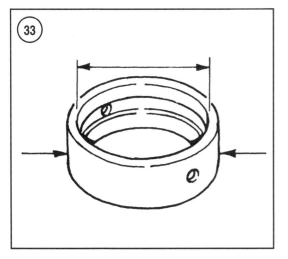

7. Measure the outside diameter of the first gear bushing (**Figure 33**). Replace the bushing if it is not within specifications.

8. Determine the first gear-to-first gear bushing clearance. Subtract the bushing outside diameter (Step 7) from the inside diameter of first gear (Step 6). Replace the worn part(s) to bring the clearance to within specifications.

9. Measure the countershaft diameter at the third gear location (B, **Figure 32**). Replace the shaft if it is not within specifications.

10. Measure the inside diameter of third gear (**Figure 30**). Replace the gear if it is not within specifications.

11. Determine the third gear-to-countershaft clearance. Subtract the countershaft diameter (Step 9) from the inside diameter of third gear (Step 10). Replace the worn part(s) to bring the clearance to within specifications.

SHIFT DRUM

The shift drum assembly (**Figure 34**) engages and disengages pairs of gears on the transmission shafts as the vehicle is upshifted and downshifted. The shift forks, which are guided by cam grooves in the shift drum, shifts the gears. The grooves are curved to guide the forks to the selected gears by cam-action.

Disassembly/Assembly

Refer to **Figure 35**.

1. Remove the clips from the shift forks (**Figure 36**).

2. Remove the guide pin from each shift fork (A, **Figure 37**).

3. Remove the shift forks from the shift drum. Identify each fork so it can be installed in its original position on the shift drum.

4. Remove the neutral switch rotor (B, **Figure 37**).

5. Clean all parts in solvent and dry with compressed air.

6. Inspect the parts as described in this section.

7. Reverse these steps to assemble the shift drum. Lubricate all parts with engine oil prior to assembly.

8. Wrap and store the assembly until it is ready for installation into the crankcase. Install the complete

5. Determine the first gear bushing-to-countershaft clearance. Subtract the shaft diameter (Step 3) from the bushing inside diameter (Step 4). Replace the worn part(s) to bring the clearance to within specifications.

6. Measure the inside diameter of first gear (**Figure 30**). Replace the gear if it is not within specifications.

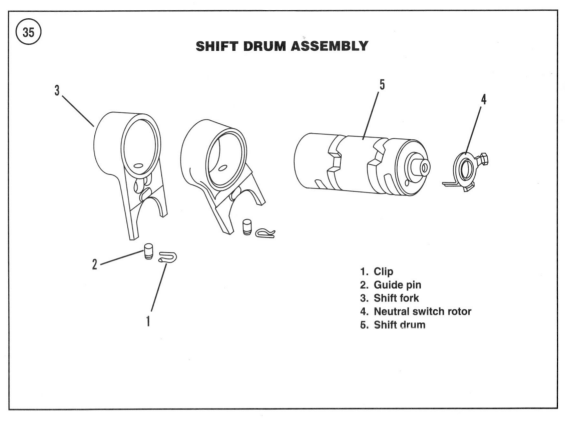

SHIFT DRUM ASSEMBLY

1. Clip
2. Guide pin
3. Shift fork
4. Neutral switch rotor
5. Shift drum

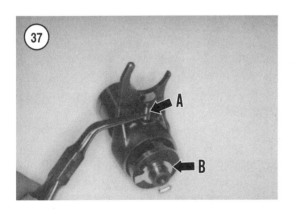

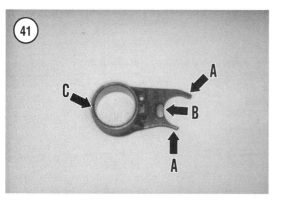

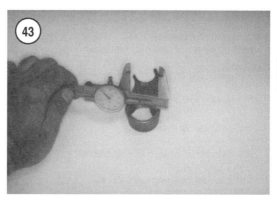

transmission assembly as described in Chapter Five, *Crankcase Assembly*.

Inspection

Record all measurements while performing the following procedure. Refer to **Table 1** for the specifications when measuring and inspecting the parts.

1. Inspect the shift drum for worn or damaged grooves, particularly at the *cam points* (**Figure 38**). Worn cam grooves prevent complete gear engagement. This can cause rough shifting and allow the transmission to disengage.

2. Visually inspect the guide pins (**Figure 39**) for wear and flat spots. If any wear is detected, replace the pins and clips. Worn pins prevent complete gear engagement. This can cause rough shifting and allow the transmission to disengage.

3. Measure the diameter of the shift drum at several locations along its length (**Figure 40**). Replace the drum if it is not within specifications.

4. Check each shift fork for:
   a. Broken or damaged fingers (A, **Figure 41**).
   b. Wear at the bearing surfaces (B, **Figure 41**).
   c. Scored or fractured bore (C, **Figure 41**).

5. Measure the finger thickness of each shift fork at the location shown in **Figure 42**. Replace the fork if it is not within specifications.

6. Measure the inside diameter of the fork bushing (**Figure 43**). Replace the fork if it is not within specifications.

Tables 1 and 2 are on the following page.

Table 1 TRANSMISSION SERVICE SPECIFICATIONS

	New mm (in.)	Service limit mm (in.)
Mainshaft assembly		
Shaft diameter at second gear	16.966-16.984 (0.6679-0.6686)	16.95 (0.667)
Second gear inside diameter	17.032-17.059 (0.6705-0.6716)	17.1 (0.673)
Second gear–to–main shaft clearance	0.048-0.093 (0.0018-0.0036)	0.1 (0.004)
Shaft diameter at fourth gear	16.966-16.984 (0.6679-0.6686)	16.95 (0.667)
Fourth gear inside diameter	17.016-17.043 (0.6699-0.6709)	17.1 (0.673)
Fourth gear–to–main shaft clearance	0.032-0.077 (0.0012-0.0030)	0.1 (0.004)
Countershaft assembly		
Shaft diameter at first gear bushing	19.959-19.980 (0.7857-0.7866)	19.94 (0.785)
First gear bushing–to–shaft clearance	0.020-0.062 (0.0008-0.0024)	0.1 (0.004)
First gear bushing inside diameter	20.0-20.021 (0.7874-0.7882)	20.08 (0.7905)
First gear inside diameter	23.020-23.053 (0.9062-0.9075)	23.10 (0.9094)
First gear bushing outside diameter	22.979-23.0 (0.9046-0.9055)	22.93 (0.9027)
First gear–to–bushing clearance	0.020-0.074 (0.0007-0.0029)	0.1 (0.004)
Shaft diameter at third gear	19.959-19.980 (0.7857-0.7866)	19.94 (0.785)
Third gear inside diameter	20.020-20.053 (0.7881-0.7894)	20.10 (0.791)
Third gear–to–shaft clearance	0.04-0.094 (0.0016-0.0037)	0.1 (0.004)
Shift drum assembly		
Shift drum diameter	33.95-33.975 (1.3366-1.3375)	33.93 (1.3358)
Shift fork finger thickness	4.86-4.94 (0.191-0.194)	4.6 (0.18)
Shift fork bushing inside diameter	34.075-34.1 (1.3415-1.3425)	34.14 (1.344)

Table 2 TRANSMISSION GENERAL SPECIFICATIONS

Transmission	4-speed constant mesh
Primary reduction	4.058 (69/17)
Final reduction	3.846 (50/13)
Gear ratios	
First gear	2.833 (34/12)
Second gear	1.937 (31/16)
Third gear	1.3 (26/20)
Fourth gear	0.958 (23/24)

CHAPTER EIGHT

FUEL AND EXHAUST SYSTEMS

This chapter describes service procedures for the following components.

1. Air cleaner.
2. Intake manifold.
3. Carburetor.
4. Throttle housing and cable.
5. Fuel tank.
6. Exhaust pipe and muffler.

Read this chapter before attempting repairs to these components. Become familiar with the procedures, photos and illustrations to understand the skill and equipment required. Refer to Chapter One for tool usage and techniques.

SERVICE PRECAUTIONS AND PRACTICES

When working on the fuel and exhaust systems, observe the following shop and safety practices.

> *WARNING*
> *Gasoline and most cleaning solvents are extremely flammable. Do not smoke or use electrical tools in the vicinity of the work area. Heating appliances, and items with a pilot light, should be shut off. If gasoline can be smelled in the work area, a potential hazard exists.*

1. Turn off the fuel valve.
2. Never work on a hot engine.
3. Wipe up fuel and solvent spills immediately.
4. Work in a well-ventilated area.
5. Wear eye protection when using compressed air and when spraying solvents and degreasers.
6. Keep a fire extinguisher in the shop, rated for class B (fuel) and class C (electrical) fires.

AIR CLEANER

Removal/Installation

Refer to Chapter Three for air filter cleaning and PAIR system (Pulse Secondary Air Injection System) (**Figure 1**) maintenance. The PAIR system is installed on 1999 and 2000 models only. Refer to the following procedure to remove the air cleaner housing from the vehicle.

Refer to **Figure 2**.

1. Remove the seat as described in Chapter Thirteen.
2. Loosen the connecting band screw at the carburetor.
3. For 1999 and 2000 models, remove the PAIR system hoses.
4. Remove the two mounting bolts.
5. Remove the three plastic rivets.
6. Lift the air cleaner housing from the vehicle.
7. Reverse these steps to install the air cleaner housing.

Air Intake Restrictor

The air intake restrictor (**Figure 3**) reduces engine performance. Use this device if the vehicle is operated by an individual with limited riding experience. The engine is limited to approximately one-half its potential performance when the restrictor is in place and the throttle level limiter is adjusted to its slowest position. See *Throttle Control* in this chapter. Remove or install the restrictor as follows:

1. Remove the seat as described in Chapter Thirteen.
2. Unlatch the four retainer clips on the air cleaner housing (**Figure 4**).
3. Remove or install the restrictor cap (**Figure 5**) on the air intake.
4. Reverse the above steps to install the air cleaner housing and seat.
5. Test the vehicle to determine if it performs as desired.

CARBURETOR AND INTAKE MANIFOLD

Removal/Installation

1. Park the vehicle on a flat surface and set the parking brake.
2. Turn off the fuel valve.
3. Remove the front fender assembly as described in Chapter Thirteen.
4. Clamp the fuel lines to prevent fuel leakage (A, **Figure 6**). If clamps are not available, drain the fuel into a suitable container.
5. Back the hose clamps off from the ends of the fuel lines (B, **Figure 6**), then remove the lines from the fuel valve.

NOTE
Use a shop rag to absorb any fuel remaining in the lines.

6. Unscrew the carburetor top (**Figure 7**) and pull the throttle valve assembly from the carburetor (**Figure 8**). The carburetor top is part of the throttle cable and cannot be removed. To remove the gasket, spring and throttle valve assembly from the cable (**Figure 9**), compress the spring and remove the cable through the slot in the throttle valve.

CAUTION
Handle the throttle valve and needle with care. Do not bend or damage the needle.

7. Remove the air vent tube from the carburetor (**Figure 10**).
8. Remove the drain tube (A, **Figure 11**).
9. Loosen the air cleaner tube clamp (B, **Figure 11**).
10. Remove the two carburetor mounting bolts (A, **Figure 12**), then remove the intake manifold cover (B).
11. Tilt the carburetor down and remove it from the engine. Account for the gasket and O-ring fitted to the carburetor intake.
12. If it is necessary to remove the intake manifold, perform the following procedure.
   a. For 1999 and 2000 models, remove the PAIR system vacuum tube from the manifold (**Figure 13**).
   b. Remove the two bolts securing the intake manifold (**Figure 14**), then remove the manifold.
   c. Account for the manifold gaskets and the O-ring in the carburetor opening.

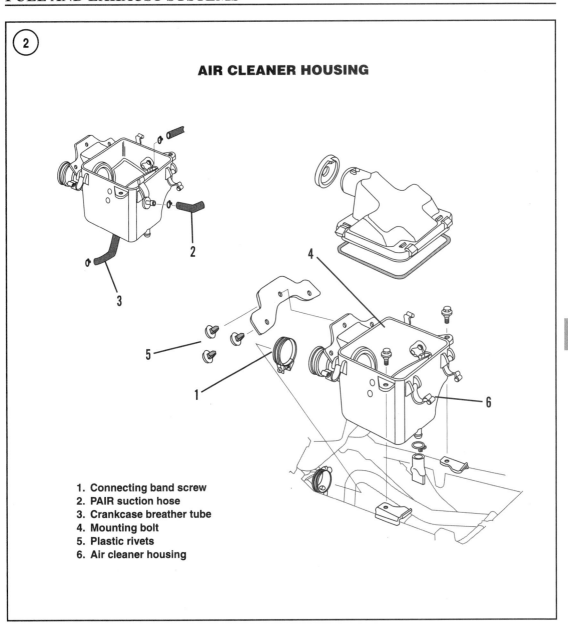

2

AIR CLEANER HOUSING

1. Connecting band screw
2. PAIR suction hose
3. Crankcase breather tube
4. Mounting bolt
5. Plastic rivets
6. Air cleaner housing

8

3

4

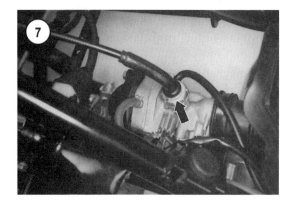

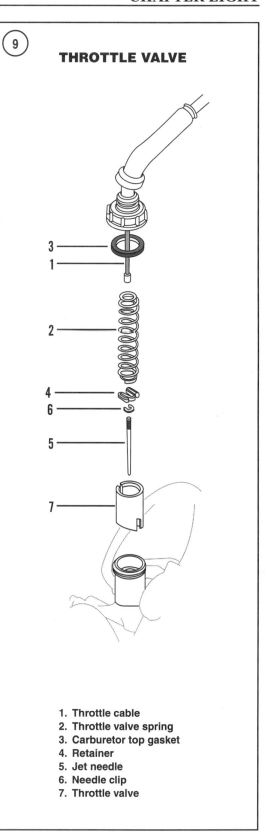

THROTTLE VALVE

1. Throttle cable
2. Throttle valve spring
3. Carburetor top gasket
4. Retainer
5. Jet needle
6. Needle clip
7. Throttle valve

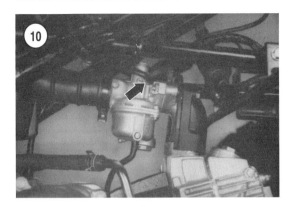

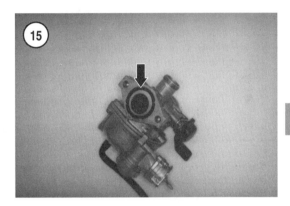

8

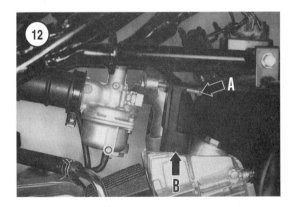

13. Cover the openings to the engine and air cleaner housing.

14. Inspect the parts as described in this section.

15. Reverse these steps to install the intake manifold and carburetor. Note the following:

    a. Install a new O-ring around the carburetor intake opening (**Figure 15**).

    b. Install new gaskets (**Figure 16**) at both connection points of the intake manifold.

    c. Tighten all bolts and screws securely.

16. After completing installation:

a. Turn on the fuel valve and inspect the carburetor for leaks or fuel flowing from the drain tube (**Figure 17**). If fuel flows from the drain tube, the float valve is either stuck or not seating completely. Turn off the fuel valve and tap the float chamber with a screwdriver. If the float is lightly stuck, this may loosen the float. Turn on the fuel valve and check for leaks. If leaking continues, remove the carburetor and examine the float, float valve and valve seat.

b. Check the throttle free play as described in Chapter Three.

c. Adjust the idle speed as described in Chapter Three.

d. Adjust the pilot air screw as described in this chapter.

e. If necessary, adjust for high altitude as described in this chapter.

Carburetor Identification

Figure 18 shows a typical view of both types of carburetors that are used on the vehicle. Differences in the jetting are due to the PAIR system (Pulse Secondary Air Injection System) fitted to 1999 and 2000 models. Refer to **Table 1** for the identification number of each carburetor. If carburetor replacement parts are required, supply the dealership with the correct carburetor identification number.

Disassembly

Refer to **Figure 18**.

> *NOTE*
> *The choke lever (A, **Figure 19**) cannot be removed from the carburetor body.*

1. While counting the number of turns, *lightly* seat the pilot air screw into the carburetor body. (B, **Figure 19**). Record the number of turns for reference when adjusting the carburetor.

2. Remove the pilot air screw (**Figure 20**), and the spring, washer and O-ring fitted to the screw (**Figure 21**).

3. Remove the throttle stop screw (**Figure 22**).

4. Remove the screws from the fuel valve (**Figure 23**).

5. Remove the fuel valve and O-ring (**Figure 24**).

6. Remove the fuel cup (A, **Figure 25**) and O-ring seal.

7. Remove the screws from the float chamber (B, **Figure 25**).

8. Remove the float chamber and O-ring (**Figure 26**).

9. Remove the float pin from the float (**Figure 27**).

10. Remove the float and float valve (**Figure 28**).

11. Remove the slow jet (**Figure 29**).

12. Remove the main jet (**Figure 30**).

13. Remove the needle jet holder (**Figure 31**).

14. Remove the needle jet (**Figure 32**).

15. Clean and inspect the parts as described in this chapter.

Assembly

Refer to **Figure 18**.

1. Install the needle jet.

> *NOTE*
> *The rounded end of the jet must face down as shown in **Figure 33**.*

2. Install the needle jet holder (**Figure 31**) and main jet (**Figure 30**).

3. Install the slow jet (**Figure 29**).

4. Insert the float valve into the float (**Figure 34**).

5. Align the float in the fuel chamber, then insert the float pin (**Figure 27**).

6. Install a new O-ring on the float chamber, aligning the O-ring tab in the float chamber (**Figure 26**). Screw the float chamber to the carburetor (B, **Figure 25**).

7. Install a new O-ring, then screw the fuel cup (A, **Figure 25**) into place.

8. Install a new O-ring, then screw the fuel valve (**Figure 24**) into place.

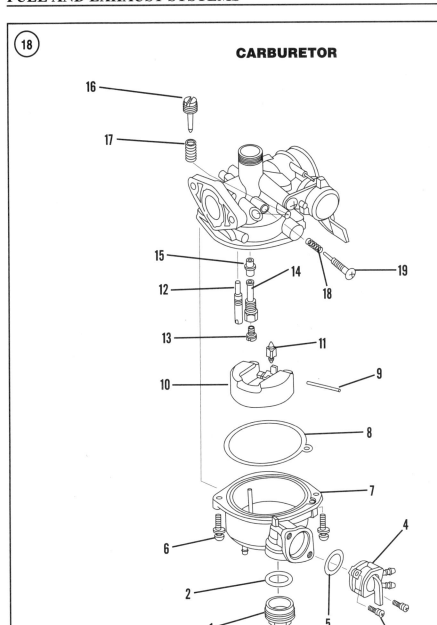

CARBURETOR

18

8

1. Fuel cup
2. O-ring
3. Screw
4. Fuel valve
5. O-ring
6. Screw
7. Float chamber
8. O-ring
9. Float pin
10. Float
11. Float valve
12. Slow jet
13. Main jet
14. Needle jet holder
15. Needle jet
16. Air pilot screw
17. Spring
18. Spring
19. Throttle stop screw

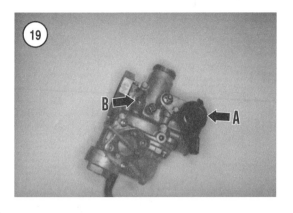

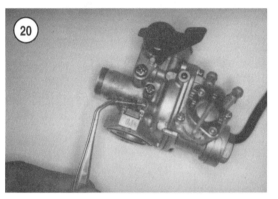

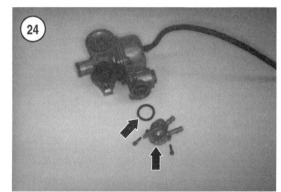

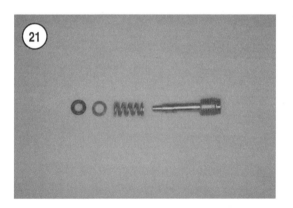

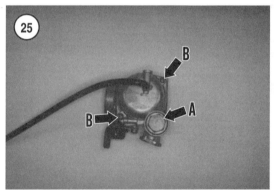

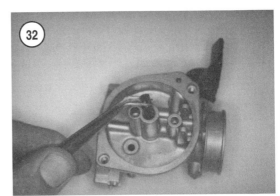

8

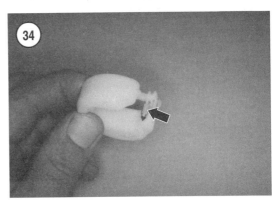

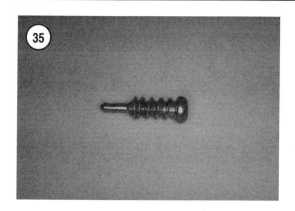

9. Place the spring on the throttle stop screw (**Figure 35**), then install the screw (**Figure 22**).

10. Place the spring, washer and new O-ring on the pilot air screw (**Figure 21**), then install the screw (**Figure 20**).

> *NOTE*
> *Lightly seat the screw, then back the screw out the number of turns recorded during disassembly. If the number of turns is not known, refer to **Table 2** for the initial setting.*

11. If the throttle valve assembly (**Figure 8**) was disassembled, perform the following procedure.

    a. Place the needle clip in the third groove of the jet needle (6, **Figure 9**).

    b. Insert the needle through the throttle valve, then clip the retainer (4, **Figure 9**) into place.

    c. Route the end of the throttle cable through the carburetor top gasket and throttle valve spring (2, **Figure 9**). Compress the spring and route the cable through the throttle valve, seating the end of the cable in the bottom of the throttle valve.

> *CAUTION*
> *Handle the throttle valve and needle with care. Do not bend or damage the needle.*

12. Adjust the carburetor as described in this chapter.

Cleaning and Inspection

Use a commercial cleaner specifically for carburetors, since the cleaner contains agents for removing fuel residues and buildup. Use a cleaner that is

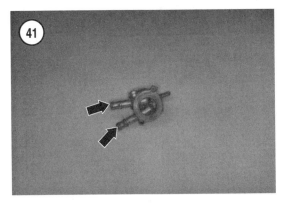

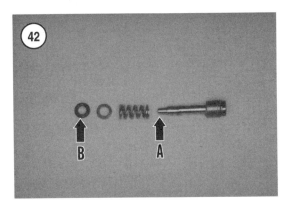

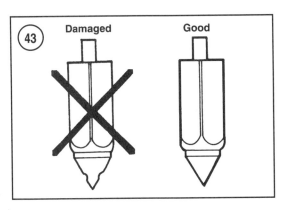

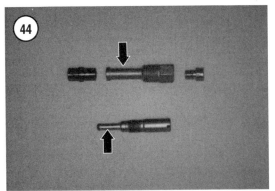

harmless to rubber and plastic parts. Follow the manufacturer's instructions when using the cleaner.

Because of heat and age, O-rings eventually lose their flexibility and do not seal properly. Replace all O-rings and gaskets when rebuilding a carburetor.

> *CAUTION*
> *Do not attempt to clean the jet orifices or seats with wire or drill bits. These items can scratch the surfaces, and alter flow rates or cause leakage.*

1. Clean all the parts in carburetor cleaner.
2. When all parts are clean, wash the parts again in hot soapy water. Rinse in cold water and dry with compressed air.
3. Inspect the float chamber overflow tube for blockage (**Figure 36**). Clean with compressed air.
4. Inspect and clean all passages with compressed air (**Figures 37-40**).
5. Inspect the fuel valve (**Figure 41**) and clean the passages with compressed air.
6. Inspect the pilot air screw assembly (**Figure 42**) as follows:
   a. Inspect the tip of the screw (A, **Figure 42**). It should be smooth and evenly tapered. If it is stepped or dented (**Figure 43**), replace the screw.
   b. Inspect the O-ring (B, **Figure 42**) for splitting and/or hardness. The O-ring helps prevent air leakage around the pilot air screw. Replace the O-ring if it is not flexible and in good condition.
7. Inspect the throttle stop screw (**Figure 35**). Replace the screw if it is bent or damaged.
8. Inspect the slow jet and main jet holder for wear or damage. Check that all the small holes in the parts (**Figure 44**) are clean and undamaged.

9. Inspect the float assembly as follows:

   a. Inspect the tip of the float valve (A, **Figure 45**). If it is stepped or dented (**Figure 43**), replace the float valve.

   b. Inspect the float (B, **Figure 45**) for leakage. Replace the float if fuel is detected inside the float.

   c. Inspect the float valve seat (C, **Figure 45**). The seat should be clean and undamaged or the float valve will not seat properly and the carburetor will overflow.

   d. Install the float valve, float and float pin so the float level can be measured.

   e. Invert the carburetor so the float rests in the closed position, then measure the distance from the edge of the float chamber to the bottom of the float (**Figure 46**). Refer to **Table 1** for the specification. If it does not meet the specification, replace the float. The float is not adjustable.

10. Inspect the jet needle (5, **Figure 9**). The needle should be smooth and evenly tapered. If it is stepped, dented, worn or bent, replace the needle.

11. Inspect the fit of the throttle valve (7, **Figure 9**) in the carburetor body. The throttle valve should fit snugly, but easily slide through the bore.

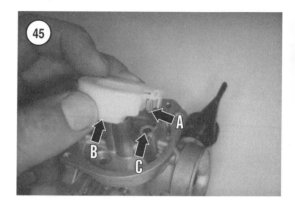

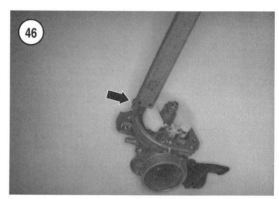

CARBURETOR ADJUSTMENTS

Idle Speed

Refer to Chapter Three for adjustment.

Pilot Air Screw

The pilot air screw (A, **Figure 47**) is preset by the manufacturer and does not need routine adjustment. The only time the screw needs adjusting is when the carburetor has been overhauled, a new pilot air screw has been installed or the screw setting is unknown because of tampering.

1. Turn the pilot air screw in until it *lightly* seats.

2. Turn the pilot air screw out the number of turns specified in **Table 2**.

3. Check that the air cleaner is clean.

4. Attach a tachometer to the engine following the manufacturer's instructions.

5. Start the engine and allow it to warm up.

WARNING
Do not run the engine in an enclosed area. Carbon monoxide can build up and cause unconsciousness and death.

6. Adjust the throttle stop screw (B, **Figure 47**) to set the engine idle speed to the specification in **Table 2**.

7. Raise and lower the engine speed a few times to ensure that it returns to the idle speed.

8. Set the pilot air screw as follows:

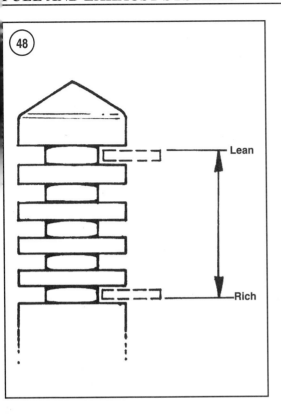

Lean

Rich

a. Turn the pilot air screw *in* until the engine speed begins to decrease. Note the slot position of the screw head.

b. Turn the screw *out* until the engine speed begins to decrease. Note the slot position of the screw head.

c. Turn the screw *in* until the slot in the screw head is between the two points observed in substeps a and b.

9. If necessary, reset the engine idle speed to the specification in **Table 2**.

10. Turn the engine off and disconnect the tachometer.

High Altitude Jetting

When the vehicle will be operated at altitudes above 5000 ft. (1500 m), replace the carburetor main jet. Refer to **Table 1** for the high-altitude jet number. Install and adjust the carburetor jet as follows:

> *CAUTION*
> *If the vehicle is operated at altitudes below 5000 ft. (1500 m) with the high-altitude jet in the carburetor, en-*

gine overheating and possible damage may occur. Always install the standard jet for altitudes below 5000 ft. (1500 m).

1. Remove the carburetor as described in this chapter.

2. Remove the float chamber as described in this chapter.

3. Remove the main jet from the needle jet holder (**Figure 30**).

4. Install the high-altitude jet into the needle jet holder. See **Table 1**.

5. Turn the pilot air screw *out* an eighth turn from its standard setting.

> *NOTE*
> *If the carburetor is refitted with the standard jet, turn the pilot air screw in eighth turn, back to its standard setting.*

6. Install the float chamber as described in this chapter.

7. Install the carburetor as described in this chapter.

8. Adjust the idle speed at the operating altitude. See Chapter Three for adjustment procedures.

Jet Needle Adjustment

The jet needle (5, **Figure 9**) controls the fuel from a fourth to three-fourths throttle. As the throttle is opened and closed, the tapered needle regulates the amount of fuel drawn past the needle jet. Adjust the position of the needle in the jet by removing the needle clip and positioning it on a higher or lower groove in the needle.

Raising the clip (**Figure 48**) lowers the needle into jet, causing a lean fuel mixture. Lowering the clip (**Figure 48**) raises the needle from the jet, causing a rich fuel mixture.

Adjust the needle according to the loads or climate in which it is operated. Do not adjust the needle in an attempt to correct other problems that may exist with the carburetor. Engine damage can occur if riding conditions do not warrant an overly rich or lean fuel mixture.

Remove and install the jet needle as described in this chapter.

8

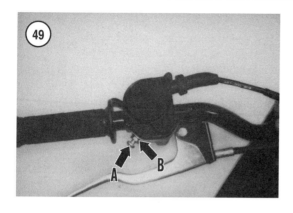

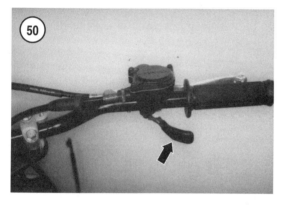

THROTTLE CONTROL AND CABLE

Throttle Lever Adjustment

Refer to Chapter Three for adjustment.

Throttle Limiter

The throttle limiter (A, **Figure 49**) screw can be adjusted to keep top speed and performance within a range that is safe for the operator. The limiter regulates the overall movement of the throttle lever (**Figure 50**). The vehicle will perform at about one-half its potential when the limiter is adjusted to its maximum *slow* position and the air intake restrictor is in place. See *Air Cleaner* in this chapter. Adjust the limiter as follows:

1. Remove the handlebar cover as described in Chapter Thirteen.
2. Loosen the locknut (B, **Figure 50**) on the limiter screw.
3. Turn the limiter screw clockwise to reduce throttle movement (less performance) or counterclockwise to increase throttle movement (more performance).

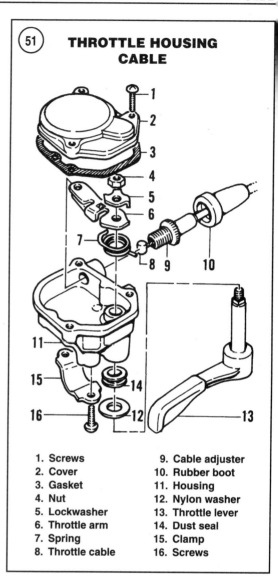

THROTTLE HOUSING CABLE

1. Screws	9. Cable adjuster
2. Cover	10. Rubber boot
3. Gasket	11. Housing
4. Nut	12. Nylon washer
5. Lockwasher	13. Throttle lever
6. Throttle arm	14. Dust seal
7. Spring	15. Clamp
8. Throttle cable	16. Screws

4. Hold the screw in place and tighten the locknut.
5. Install the handlebar cover as described in Chapter Thirteen.
6. Test the vehicle to determine if it performs as desired.

NOTE
If the limiter screw is completely removed, replace it with the short screw provided with the Honda owners packet. If the screw is not available, find a short screw with the same thread pitch. Leaving the hole open allows dirt and moisture into the housing and eventually causes damage.

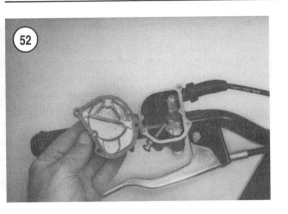

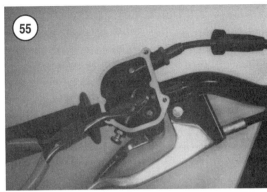

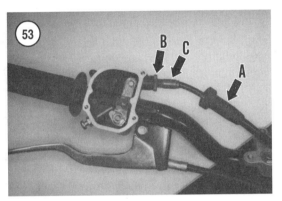

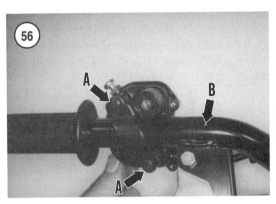

8

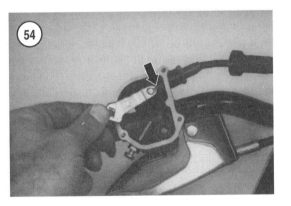

Throttle Housing
Disassembly/Inspection/Assembly

Disassemble and inspect the throttle housing if the throttle lever does not return, indicating loss of spring action, or if the throttle lever binds or drags.

Refer to **Figure 51**.

1. Remove the handlebar cover as described in Chapter Thirteen.

2. Remove the screws from the cover, then remove the cover and gasket (**Figure 52**).

3. Slide the rubber boot off the cable adjuster (A, **Figure 53**).

4. Loosen the cable adjuster locknut (B, **Figure 53**), then turn the cable adjuster in (C) to gain maximum free-play in the cable.

5. Pry the locking tabs away from the throttle arm retaining nut, then remove the nut and lockwasher. Install a new lockwasher during assembly.

6. Lift the throttle arm from the pivot, then release the cable through the slot on the bottom of the throttle arm (**Figure 54**).

7. Remove the return spring from the housing (**Figure 55**).

8. Remove the throttle lever, washer and dust seal from the bottom of the housing.

9. Remove the two screws from the handlebar clamp (A, **Figure 56**).

10. Inspect the throttle assembly for the following.

    a. Corrosion due to water leakage around the gasket, throttle limiter screw or dust seals.

    b. Broken or fatigued return spring.

    c. Frayed or kinked throttle cable.

    d. Worn throttle cable end.

    e. Worn plastic washer.

11. To begin installation, loosely screw the clamp to the housing (A, **Figure 56**). Align the protrusion on the housing with the punch mark on the handlebars (B, **Figure 56**). Tighten the clamp screws.

12. Lubricate the inside of the dust seal with lithium-based multipurpose grease (NLGI No. 2).

13. Place the plastic washer and dust seal on the throttle lever, then insert the throttle lever through the bottom of the housing.

14. Insert the return spring into the housing, arranging the spring so the hook is facing up and located as shown in **Figure 57**.

15. Apply lithium-based multipurpose grease (NLGI No. 2) on the cable end (**Figure 58**), then attach the cable to the throttle arm.

16. Hook the return spring to the throttle arm (A, **Figure 59**).

17. Fit the square shoulder on the throttle lever shaft through the square hole in the throttle arm.

18. Place a new lockwasher on the throttle lever shaft, then tighten the nut to the shaft (B, **Figure 59**).

19. Bend the tabs on the lockwasher to prevent the nut from loosening (C, **Figure 59**).

20. Place a new gasket on the cover (**Figure 52**), then screw the cover into place. Torque the screws to the specification in **Table 3**.

21. Adjust the cable as described in Chapter Three.

22. If necessary, adjust the throttle limiter screw as described in this section.

Cable Replacement

1. Park the vehicle on a flat surface and set the parking brake.

2. Remove the handlebar cover and front fender assembly as described in Chapter Thirteen.

3. Disconnect the cable and carburetor top from the throttle valve as described in *Carburetor Removal* in this chapter.

4. Disconnect the cable end from the throttle lever as described in *Throttle Housing Disassembly* in this section.

5. Disconnect any cable retainers on the frame so the cable can be removed. Note how the cable is routed so the new cable can be installed in the same location.

6. Route the new cable from the carburetor to the throttle housing.

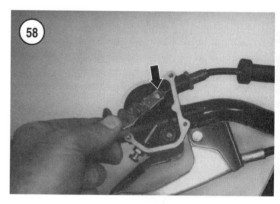

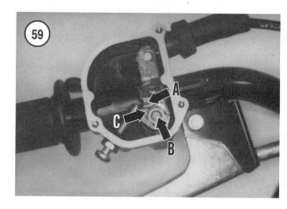

7. Attach the cable and carburetor top to the throttle valve and carburetor as described in *Carburetor Installation* in this chapter.

8. Attach the cable end to the throttle lever as described in *Throttle Housing Assembly* in this section.

9. Secure the cable to the frame with any cable retainers that were removed.

10. Adjust the cable free play as described in Chapter Three.

11. Start the engine.

a. Check the throttle lever action for proper increase and decrease in engine speed.

b. Check that there is no increase in speed when the handlebars are turned full left and right.

12. Correct any problems that are detected in Step 11.

13. Install the handlebar cover and front fender assembly as described in Chapter Thirteen.

14. Test ride the vehicle for proper operation.

FUEL TANK

Removal/Installation

1. Park the vehicle on a flat surface and set the parking brake.

2. Turn off the fuel valve.

3. Remove the front fender assembly as described in Chapter Thirteen.

4. Pull the fuel line breather tube from the steering shaft (A, **Figure 60**).

5. Clamp the fuel lines to prevent fuel leakage (A, **Figure 61**). If clamps are not available, drain the fuel into a suitable container.

6. Back the hose clamps off from the ends of the fuel lines (B, **Figure 61**), then remove the lines from the fuel valve.

> *NOTE*
> *Use a shop rag to absorb any fuel remaining in the lines.*

7. Remove the fuel tank holder bands (B, **Figure 60**) from both sides of the tank.

8. Remove the fuel tank mounting bolts (**Figure 62**) and the collars under the bolts.

> *NOTE*
> *Note how the fuel lines are routed to the fuel valve before removing the tank. Avoid snagging the clamps while removing the tank.*

9. Slowly lift the fuel tank from the vehicle (**Figure 63**).

10. Reverse these steps to install the fuel tank. Note the following:

a. Replace the fuel line hose clamps if they are distorted.

b. The upper fuel line on the tank connects to the upper fitting on the fuel valve.

c. Check that the fuel lines are not kinked or stretched when they are installed.

d. Turn on the fuel valve and check for leaks before installing the front fender assembly.

EXHAUST PIPE AND MUFFLER

Removal/Installation

Do not attempt to remove the exhaust pipe or muffler while the engine is hot.

1. Park the vehicle on a flat surface and set the parking brake.

2. Remove the rear fender assembly as described in Chapter Thirteen.

3. Remove the muffler band bolt (A, **Figure 64**).

4. Remove the muffler mounting bolt and washer (**Figure 65**).

5. Remove the muffler from the exhaust pipe. Account for the muffler gasket that is installed in the joint. Install a new gasket during reassembly.

NOTE
Do not hammer on the muffler if it is stuck to the exhaust pipe. Twist the muffler off the pipe. If necessary, ap-

ply penetrating oil around the connection.

6. Remove the exhaust pipe mounting bolt (B, **Figure 64**).

7. Remove the two exhaust pipe joint nuts (**Figure 66**), then remove the pipe from the vehicle.

NOTE
If the nuts are rusted to the studs, apply penetrating oil.

8. Remove the exhaust pipe gasket (**Figure 67**) from the cylinder head.

9. Reverse these steps to install the exhaust system. Note the following:

a. Install a new exhaust pipe gasket and muffler gasket.

b. Seat and bolt the exhaust pipe squarely in the cylinder head. Tighten the two exhaust pipe joint nuts (**Figure 66**) before tightening the exhaust pipe mounting bolt (B, **Figure 64**).

c. Torque all fasteners to the specifications in **Table 3**.

d. Install the rear fender assembly as described in Chapter Thirteen.

Table 1 CARBURETOR SPECIFICATIONS

Identification number	
1993-1998	PB1AA
1999-2000	PB5FA
Main jet number	
Standard	80
High altitude	78
Slow jet	
1993-1998	40
1999-2000	40 × 40
Jet needle clip position	3rd groove
Float level	10.7 mm (0.42 in.)

Table 2 CARBURETOR ADJUSTMENT SPECIFICATIONS

Pilot air screw initial opening	
1993-1998	1-3/8 turns out
1999-2000	2-1/2 turns out
Idle speed	1600 ± 100 rpm

Table 3 TORQUE SPECIFICATIONS

	N•m	in.-lb.	ft.-lb.
Exhaust pipe joint nuts	14	–	10
Muffler band bolt	23	–	17
Muffler mounting bolt	69	–	51
Throttle housing cover screws	4	13	–
5 mm screw	4	13	–
6 mm screw	9	80	–
6 mm flange bolt (8 mm head)	9	80	–
6 mm flange bolt (10 mm head) and nut	12	106	–
8 mm flange bolt and nut	27	–	20

8

CHAPTER NINE

ELECTRICAL SYSTEM

This chapter describes service procedures for the capacitor discharge ignition (CDI) system. The system is essentially maintenance free. The spark plug is the only part that requires routine replacement. Since the system uses a permanent magnet alternator, a battery is not required.

Refer to the *Lubrication, Maintenance and Tune-Up* section for spark plug recommendations and gapping. Refer to the *Troubleshooting* section for performance problems and possible causes related to the electrical system.

BASIC SYSTEM OPERATION

The alternator consists of a stator (A, **Figure 1**), permanent magnet flywheel (B) and ignition pulse generator (C). When the engine is running, the flywheel revolves around the stator coils and produces alternating current (AC). The current is converted to direct current (DC) by the ignition control module (A, **Figure 2**) and is stored in a capacitor.

When the flywheel is in the correct position for ignition, the ignition pulse generator signals the control module to release the stored charge to the coil (B, **Figure 2**). The charge of current into the coil primary windings induces a much higher voltage in the secondary windings which fires the spark plug.

ALTERNATOR

Removal/Installation

It is not necessary to remove the alternator assembly to test the exciter coil or ignition pulse generator coil. Refer to *Alternator and Switch Testing* in this chapter for test procedures.

Refer to **Figure 3**.

1. Park the vehicle on a level surface. Set the parking brake and place the transmission in neutral.
2. Remove the rear fender assembly as described in Chapter Thirteen.
3. Remove the recoil starter as described in Chapter Five.
4. Remove the left crankcase cover as described in *Engine Removal* in Chapter Five.
5. Attach a holding tool (A, **Figure 4**) to the flywheel (B) to prevent the flywheel from moving.

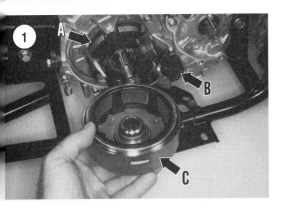

The tool shown is a *Yamaha* rotor holding tool (part No. YU-01235). The Honda holding tool (part No. 07725-0030000) can be obtained from a dealership. A strap-style rotor holder (part No. 07725-0040000) will also work to hold the flywheel.

6. Remove the flywheel nut and lockwasher (**Figure 5**).

7. Remove the flywheel as follows:

   a. Thread the outer part of the flywheel puller (A, **Figure 6**) (part No. 07933-0010000) into the flywheel.

   b. Thread the inner puller shaft (B, **Figure 6**) into the outer part (**Figure 7**).

   c. Hold the outer part with a wrench and tighten the inner puller shaft to remove the flywheel (**Figure 8**).

CAUTION
Do not hammer on the puller shaft or try to pry the flywheel off the shaft. Damage could occur to the rotor and crankshaft components.

   d. Account for the Woodruff key between the rotor and crankshaft.

8. Disconnect the alternator and neutral switch wires (**Figure 9**).

9. Remove the rubber caps from the neutral and top gear switches (**Figure 10**).

10. Press the retainers (A, **Figure 11**) and remove the wires from the switches.

11. If the engine crankcases will be separated, remove the bolt (B, **Figure 11**) and setting plate (C), remove the switches from the crankcase (**Figure 12**).

NOTE
The top switch (neutral) is marked with 14 on the switch. During assembly, reconnect this switch to the light green/red wire. The bottom switch (top gear) is marked with 15 on the switch. During assembly, reconnect this switch to the pink wire.

12. Remove the bolt and wire clamp (D, **Figure 11**).

13. Remove the bolts from the ignition pulse generator and wire clamp (A, **Figure 13**).

14. Remove the bolts from the stator (B, **Figure 13**).

15. Remove the stator and ignition pulse generator from the engine (**Figure 14**).

16. Reverse these steps to install the stator and flywheel. Note the following:

   a. Check that the wire grommets are properly seated and no wires are pinched when assembling parts.

   b. Apply dielectric grease to the electrical connections to prevent the entry of moisture.

   c. Lubricate the flywheel nut with engine oil and torque it to the specification in **Table 2**.

   d. Check that the transmission is in neutral before aligning the neutral indicator to the crankcase mark.

ALTERNATOR AND SWITCH TESTING

Before performing any of the tests in this section, remove the front fender assembly as described in Chapter Thirteen. Note the following:

   a. All tests are performed with an ohmmeter.

   b. The tests can be made at the wire connections at the ignition control module (A, **Figure 15**)

9

③

LEFT CRANKCASE COVER AND ALTERNATOR

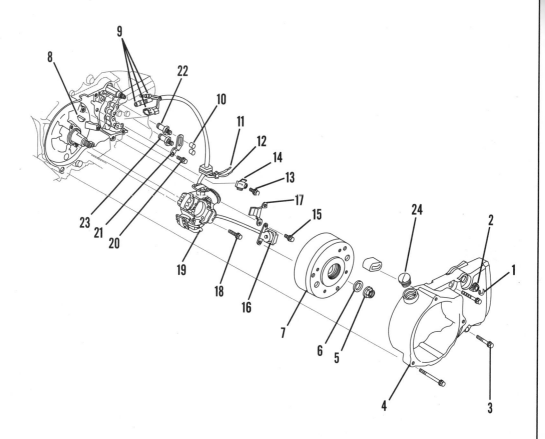

1. Circlip	13. Bolt
2. Neutral indicator	14. Wire clamp
3. Bolt	15. Bolt
4. Left crankcase cover	16. Ignition pulse generator
5. Flywheel nut	17. Wire clamp
6. Lockwasher	18. Bolt
7. Flywheel	19. Stator
8. Woodruff key	20. Bolt
9. Alternator and neutral	21 Setting plate
switch connectors	22. Neutral switch
10. Rubber cap	23. Top gear switch
11. Neutral switch wire	24. Timing hole cap
12. Top gear switch wire	

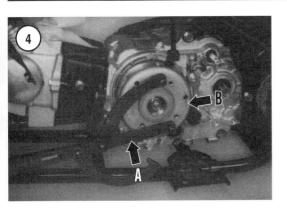

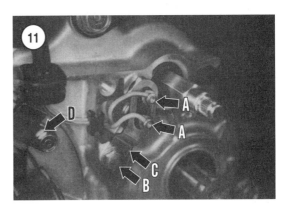

9

and the connections under the rubber cover (B). Remove the connector from the back of the control module and disconnect the wires under the cover.

c. All measurements in **Table 1** are based on an ambient temperature of 20° C (68° F).

d. Use the frame ground bolt (C, **Figure 15**) as a ground when performing the tests. If a ground (green) wire is suspected to be faulty, check for continuity between the wire and the frame ground bolt. There should be continuity.

e. Refer to the wiring diagram at the back of the manual as needed.

f. When reassembling the connections, apply dielectric grease to all connectors to prevent the entry of moisture.

g. Always recheck a component considered to be faulty after removal from the vehicle.

WARNING
Perform all tests with the engine off. The ignition control module can be damaged internally if any wires are disconnected while the engine is running. The ignition control module can also be damaged if dropped or impacted.

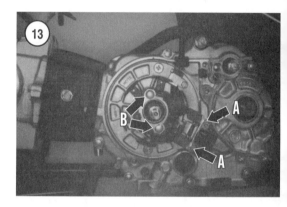

Ignition Pulse Generator

1. Set the ohmmeter to R × 100.
2. Measure the resistance between the blue/yellow wire and ground.
3. Refer to **Table 1** for the resistance reading.
4. Replace the ignition pulse generator if it is not within specification.

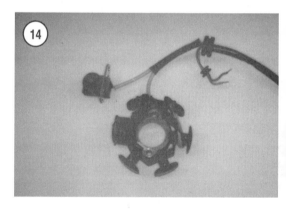

Alternator Exciter Coil

1. Set the ohmmeter to R × 100.
2. Measure the resistance between the black/red wire and ground.
3. Refer to **Table 1** for the resistance reading.
4. Replace the exciter coil if it is not within specification.

Ignition Switch and Engine Stop Switch

The following test checks the connections between the ignition switch (A, **Figure 16**) and engine stop switch (B).

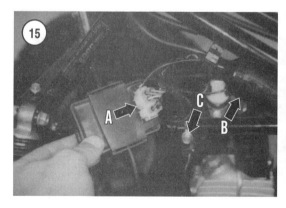

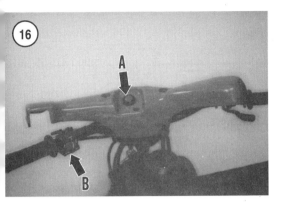

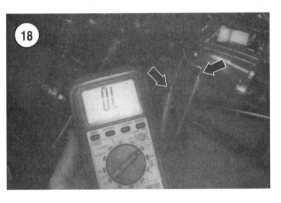

1. Connect the ohmmeter to the black/white wire and ground.

   a. There should be continuity with the ignition switch OFF and/or the engine stop switch OFF.

   b. There should be no continuity with the ignition switch ON and the engine stop switch in the RUN position.

2. If the switches do not pass the tests, check the wire connections between the two switches. If necessary, check each switch individually as described in Steps 3 and 4.

3. Check the ignition switch as follows:

   a. Connect the ohmmeter to the black/white and green wires on the ignition switch (**Figure 17**).

   b. There should be continuity only when the switch is OFF.

   c. If necessary, replace the switch as described in this chapter.

4. Check the engine stop switch as follows:

   a. Connect the ohmmeter to the black/white and green wires on the engine stop switch (**Figure 18**).

   b. There should be continuity only when the switch is OFF. Check both OFF positions.

   c. If necessary, replace the switch as described in this chapter.

Neutral Switch

1. Connect the ohmmeter to the light green/red wire and ground.

   a. There should be continuity with the transmission in neutral.

   b. There should be no continuity with the transmission in any gear.

2. If necessary, replace the switch.

Top Gear Switch

1. Connect the ohmmeter to the pink wire and ground.

   a. There should be continuity with the transmission in fourth gear.

   b. There should be no continuity with the transmission in any gear.

2. If necessary, replace the switch.

IGNITION COIL AND LEADS

Before performing any of the tests in this section, remove the front fender assembly as described in Chapter Thirteen. Note the following:

1. All tests are performed with an ohmmeter.

2. Perform the tests at the coil terminals. Disconnect the coil wires from the coil terminals (A and B, **Figure 19**) before beginning the tests. Note that the green wire (A) is on the left terminal of the coil.

3. All specifications in **Table 1** are based on an ambient temperature of 20° C (68° F).

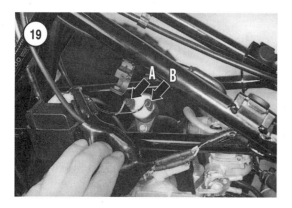

4. Refer to the wiring diagram at the back of the manual as needed.

5. When reassembling the connections, apply dielectric grease to the connectors to prevent the entry of moisture.

Primary Coil Test

Refer to **Figure 20**.
1. Set the ohmmeter to R × 1.
2. Connect the meter probes to both coil terminals and measure the resistance.
3. Refer to **Table 1** for the resistance reading.
4. Replace the coil if it is not within specification.

Secondary Coil Test

Refer to **Figure 20**.
1. Set the ohmmeter to R × 1000.
2. Remove the spark plug cap from the spark plug.
3. Insert a meter probe into the cap, touching it to the metal connector.
4. Connect the second meter probe to the left (green) coil terminal and measure the resistance.
5. Refer to **Table 1** for the resistance reading.
6. If the resistance reading is not within specification, perform the following:
   a. Remove the spark plug cap from the ignition wire.
   b. Insert a meter probe into the ignition wire (**Figure 20**).
   c. Connect the second meter probe to the left (green) coil terminal and measure the resistance.
   d. Refer to **Table 1** for the resistance reading.
   e. If the resistance reading is within specification, the spark plug cap is defective.

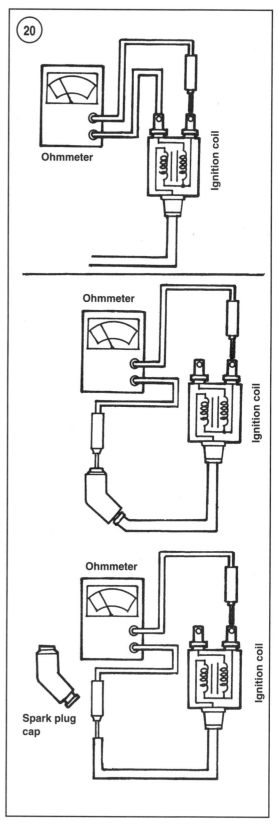

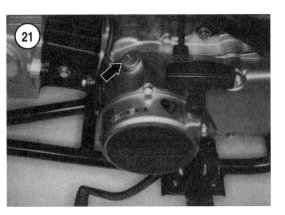

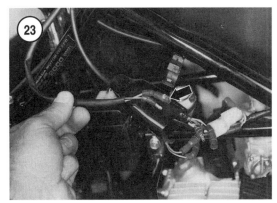

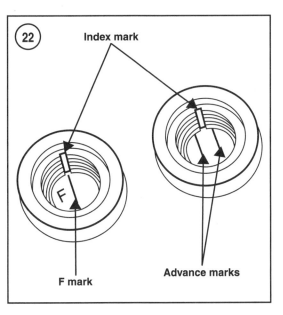

Index mark

F mark

Advance marks

f. If the resistance reading is not within specification, replace the coil and ignition wire.

IGNITION TIMING

The ignition timing is electronically controlled by the ignition control module. No adjustment is possible to the ignition timing. Check the timing to verify the ignition control module is functioning properly.

1. Warm up the engine to operating temperature.

2. Remove the timing hole cap (**Figure 21**).

3. Connect a timing light and tachometer following the manufacturer's instructions.

4. Start the engine and allow it to idle at the speed specified in **Table 1**.

5. Aim the timing light into the timing hole and observe the timing mark. The F mark should be aligned with the index mark in the hole (**Figure 22**).

6. Raise the engine speed to 3050 rpm and observe the timing marks. The index mark should be between the two advance lines (**Figure 22**).

7. If either timing check is incorrect, the ignition control module is defective and must be replaced.

8. Shut off the engine and disconnect the test equipment.

9. Screw the cap into the timing hole.

IGNITION SWITCH

Removal/Installation

1. Remove the handlebar cover as described in Chapter Thirteen.

2. Disconnect the black/white and green switch wires below the fuel tank (**Figure 23**).

NOTE
Check that the proper wires are disconnected. The black/white and green wire combination is also used for the engine stop switch.

3. Squeeze the switch tabs located under the handlebar cover (**Figure 24**).

4. Remove the switch and wiring through the top of the handlebar cover (**Figure 25**).

5. Reverse these steps to install the ignition switch. Note the following:

   a. Align the tab on the switch with the notch in the cover hole.

   b. Push on the switch to lock the tabs under the handlebar cover (**Figure 26**).

9

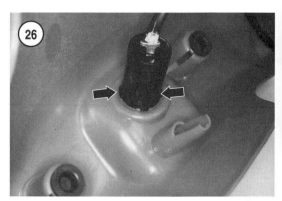

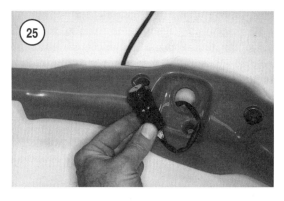

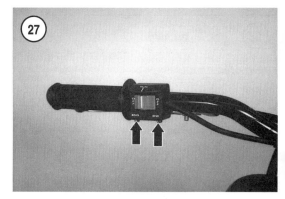

c. Route the wiring so it is not pinched or near hot surfaces.

d. Apply dielectric grease to the connectors to prevent the entry of moisture.

ENGINE STOP SWITCH

Removal/Installation

1. Remove the handlebar cover as described in Chapter Thirteen.

2. Disconnect the black/white and green switch wires below the fuel tank (**Figure 23**).

NOTE
Check that the proper wires are disconnected. The black/white and green wire combination is also used for the ignition switch.

3. Remove the screws from the switch (**Figure 27**).

4. Remove the switch and wiring from the vehicle.

5. Reverse these steps to install the switch. Note the following:

   a. Route the wiring so it is not pinched or near hot surfaces.

   b. Apply dielectric grease to the connectors to prevent the entry of moisture.

Table 1 ELECTRICAL SYSTEM SPECIFICATIONS

Idle speed	1600 ± 100 rpm
Ignition timing F mark	
1993-1998	7° BTDC @ 1600 rpm
1999-2000	7° BTDC @ 1500 rpm
Ignition timing full advance	30° BTDC @ 3050 rpm
Ignition coil resistance @ 20° C (68° F)	
Primary coil	0.19-0.23 ohms
Secondary coil with spark plug cap	7.8-8.4K ohms
Secondary coil without spark plug cap	2.8-3.4K ohms
Alternator exciter coil resistance @ 20° C (68° F)	400-800 ohms
Ignition pulse generator resistance @ 20° C (68° F)	50-200 ohms

Table 2 TORQUE SPECIFICATIONS

	N•m	in.-lb.	ft.-lb.
Flywheel nut	40	–	29
Timing hole cap	3	27	–
5 mm bolt and nut	5	44	–
6 mm bolt and nut	10	88	–
8 mm bolt and nut	22	–	16
6 mm flange bolt (8 mm head)	9	80	–
6 mm flange bolt (10 mm head) and nut	12	106	–
8 mm flange bolt and nut	27	–	20

9

CHAPTER TEN

FRONT SUSPENSION AND STEERING

This chapter describes repair of the front wheels, front suspension and steering components.

FRONT WHEEL

Removal/Installation

1. Park the vehicle on level ground and set the parking brake.
2. Remove the wheel center cap (A, **Figure 1**).
3. Loosen the lug nuts (B, **Figure 1**).
4. Raise and support the vehicle with wooden blocks placed under the frame. The front wheels must be off the ground.
5. Remove the lug nuts, then the wheel, from the brake drum.
6. If tire repair is required, perform the repair as described in this chapter.
7. Clean the lug nuts and brake drum studs. If studs are broken or damaged, replace the studs.
8. Install the wheel on the brake drum studs.
9. Finger-tighten the lug nuts.
10. Lower the vehicle to the ground, then equally tighten the lug nuts in a crossing pattern. Tighten the lug nuts in several stages to the torque specification listed in **Table 4**.
11. Raise the vehicle and spin the wheel, checking that the wheel runs true.
12. Lower the vehicle to the ground.

STEERING KNUCKLE

Removal/Inspection/Installation

Refer to **Figure 2**.

1. Remove the front wheel as described in this chapter.
2. Remove the brake assembly as described in Chapter Twelve.
3. Remove the cotter pin (**Figure 3**) from the tie rod end.
4. Remove the nut (A, **Figure 4**) from the tie rod as follows:

   a. Hold the tie rod end using a 14 mm open end wrench installed on the flats below the steering knuckle (B, **Figure 4**).

   b. Remove the nut from the tie rod end.

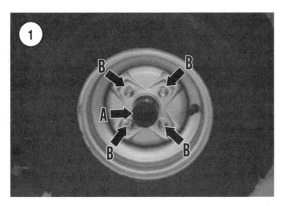

c. Remove the tie rod end from the steering knuckle.

5. Remove the cotter pin and nut (A, **Figure 5**) from the kingpin bolt (B).

6. Remove the bolt (C, **Figure 5**) securing the front brake cable bracket to the steering knuckle.

7. Remove the kingpin bolt from the steering knuckle.

8. Remove the steering knuckle (**Figure 6**) and inspect the steering knuckle for the following:

a. Inspect the axle where it contacts the wheel bearings (A, **Figure 7**). Check for scoring, galling and wear.

b. Inspect the bores for the kingpin bolt and tie rod end (B, **Figure 7**). Check for fractures and damage caused by the tie rod end or kingpin bolt.

9. Reverse these steps to install the steering knuckle. Note the following:

a. Install new nuts on the kingpin bolt and tie rod end.

b. Torque all nuts and bolts to the specifications in **Table 4**.

c. For nuts that are secured with a cotter pin, if necessary, tighten the nut after torque is reached to align the holes for a new cotter pin. Do not loosen a torqued nut to align the cotter pin holes.

CONTROL ARM

Removal/Installation

Refer to **Figure 2**.

1. Remove the front wheel as described in this chapter.

2. Remove the brake assembly as described in Chapter Twelve.

3. Remove the steering knuckle as described in this chapter.

4. Remove the lower mounting nut and bolt from the shock absorber.

5. Remove the nuts from the control arm pivot bolts (**Figure 8**).

6. Remove the control arm bolts from the control arm. Identify each bolt so it can be reinstalled in the same control arm pivot.

7. Remove and inspect the control arm.

8. Reverse these steps to install the control arm. Note the following:

a. Install new nuts on the control arm bolts.

b. Torque all nuts and bolts to the specifications in **Table 4**.

Inspection

1. Inspect all welded joints on the control arm (**Figure 9**). Check for fractures, bending or other damage. If damage is detected, replace the control arm, or have a dealership or machine shop weld and test the strength of the control arm.

2. Inspect the control arm pivots (**Figure 10**) and pivot bolts. Insert each bolt in its pivot and check for play. If play is evident, replace the pivot bolt. If play continues to be evident, replace the control arm. Honda does not indicate that the control arm bushings are replaceable.

3. Inspect the kingpin and bushings as follows:

a. Remove the dust seals (A, **Figure 11**) from the control arm, then push the kingpin (B) out of the bushing. Clean the kingpin and kingpin bushings.

b. Use a vernier caliper and measure the diameter of the kingpin at several points along its length. Refer to **Table 1** to determine if the kingpin is still within the service limit. Replace the pin if worn beyond the service limit

c. Use a vernier caliper and measure the inside diameter of the kingpin bushings. Refer to **Table 1** to determine if the bushings are within the service limit. Replace both bushings if either one is not within the service limit. Refer to the procedure in this chapter for bushing replacement.

10

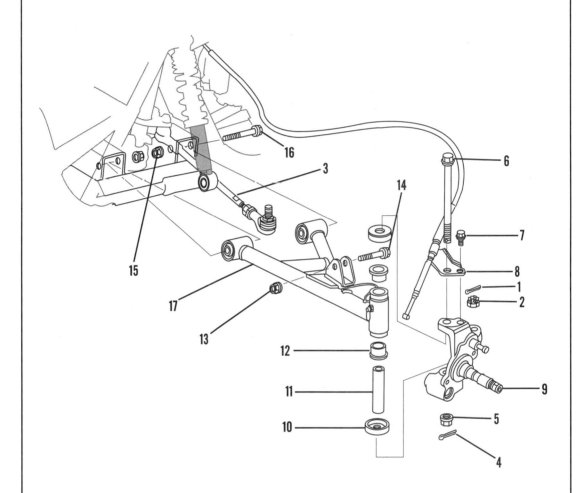

② **STEERING KNUCKLE AND CONTROL ARM**

1. Cotter pin
2. Tie rod ball joint nut
3. Tie rod
4. Cotter pin
5. Kingpin nut
6. Kingpin bolt
7. Cable bracket bolt
8. Cable bracket
9. Steering knuckle
10. Dust seal
11. Kingpin
12. Kingpin bushing
13. Shock absorber nut
14. Shock absorber bolt
15. Control arm nut
16. Control arm bolt
17. Control arm

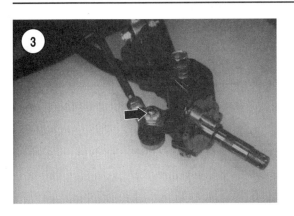

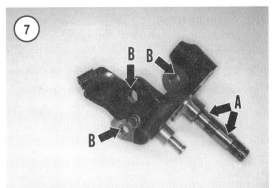

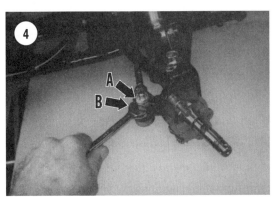

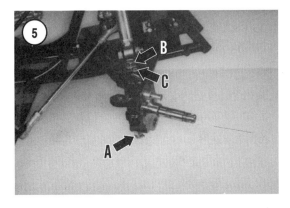

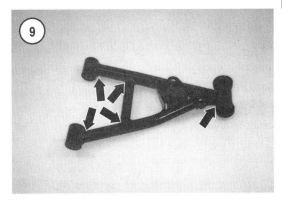

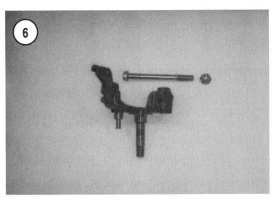

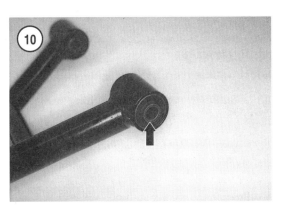

10

d. Apply molydisulfide grease to the bushings and kingpin, then insert the kingpin into the bushings.

e. Pack molydisulfide grease in the lips of the seals, then install the seals over the bushings.

4. Attach a grease gun to the nipple (C, **Figure 11**) and lubricate the kingpin and bushings with molydisulfide grease.

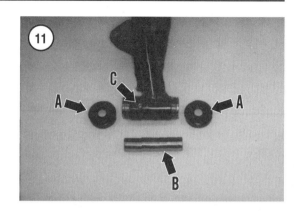

KINGPIN BUSHINGS

Replacement

Bushings will be damaged during removal. Always install new bushings. Refer to **Figure 2**.

1. Insert a blind bearing puller into the bushing (**Figure 12**).

2. Tighten the puller against the bushing (**Figure 13**).

3. Support the control arm in a hydraulic press, leaving the bearing puller (A, **Figure 14**) and bushing free to move down when pressure is applied.

4. Insert a driver through the upper bushing and rest it on the end of the bearing puller (B, **Figure 14**).

5. Press the bushing and puller from the control arm (**Figure 15**).

6. Press the second bushing from the control arm, using an appropriate-size driver.

7. Clean the bushing bores.

8. Support the control arm in the press and position a new bushing squarely over the bore (A, **Figure 16**).

9. Press and seat the bushing into the control arm. Use a driver that fits over the entire end of the bushing (B, **Figure 16**).

> *NOTE*
> *Bushings can be driven using the Honda driver (part No. 07749-0010000) and 32 × 35 mm attachment (part No. 07746-0010100). Order the parts from a dealership.*

10. Press in the second bushing.

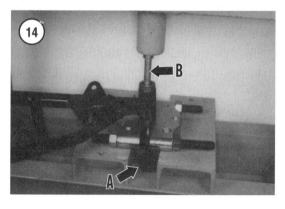

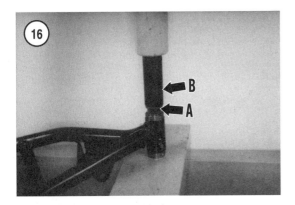

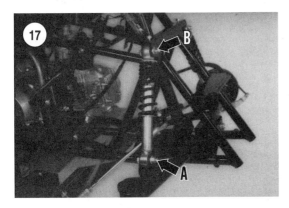

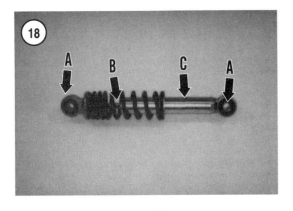

SHOCK ABSORBERS

Removal/Inspection/Installation

The front shock absorbers cannot be repaired. Replace shock absorbers as a pair if they are damaged. The shock absorbers cannot be adjusted.

1. Raise and support the vehicle with wooden blocks placed under the frame. The weight of the vehicle must be off the front wheels.

2. Remove the lower mounting nut and bolt (A, **Figure 17**).

3. Remove the upper mounting nut and bolt (B, **Figure 17**).

4. Remove the shock absorber and inspect the following:

    a. Inspect the bushings (A, **Figure 18**) and mounting bolts for wear and looseness. Fit the mounting bolts in the bushings and check for play. Replace worn or damaged parts.

    b. Inspect the rod seal for leakage (B, **Figure 18**). Replace the unit if leakage is evident.

    c. Inspect the body for (C, **Figure 18**) major dents or fractures. Replace the unit if damage is evident.

5. Reverse these steps to install the shock absorbers. Note the following:

    a. Install new nuts on the mounting bolts.

    b. Torque the nuts to the specifications in **Table 4**.

TIE RODS

Removal/Installation

The brake assembly is shown removed in the following procedure for clarity.

1. Remove the front wheel as described in this chapter.

2. Remove the cotter pin (**Figure 19**) from the tie rod end at the wheel.

3. Remove the nut (A, **Figure 20**) from the tie rod as follows:

    a. Hold the tie rod end using a 14 mm open end wrench installed on the flats below the steering knuckle (B, **Figure 20**).

    b. Remove the nut from the tie rod end.

    c. Remove the tie rod end from the steering knuckle.

10

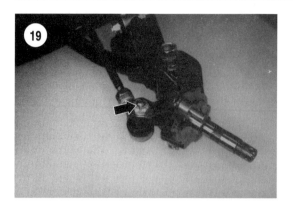

4. Repeat Step 3 to remove the tie rod from the steering shaft (**Figure 21**).

5. Reverse these steps to install the tie rods. Note the following:

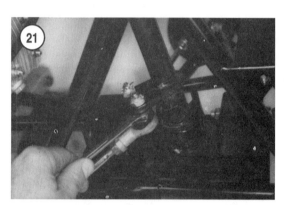

   a. Install the tie rods so the tie rod flats (**Figure 22**) are nearest the wheel.

   b. Torque all nuts to the specifications in **Table 4**.

   c. For nuts that are secured with a cotter pin, if necessary, tighten the nut after torque is reached to align the holes for a new cotter pin. Do not loosen a torqued nut to align the cotter pin holes.

6. Check wheel alignment as described in this chapter.

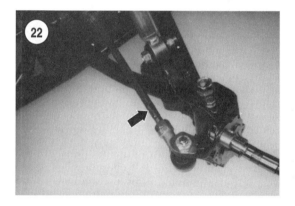

Inspection

> *NOTE*
> *The tie rod ends are sealed and non-serviceable. Do not immerse the tie rod ends in solvent or any other liquid that could penetrate the boots and seals. Wipe the ends with a shop cloth prior to inspection.*

1. Inspect the tie rod (A, **Figure 23**) for straightness. Replace the rod if it is bent.

2. Inspect the boots (B, **Figure 23**) for tears. Replace the tie rods ends if the boots are damaged or missing.

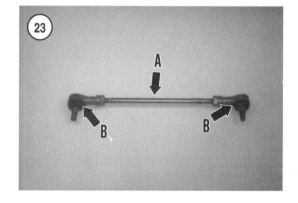

3. Grasp each ball joint (**Figure 24**) and swivel it in all directions. Check for roughness and play. Replace the end if wear is detected.

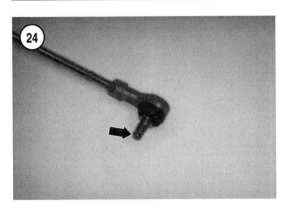

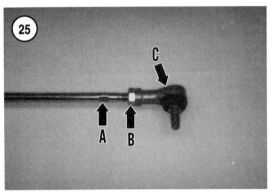

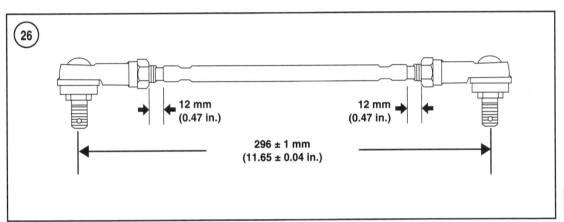

10

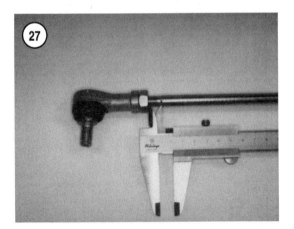

Tie Rod Ends Disassembly/Assembly

NOTE
The outer tie rod end has right-hand threads. The inner tie rod end has left-hand threads. Remember which direction each set of parts must be turned when loosening and tightening the parts.

1. Hold the tie rod with a wrench placed on the tie rod flats (A, **Figure 25**).

2. Loosen the locknut (B, **Figure 25**).

3. Remove the tie rod end (C, **Figure 25**).

4. Clean the tie rod threads.

5. Thread the correct tie rod end onto the tie rod.

NOTE
*Install the unmarked tie rod end (right-hand thread) nearest the tie rod flats. It is secured with the silver locknut. Install the **L** marked tie rod end (left-hand thread) at the opposite end of the tie rod. It is secured with the gold locknut.*

6. Repeat the procedure for the second tie rod end.

7. Adjust the length of the tie rod as follows:

    a. Adjust each tie rod end locknut until the dimension in **Figure 26** is achieved. Measure from the locknut to the groove on the tie rod (**Figure 27**). The difference between the two measurements should be less than 3 mm (0.12

in.). Keep the ends aligned and pointing in the same direction when making adjustments.

b. When the measurements are correct, hold the tie rod and torque the locknuts (**Figure 28**) to the specification in **Table 4**.

c. Straighten the ball joints and check the dimension between the tie rod ends (**Figure 26**). If necessary, adjust the tie rod ends to bring all measurements to within specifications.

d. Check toe-in adjustment as described in this section.

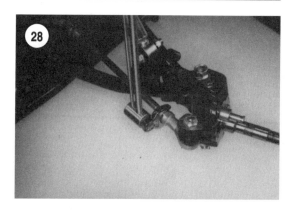

Toe-In Adjustment

To maintain stable steering and minimize tire wear, set the front wheels for toe-in. When correctly set, the front of the tires will point in slightly, while the rear of the tires will point out (**Figure 29**). Check toe-in by accurately measuring the distance between the tires at the front and rear. If toe-in is incorrect, adjust the tie rods to bring the measurement to within specification.

Proper toe-in adjustment cannot be achieved if the tie rods, wheel bearings or kingpin bushings are worn. Replace worn parts before adjusting toe-in.

1. Inflate all tires to the recommended pressure in **Table 3**.

2. Park the vehicle on level ground with the wheels pointing straight ahead. Set the parking brake.

3. On both front tires, make a chalk mark at the center of the tread (**Figure 30**). The mark should be level with the centerline of the axle.

4. Measure the distance between the tires as shown in A, **Figure 29**. Record the measurement.

5. Release the parking brake and roll the vehicle straight back until the marks are at the back of the wheel and level with the axle. Set the parking brake.

6. Measure the distance between the tires as shown in B, **Figure 29**. Record the measurement.

7. Subtract measurements.

a. If the difference is 14 ± 1 mm (9/16 ± 1/16 in.), toe-in is correct.

b. If toe-in is not correct, perform Step 8.

8. Adjust *both* tie rods equally as follows:

NOTE
The outer tie rod end has right-hand threads. The inner tie rod end has left-hand threads. Remember which

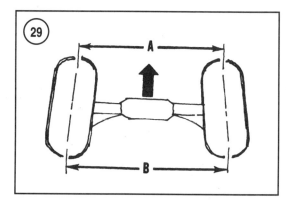

direction each set of parts must be turned when loosening and tightening the parts.

a. Loosen the tie rod locknuts (**Figure 31** and A, **Figure 32**).

b. Turn each tie rod with a wrench installed on the flats on the rod (B, **Figure 32**).

c. Recheck the measurements.

d. Torque the locknuts to the specification in **Table 4**.

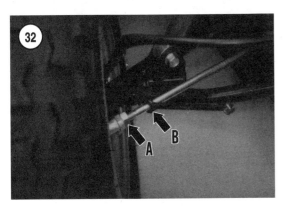

STEERING SHAFT

Removal/Installation

Refer to **Figure 33**.

1. Remove the handlebar cover, front fender and cover assembly as described in Chapter Thirteen.

> *NOTE*
> *Remove the front cover in order to gain access to the steering shaft. Removal of the handlebar cover and front fender is optional, but it is easier to access the fasteners with the bodywork removed.*

2. Remove the nuts (**Figure 34**) securing the handlebar to the steering shaft. Lay the handlebar back and secure it with duct tape. Avoid kinking the cables.

3. Remove the cotter pin and nut from the end of the steering shaft (**Figure 35**).

4. Remove the tie rod ends (**Figure 36**) from the steering shaft as described in this chapter.

5. Remove the bolts (**Figure 37**) from the steering shaft holders.

6. Lift and remove the steering shaft from the vehicle.

7. Reverse these steps to install the steering shaft. Note the following:

   a. Torque all nuts and bolts to the specification in **Table 4**.

   b. For nuts that are secured with a cotter pin, if necessary, tighten the nut after torque is reached to align the holes for a new cotter pin. Do not loosen a torqued nut to align the cotter pin holes.

Inspection

Refer to **Figure 33**.

1. Clean the steering shaft.

2. Inspect the steering shaft for the following:

   a. Enlarged tie rod attachment holes.

   b. Cracked cotter pin hole.

   c. Damaged threads.

   d. Worn or damaged steering shaft bushing.

3. Inspect the steering shaft holders for cracks or other damage.

4. Inspect the steering shaft bushing for wear and deterioration. Remove and clean the bushing. Apply lithium-based grease to the interior and exterior of the bushing, then reinstall the bushing on the steering shaft. Check that the *UP* mark on the bushing faces up.

5. Inspect the bearing holder, dust seal and bearing (**Figure 38**) for the following:

   a. Inspect the seal for wear and deterioration.

   b. Inspect the bearing by turning its inner race. The bearing should turn smoothly and have minimal or no play.

   c. If necessary, replace the bearing and seal as described in this section.

Steering Shaft Bearing and Seal Replacement

Refer to **Figure 33**.

1. Pry the seal out of the bearing holder.

2. Remove the internal circlip from the bearing holder.

3. Lift the bearing from the holder.

4. Clean the circlip and the bearing holder bore.

5. Apply lithium-based grease to the new bearing and inside the race.

10

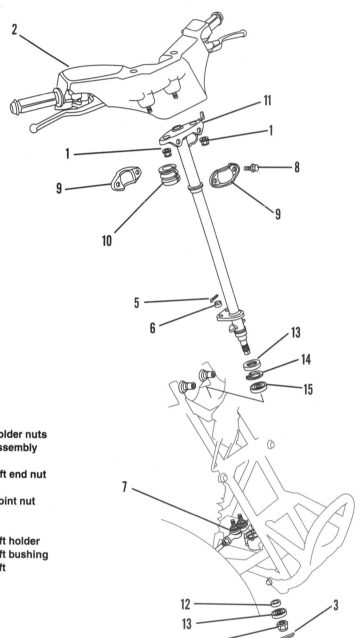

STEERING SHAFT

1. Handlebar holder nuts
2. Handlebar assembly
3. Cotter pin
4. Steering shaft end nut
5. Cotter pin
6. Tie rod ball joint nut
7. Tie rod
8. Holder bolt
9. Steering shaft holder
10. Steering shaft bushing
11. Steering shaft
12. Collar
13. Dust seal
14. Circlip
15. Bearing

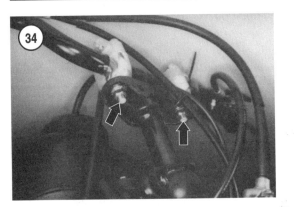

6. Insert the new bearing into the bearing holder. Install the bearing so the manufacturer's marks and numbers face up.

7. Install the circlip in the bearing holder. Check that the rounded edge of the circlip faces toward the bearing.

8. Apply lithium-based grease to the seal. Pack grease in the lip of the seal.

9. Place the seal squarely over the bore in the bearing holder, then drive the seal into place. Use a driver or socket that fits to the outer edge of the seal.

HANDLEBAR

Removal/Adjustment

The handlebar and controls should be tight and not move or pivot when pressure is applied. To reposition the handlebar, loosen the bolts securing the upper holders (**Figure 39**). Tilt the handlebar to the desired position, then retighten the bolts.

If the handlebar is damaged and requires replacement, remove the components shown in **Figure 39**, then remove the bolts from the upper holder. Position and tighten the new handlebar into place, then install the controls and grips.

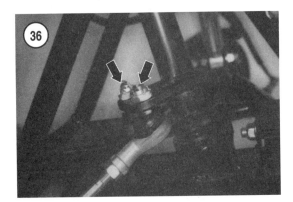

TIRES AND WHEELS

The vehicle is equipped with tubeless, low pressure tires. The tires are designed for off-road use. Riding on paved surfaces will rapidly wear the tires. If a puncture occurs, a tire plug may be used temporarily. A tire plug is not designed to be a permanent repair. Repair the tire as soon as possible. The procedures provided in this section detail how to re-

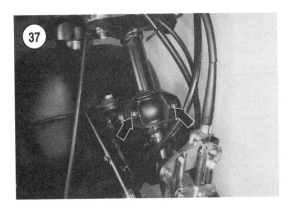

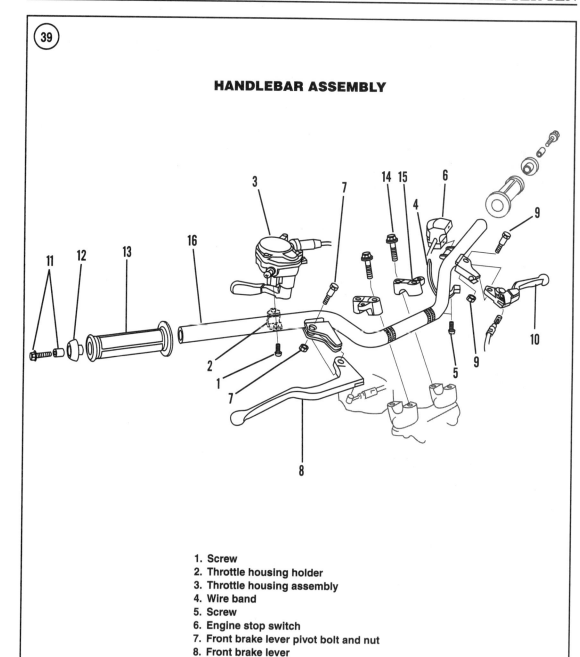

HANDLEBAR ASSEMBLY

1. Screw
2. Throttle housing holder
3. Throttle housing assembly
4. Wire band
5. Screw
6. Engine stop switch
7. Front brake lever pivot bolt and nut
8. Front brake lever
9. Parking brake lever pivot bolt and nut
10. Rear/parking brake lever assembly
11. Bolt and collar
12. Handlebar end guard
13. Handlebar grip
14. Bolt
15. Handlebar upper holder
16. Handlebar

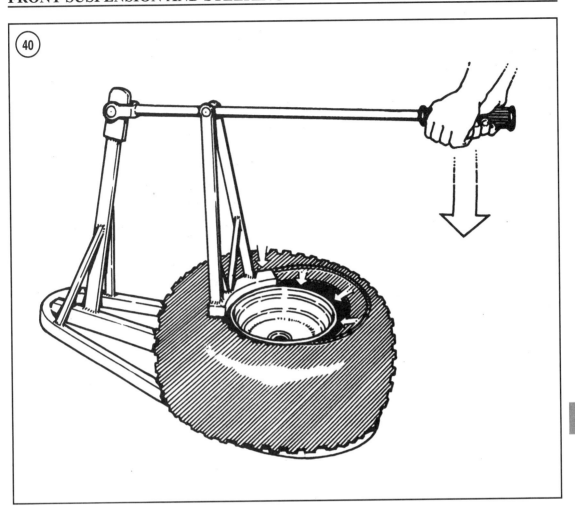

10

move a tire from the rim and how to make a permanent cold patch tire repair.

Tire Changing

The following tools are required to remove and install the tire on the wheel rim.
  a. Bead breaker tool.
  b. Tire irons.
  c. Rim protectors.
1. Remove the valve stem cap and core, and deflate the tire.
2. Lubricate the tire bead and rim flanges with a rubber lubricant. Press the sidewalls down to allow the lubricant to penetrate the bead. Also lubricate the sidewall where the bead breaker will make contact.
3. Position the wheel under the bead breaker tool (**Figure 40**).

4. With the tool seated against the rim, press down on the lever to break the tire bead from the rim. Work around the rim, using the bead breaker and hand pressure to break the tire free.
5. Turn the rim over and repeat Steps 2-4.
6. Relubricate the tire beads and rim flanges to prepare for using the tire irons.
7. Place rim protectors or other padding, such as a split rubber hose, on the rim edge. Position the protectors where the tire irons will be inserted (**Figure 41**).

CAUTION
Failure to use rim protectors may damage the bead seating area and cause air leakage at the bead. Rim replacement would then be required.

8. Insert the tire irons between the rim and tire as shown in **Figure 41**. Pry the tire bead over the rim.

If removal is difficult, move the tire irons closer together and remove smaller sections at a time.

9. When the upper sidewall is free, lift the lower sidewall up so it can be removed as described in Steps 6-8.

10. Clean and inspect the rim sealing surfaces (**Figure 42**). The sealing surface must be straight, clean and smooth in order to seal properly.

11. Replace the valve stem as follows:

   a. Remove the valve stem by pulling it out from inside the rim.

   b. Lubricate the *new* valve stem with tire lubricant.

   c. Insert the valve stem through the rim hole, then pull it out until it snaps into place (**Figure 43**).

12. Inspect the tire bead and rim for cleanliness.

13. Check the tire sidewall for the *direction arrow* and orient the tire so the arrow will point forward when the tire is mounted.

> *WARNING*
> *The sidewall arrow on the tire must be oriented properly when the tire is mounted. If the tire is installed with the arrow pointing to the rear, the tire may fail during operation.*

14. Place the rim with the valve stem facing down.

15. Check the tire orientation, then wet the tire bead with water.

> *NOTE*
> *Tire lubricants applied to the bead during installation can cause the tire to slip on the rim and result in a loss of air pressure. Only use water as a lubricant during tire installation.*

16. Hand-fit as much of the tire as possible onto the rim (**Figure 44**).

17. Use the rim protectors and tire irons to finish installing the bead (**Figure 45**). Push the bead to the opposite side of the rim so the second bead can be installed.

18. Repeat Steps 16 and 17 to install the second bead.

19. Install the valve stem core, if removed.

20. Apply water to the rim beads, then inflate the tire to the maximum pressure for seating the tire beads (**Table 3**).

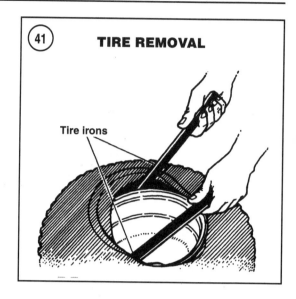

41 **TIRE REMOVAL**

Tire irons

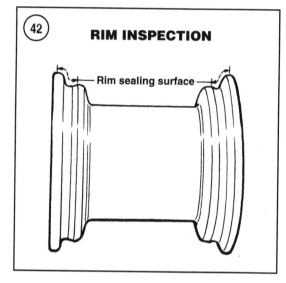

42 **RIM INSPECTION**

Rim sealing surface

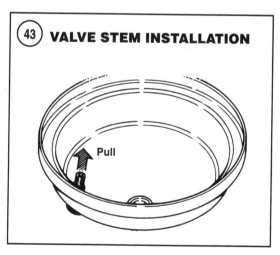

43 **VALVE STEM INSTALLATION**

Pull

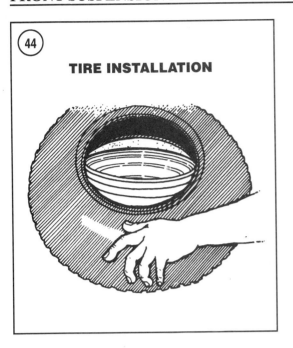

44

TIRE INSTALLATION

45

TIRE BEAD INSTALLATION

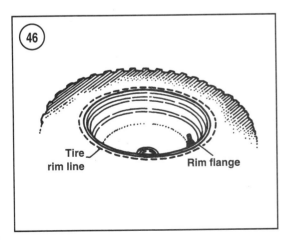

46

Tire
rim line

Rim flange

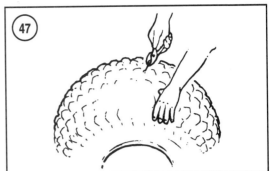

47

WARNING
Do not inflate the tire past the recommended bead seating pressure. Tire explosion and personal injury is possible. When using an air compressor to inflate the tire, attach and remove the air hose from the valve stem quickly, then check the pressure. Over-inflation can occur quickly when using an air compressor.

21. Check the rim lines on both sides of the tire to ensure the beads are seated. If the beads are seated correctly, the rim lines will be parallel with the rim flanges as shown in **Figure 46**. If the beads are not seated correctly, deflate the tire and break the bead so additional water can be applied to the tire bead. Reinflate the tire and check the beads.

22. After seating the tire properly, follow substeps a-d:

    a. Remove the valve core to deflate the tire.

    b. Wait one hour to allow adjustment of the tire on the rim.

    c. Install the valve core and inflate the tire to the operating pressure listed in **Table 3**.

    d. Apply water to the beads and valve stem, and check for leaks.

23. Install the wheel on the vehicle as described in this chapter.

Cold Patch Repair

Follow the manufacturer's instructions when using a repair kit. If instructions are not available, use the following procedure.

1. Remove the tire as described in this section.

2. Mark the puncture location with chalk or a crayon, then remove the object puncturing the tire (**Figure 47**).

10

3. Working from inside the tire, roughen the area around the puncture (**Figure 48**). The roughened area should be larger than the patch to be applied. If the repair kit does not provide a tool to roughen the area, use coarse sandpaper or any object that will lightly scrape and roughen the surface.

4. Clean the roughened area with a nonflammable and non-oily solvent.

5. Apply a small amount of the repair adhesive to the roughened area. Allow the adhesive to dry for about 30 seconds.

6. Remove the backing from the patch.

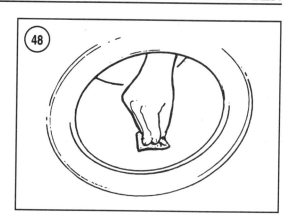

CAUTION
To ensure good adhesion of the patch,
do not touch the newly exposed sur-
face of the patch.

7. Center the patch over the puncture, then press the patch into place. Do not attempt to raise or slide the patch once it contacts the adhesive.

8. If a roller is available (**Figure 49**) burnish the patch. Make sure the edges are sealed tightly. If a roller is not available, use a smooth hard object, such as the end of a screwdriver handle.

9. Install the tire on the rim as described in this section.

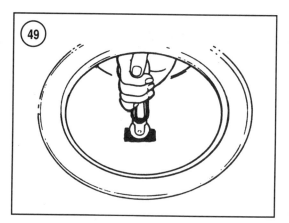

Table 1 STEERING AND FRONT SUSPENSION SPECIFICATIONS

	New mm (in.)	Service limit mm (in.)
Kingpin diameter	17.966-17.984 (0.7073-0.7080)	17.9 (0.705)
Kingpin bushing inner diameter	18.045-18.075 (0.7104-0.7116)	18.17 (0.715)
Front suspension	Swing axle type	–
Front wheel travel	65 (2.56)	–
Steering		
Camber angle	2°	–
Caster angle	4°	–
Toe-in	14 ± 1 (9/16 ± 1/16)	–
Trail	16 (5/8)	–

Table 2 TIRE SPECIFICATIONS

Tires	
Type	Tubeless
Size	
Front	AT20 × 7-8
Rear	AT19 × 8-8
Minimum usable tread depth	4 mm (0.16 in)

Table 3 TIRE INFLATION PRESSURES

	Front psi (kPa)	Rear psi (kPa)
Recommended operating pressure	2.9 (20)	2.9 (20)
Maximum pressure	3.3 (23)	3.3 (23)
Minimum pressure	2.5 (17)	2.5 (17)
Bead seating pressure	36 (250)	36 (250)

Table 4 TORQUE SPECIFICATIONS

	N•m	in.-lb.	ft.-lb.
Control arm pivot bolt	45	–	33
Front brake cable bracket bolt	12	106	–
Front shock absorber mounting bolt	25	–	18
Kingpin bolt nut	60	–	44
Steering shaft end nut	70	–	52
Steering shaft holder bolt	33	–	24
Tie rod ball joint nut	35-43	–	26-32
Tie rod locknut	39	–	29
Wheel lug nuts	55	–	41

10

REAR SUSPENSION

This chapter describes repair of the rear axle assembly, including the wheels, shock absorber, driven sprocket, axle, bearing holder, swing arm and chain. It is not necessary to remove the rear fender assembly for many of these procedures. However, removing the fender may make removing assemblies such as the swing arm, axle or bearing holder easier.

REAR WHEEL

Removal/Installation

1. Park the vehicle on level ground and set the parking brake.
2. Remove the wheel center cap (A, **Figure 1**).
3. Loosen the lug nuts (B, **Figure 1**).
4. Raise and support the vehicle with wooden blocks placed under the frame. The rear wheels must be off the ground.
5. Remove the lug nuts, then the wheel, from the hub.
6. If tire repair is required, make the repair as described in Chapter Ten.
7. Clean the lug nuts and hub studs. If studs are broken or damaged, replace the studs.
8. Install the wheel on the hub studs.
9. Finger-tighten the lug nuts.
10. Lower the vehicle to the ground, then equally tighten the lug nuts in a crossing pattern. Tighten the lug nuts in several stages to the torque specification listed in **Table 2**.

11. Raise the vehicle so both rear wheels are off the ground.
12. Release the parking brake and spin the wheel. Check that the wheel runs true.
13. Lower the vehicle to the ground.

SHOCK ABSORBER

Removal/Installation

The vehicle is equipped with a single, rear shock absorber. The unit is nonadjustable.
1. Set the parking brake.
2. Place wooden blocks, or another stable support, under the frame. The weight of the vehicle must be off the swing arm and wheels when the shock absorber is removed.
3. Remove the lower mounting nut and bolt (**Figure 2**).
4. Remove the upper mounting nut and bolt (**Figure 3**).
5. Reverse these steps to install the shock absorber. Note the following:
   a. Install new nuts on the mounting bolts.
   b. Torque the nuts to the specification in **Table 2**.

Inspection/Repair

All the parts of the rear shock absorber except the damper body are available individually. If the

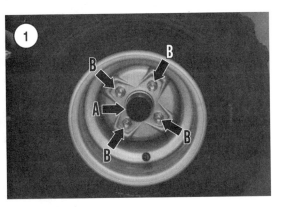

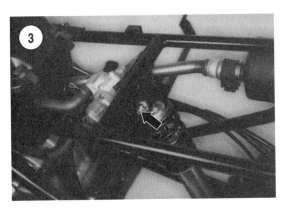

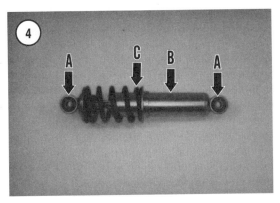

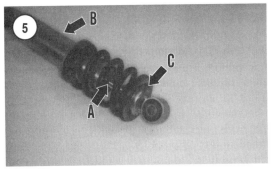

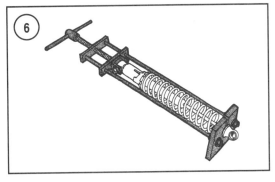

damper body leaks or is damaged, replace the entire shock absorber.

1. Inspect the shock absorber as follows:

   a. Inspect the bushings (A, **Figure 4**) and mounting bolts for wear and looseness. Fit the mounting bolts in the bushings and check for play. Replace worn or damaged parts. The bushings are a press-fit in the damper unit.

   b. Inspect the damper rod seal for leakage (A, **Figure 5**). Replace the shock absorber if leakage is evident.

   c. Inspect the body (B, **Figure 4**) for major dents or fractures. Replace the shock absorber if damage is evident.

   d. Inspect the spring for damage and fatigue. The spring should pull the damper rod out to the end of its travel. If necessary, inspect and/or replace the spring as described in the following steps.

2. Remove and inspect the spring as follows:

   a. Place the shock absorber in a spring compressor tool (**Figure 6**).

NOTE
A shock absorber compressor tool is available from Honda dealerships. Order part No. 07GME-0010000 or part No. 07959-3290001.

11

b. Compress the spring to remove the spring stopper (C, **Figure 5**).

c. Relieve the pressure on the spring, then remove it from the damper body.

d. Measure the free length of the spring (**Figure 7**). Refer to **Table 1** to determine if the measurement is within the service limit. Replace the spring if necessary.

3. Assemble the shock absorber as follows:

a. Place the spring on the damper body.

NOTE
*The small diameter coil (C, **Figure 4**) must be installed first.*

b. Place the shock absorber in the spring compressor tool and compress the spring.

c. Install the spring stopper.

d. Relieve the pressure on the spring, checking that it seats in the spring stopper.

e. Remove the shock absorber from the compressor.

DRIVEN SPROCKET

Before removing the driven sprocket, check the condition of both the drive chain and sprocket as described in Chapter Three. Using a new sprocket with a worn chain or a new chain on a worn sprocket shortens the life of the new part. Before starting repairs, determine if the chain should be replaced at the time of sprocket removal.

Removal/Installation

1. Shift the transmission into gear and set the parking brake.

2. Remove the left rear wheel as described in this chapter.

3. Remove the two bolts securing the drive chain cover (**Figure 8**), then remove the cover (**Figure 9**).

4. Remove the three bolts securing the drive chain guard (**Figures 10** and **11**), then remove the guard (**Figure 12**).

5. Remove the four nuts securing the driven sprocket to the hub (**Figure 13**). Pull the sprocket from the hub and remove the chain.

6. Clean and inspect the sprocket and nuts (**Figure 14**). Refer to Chapter Three for sprocket and chain inspection.

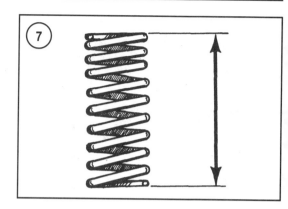

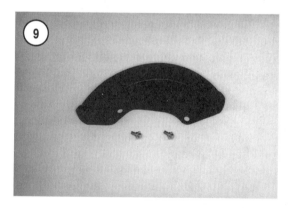

7. Pass the sprocket over the axle, then place the chain on the sprocket.

8. Install the sprocket on the hub studs, then finger-tighten the four nuts (**Figure 13**). If necessary, reposition the chain on the sprocket so it may be mounted on the studs.

9. Torque the sprocket nuts to the specification in **Table 2**. Tighten the nuts in a crossing pattern.

10. Install the drive chain guard, then tighten the three bolts (**Figures 10** and **11**).

11. Install the drive chain cover, then tighten the two bolts (**Figure 8**).

12. Install the rear wheel as described in this chapter.

13. Check chain adjustment as described in Chapter Three.

REAR AXLE

Removal

Refer to **Figure 15**.

1. Place wooden blocks, or another stable support, under the frame. The weight of the vehicle must be off the rear axle and wheels.

2. Remove the rear wheels as described in this chapter.

3. Remove the rear brake assembly as described in Chapter Twelve.

4. Remove the left rear wheel hub as follows:

   a. Remove the cotter pin and nut from the axle (**Figure 16**).

   b. Remove the lockwasher (**Figure 17**) from the axle.

   c. Pull the wheel hub (**Figure 18**) from the axle splines. Mark the hub so it can be reinstalled on the left end of the axle.

5. Remove the driven sprocket, drive chain cover and drive chain guard as described in *Driven Sprocket* in this chapter.

6. Thread an axle nut onto the right end of the axle (**Figure 19**).

> *NOTE*
> *Thread the nut on backwards. Rotate the nut until the axle is slightly below the face of the nut (**Figure 20**). Make sure the axle will not contact the hammer.*

11

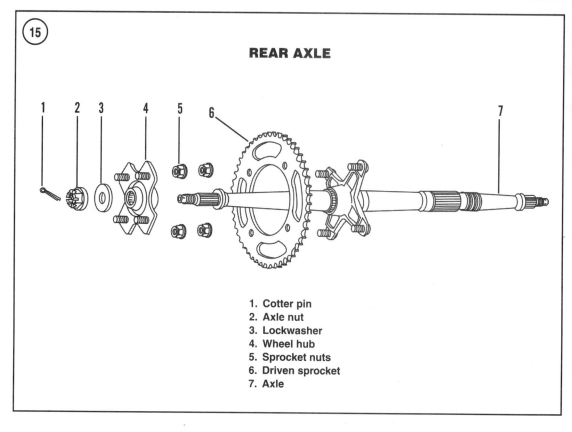

REAR AXLE

1. Cotter pin
2. Axle nut
3. Lockwasher
4. Wheel hub
5. Sprocket nuts
6. Driven sprocket
7. Axle

7. Strike the nut with a soft-faced hammer to drive the axle out of the bearing holder.

8. Inspect the axle and wheel hubs as described in this section.

Inspection

1. Clean the axle and wheel hubs. All splines must be clean for inspection.

2. Make the following checks at each end of the axle.

   a. Inspect the cotter pin hole (A, **Figure 21**). Check for cracks or fractures around the hole. Replace the axle if damage is evident.

   b. Inspect the axle nut threads (B, **Figure 21**). Check for uniform and symmetrical threads. Screw the axle nut onto the threads, and check for roughness and play. If damage is detected, replace the axle and axle nuts.

   c. Inspect the wheel hub splines (C, **Figure 21**). Check for worn, distorted and broken splines. Inspect the splines in each wheel hub (**Figure 22**) for damage. Fit each hub to its respective

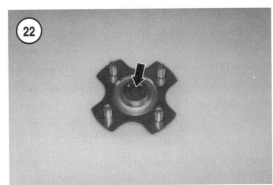

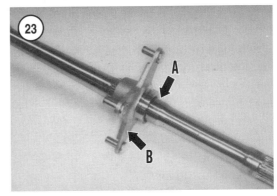

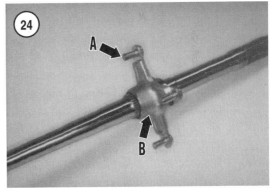

11

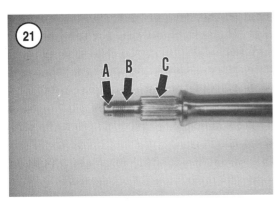

end of the axle and check for play. If play or wear is detected, replace the parts.

3. Inspect the axle where it contacts the bearings in the axle bearing holder (A, **Figure 23**). Check for scoring, galling and other damage. If damage is evident, inspect the bearings in the axle bearing holder as described in this chapter. Replace damaged parts.

4. Inspect the driven sprocket hub:

    a. Inspect the front side of the hub for loose, damaged, broken or stripped studs (A, **Figure 24**). Replace studs that are damaged.

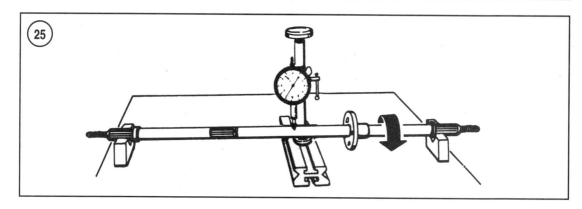

b. Inspect the front side of the hub for cracks or fractures (B, **Figure 24**).

c. Inspect the back side of the hub for cracks or fractures (B, **Figure 23**).

d. Replace the axle if hub damage is detected.

5. Check the axle for straightness using a dial indicator and V-blocks as shown in **Figure 25**. Replace the axle if runout exceeds the service limit specified in **Table 1**.

> *NOTE*
> *When measuring runout, the actual amount of runout is one-half the reading of the dial indicator.*

Installation

Refer to **Figure 15**.

1. Apply grease to the lips of the seals in both sides of the axle bearing holder (**Figure 26**).

2. Apply grease to the axle splines (**Figure 27**).

3. Working from the left side of the axle bearing holder, insert the right end of the axle through the drive chain, then carefully push the axle into the bearing holder (**Figure 28**).

4. Thread an axle nut onto the left end of the axle (**Figure 29**).

> *NOTE*
> *Thread the nut on backwards. Rotate the nut until the axle is slightly below the face of the nut (**Figure 30**). Make sure the axle will not contact the hammer.*

5. Seat the axle in the bearings as follows:

a. Align the axle with the bearing holder. Make sure the axle is aligned with the bearing race on the right side of the holder (**Figure 31**).

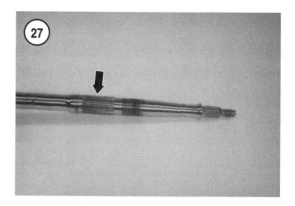

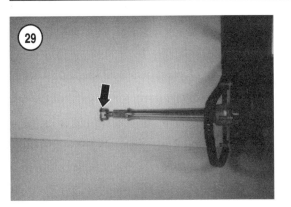

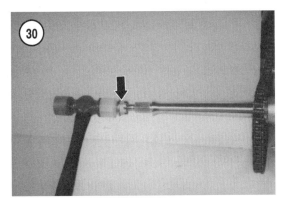

b. Strike the nut with a soft-faced hammer to drive the axle into the bearings.

c. Check that the sprocket hub is completely seated (**Figure 32**).

6. Install the driven sprocket, drive chain cover and drive chain guard as described in *Driven Sprocket* in this chapter.

7. Install the left rear wheel hub as follows:

a. Apply grease to the axle splines.

b. Slide the wheel hub onto the splines (**Figure 18**).

c. Place the lockwasher on the axle and against the wheel hub (**Figure 17**).

NOTE
*Make sure the **OUT SIDE** mark on the lockwasher is facing out.*

d. Lubricate the axle nut threads with grease.

e. Install and torque the axle nut (**Figure 33**) to the specification in **Table 2**. After the correct torque is reached, continue to turn the nut until the cotter pin hole is visible.

f. Insert and secure a *new* cotter pin into the axle (**Figure 16**).

8. Install the rear brake assembly as described in Chapter Twelve.

9. Install both rear wheels as described in this chapter.

10. Check chain adjustment as described in Chapter Three.

REAR AXLE BEARING HOLDER

Removal/Installation

Refer to **Figure 34**.

1. Remove the rear axle as described in this chapter.

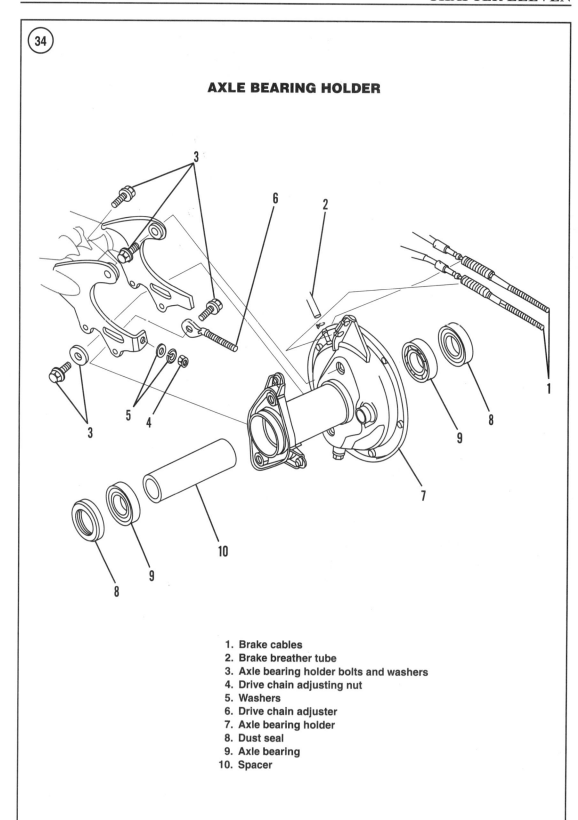

AXLE BEARING HOLDER

1. Brake cables
2. Brake breather tube
3. Axle bearing holder bolts and washers
4. Drive chain adjusting nut
5. Washers
6. Drive chain adjuster
7. Axle bearing holder
8. Dust seal
9. Axle bearing
10. Spacer

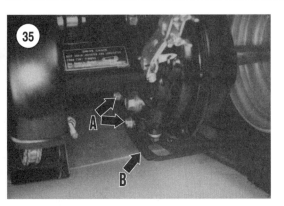

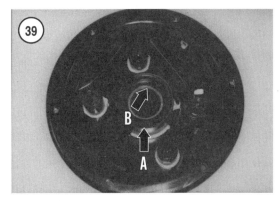

2. Remove the bolts (A, **Figure 35**) securing the skid plate (B), then remove the plate.

3. Disconnect the brake cables from the housing (A, **Figure 36**). If necessary, refer to the *Removal/Installation* procedures in Chapter Twelve for disconnecting the cables.

4. Disconnect the brake breather tube (B, **Figure 36**) from the axle bearing holder.

5. Remove the two bolts and washers (A, **Figure 37**) from each side of the axle bearing holder.

6. Remove the drive chain adjusting nut, washers and adjuster (B, **Figure 37**).

7. Remove the axle bearing holder from the swing arm (**Figure 38**).

8. Inspect the bearing holder as described in this section.

9. Reverse these steps to install the axle bearing holder. Note the following:

   a. Torque the axle bearing holder bolts to the specification in **Table 2**.

   b. Refer to Chapter Three to make final adjustments to the brake cables.

Inspection

1. Clean the axle bearing holder. Do not immerse the bearing holder in solvent unless the bearings and seals will be replaced.

2. Inspect the dust seals (A, **Figure 39**) for tears, distortion or other damage. If rust or moisture is evident on the inner bearing races or bearing spacer, leakage is occurring at the seals. Replace the seals as described in this section.

3. Inspect the bearings as follows:

   a. Turn each bearing inner race (B, **Figure 39**). Feel for roughness, noise or binding. The bearings should turn smoothly and quietly.

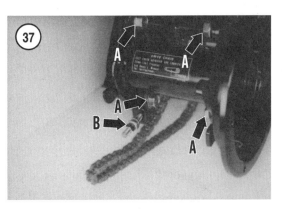

b. Check for axial and radial (**Figure 40**) play. Replace the bearings if worn or damaged. Remove and install the bearings as described in this section.

NOTE
Always replace bearings as a pair.

Seal Replacement

Dust seals prevent the entry of moisture and dirt into the bearings. Always install new seals when the bearings are replaced.

1. Pry old seals out of their recesses with a seal puller or a wide-blade screwdriver. Place a shop rag under the tool to prevent damage to the part (**Figure 41**). If a screwdriver is used to pry the seal, place a small block of wood under the tool so leverage can be applied.

2. Pack grease into the inner lip of the new seal.

NOTE
The inside diameter of the left seal is larger than the inside diameter of the right seal.

3. Clean and lubricate the bore in which the seal will be installed.

4. Place the seal *squarely* over the bore. Make sure the manufacturer's number or mark is facing out, unless specified otherwise.

5. Place a suitably-sized driver or socket over the seal (**Figure 42**). Seat the driver against the outside diameter of the seal (**Figure 43**).

6. Press the seal into place squarely.

Bearing Replacement

1. Remove the dust seals as described in this section.

2. Insert a drift into one side of the bearing holder and push the spacer between the bearings to one side.

3. Place the drift on the edge of the inner bearing race and tap it with a hammer. Work around the perimeter of the race, moving it in small increments until it is removed.

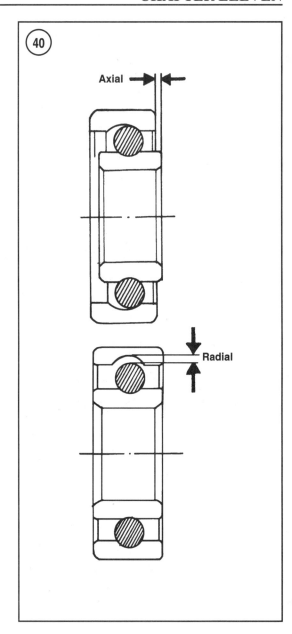

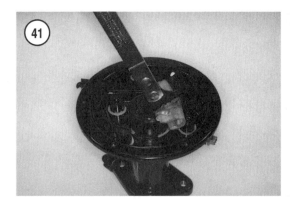

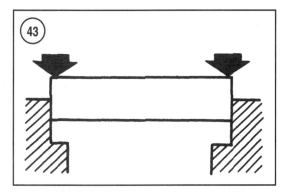

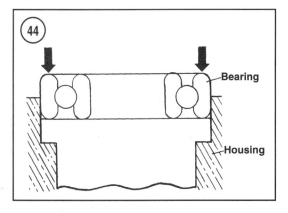

Bearing

Housing

NOTE
Striking the drift with excessive force can cause the bearing to jam against the wall of the bearing holder.

4. Remove the spacer from the bearing holder.

5. Remove the remaining bearing. Drive it out with a bearing driver or large socket that fits on the outer race of the bearing.

6. Clean and dry the bearing holder and spacer.

7. Before installing the new bearings and seals, note the following:

    a. Inspect the new bearings and determine which side faces out. This is usually the side with the manufacturer's marks and numbers. If a shield is on one side of the bearing, the shield faces out.

    b. Apply grease (NLGI No. 2) to bearings that are not lubricated by the manufacturer. Work the grease into the cavities between the balls and races.

8. Place a bearing *squarely* over the bearing bore.

9. Place a suitably-sized driver or socket over the bearing. Seat the driver against the outside diameter of the bearing (**Figure 44**).

NOTE
A driver tool (part No. 07GME-0010000) and attachment (part No. 07959-3290001) are available from Honda dealerships.

10. Press or drive the bearing into place, seating it in the holder (**Figure 45**).

NOTE
Do not press or strike the bearing directly. Bearing damage will occur.

11. Turn the holder over and install the spacer.

12. Press or drive in the remaining bearing, seating it in the holder.

13. Install the seals as described in this section.

SWING ARM

Removal/Installation

This procedure assumes the swing arm is being removed for service or replacement. Therefore, assemblies attached to the swing arm are removed.

11

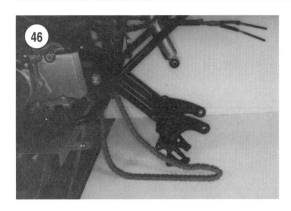

Figure 46 shows the swing arm with all assemblies removed.

1. Remove the seat and rear fender assembly as described in Chapter Thirteen.

2. Remove the rear wheels as described in this chapter.

> *NOTE*
> *Place wooden blocks, or another sta-*
> *ble support, under the frame. The*
> *weight of the vehicle must be off the*
> *swing arm.*

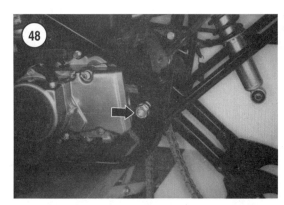

3. Remove the rear brake assembly as described in Chapter Twelve.

4. Remove the rear axle as described in this chapter.

5. Remove the rear axle bearing holder as described in this chapter.

6. Remove the lower mounting nut and bolt from the shock absorber (**Figure 47**).

7. Remove the rear brake pedal as described in Chapter Twelve.

8. Remove the swing arm pivot nut (**Figure 48**) from the left side of the swing arm.

9. Remove the swing arm pivot bolt (**Figure 49**) from the right side of the swing arm. If necessary, use a long, narrow drift to tap the bolt out of the swing arm.

10. Inspect and service the swing arm as described in this section.

11. Reverse these steps to install the swing arm assembly. Note the following:

   a. Make sure the drive chain is routed above and below the swing arm (**Figure 50**) before inserting and tightening the swing arm pivot bolt.

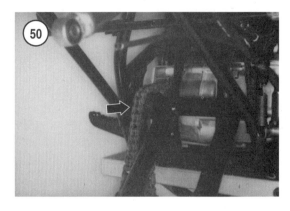

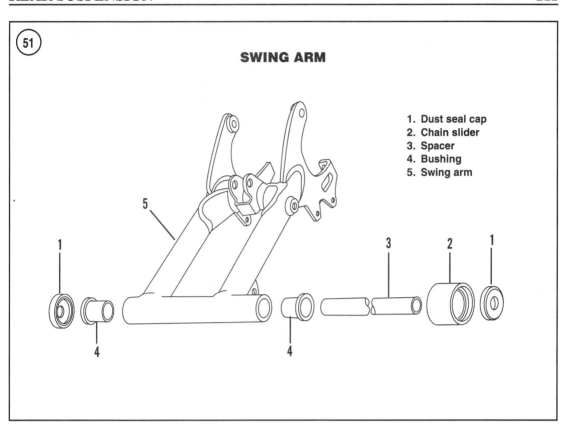

SWING ARM

1. Dust seal cap
2. Chain slider
3. Spacer
4. Bushing
5. Swing arm

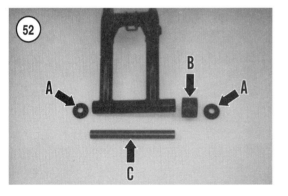

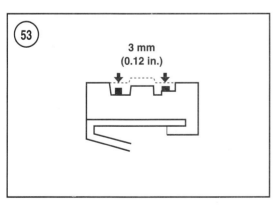

3 mm
(0.12 in.)

b. Torque the swing arm pivot nut to the specification in **Table 2**.

Inspection

Refer to **Figure 51**.

1. Remove the dust seal caps (A, **Figure 52**) from each side of the swing arm.

2. Remove the chain slider (B, **Figure 52**) from the swing arm.

3. Push the spacer (C, **Figure 52**) out of the bushings.

4. Clean and dry the swing arm and components.

5. Inspect the dust seal caps for wear or deterioration. Replace the caps if damage is evident. Always replace the caps if moisture is detected inside the swing arm pivot.

6. Inspect the chain slider for wear. It is normal for the chain to wear grooves in the slider. Trim the slider with a razor blade if groove depth exceeds 3 mm (0.12 in.) (**Figure 53**). Replace the slider if the grooves are more than 6 mm (0.24 in.) (**Figure 54**).

7. Inspect all welded joints on the swing arm (**Figure 55**). Check for fractures, bending or other dam-

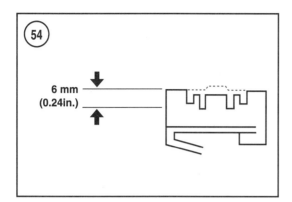

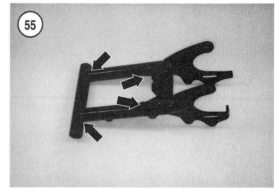

age. If damage is detected, replace the swing arm, or have a dealership or machine shop weld and test the strength of the swing arm.

8. Inspect the bushings (**Figure 56**) for scoring and wear. Insert the spacer into the bushings and check for radial play. The spacer should fit tightly, but still rotate in the bushings. Replace the bushings and spacer if play is detected. Replace the bushings as described in this section.

Bushing Replacement

Refer to **Figure 51**.

1. Replace the swing arm bushings as follows:

2. Insert an appropriately-sized drift into the swing arm. The drift must reach through the swing arm and to the bushing on the opposite side (**Figure 57** inset).

3. Drive the bushing out of the swing arm.

4. Insert the drift into the opposite side of the swing arm and drive out the remaining bushing. If possible, use a drift that fits squarely on the end of the bushing.

5. Clean the bores in the swing arm.

6. Lubricate the new bushings with molydisulfide grease.

7. Place a new bushing squarely over the bore in one side of the swing arm.

8. Press the new bushing into place (**Figure 58**) using a driver that fits squarely over the end of the bushing.

NOTE
A driver tool (part No. 07946-KA50000 or part No. 07936-3710600) is available from Honda dealerships.

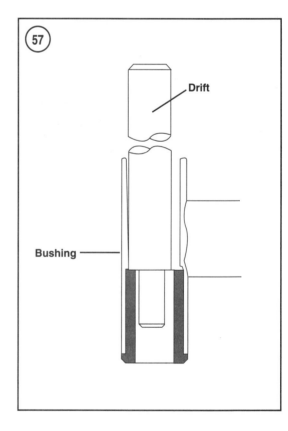

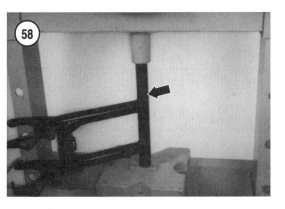

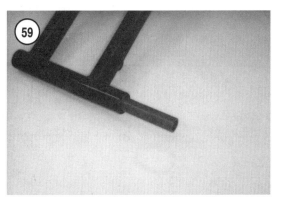

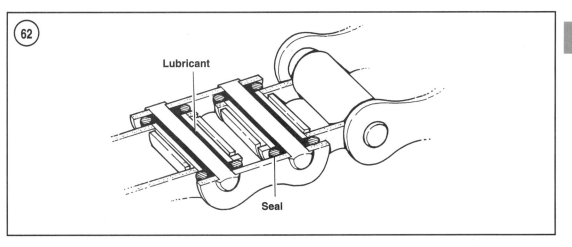

Lubricant

Seal

9. Drive the remaining bushing into the swing arm.

10. Lubricate the spacer with molydisulfide grease, then insert it into the swing arm bushings (**Figure 59**).

11. Place the chain slider (**Figure 60**) on the left side of the swing arm.

12. Pack the dust seal caps (**Figure 61**) with molydisulfide grease, then install them to each side of the swing arm.

DRIVE CHAIN

Engine power is transferred to the driven sprocket by an endless, O-ring chain. This type of chain is internally lubricated and sealed by O-rings (**Figure 62**). The chain requires regular cleaning, lubrication and adjustment as described in Chapter Three. Measurement of the chain to determine its wear is performed in Chapter Three. To replace the chain,

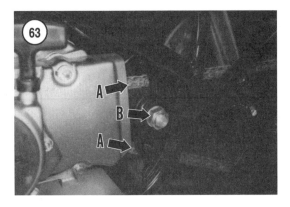

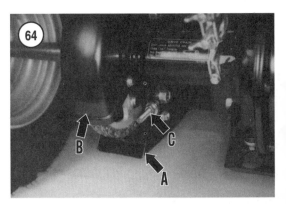

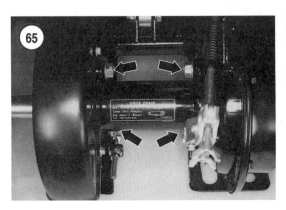

remove it using one of the methods described in this section. Refer to **Table 1** for chain specifications.

Replacement

Since the chain (A, **Figure 63**) is endless and encircles the swing arm pivot (B). Replace the chain as follows:

1. Partially disassemble the swing arm components so the old and new chains can be routed around the pivot.

2. Break the old chain, then replace it with a new chain that does not have connected ends. After the new chain is routed, attach a permanent master link to the loose chain ends.

If installing the new chain by completely or partially disassembling the components attached to the swing arm, refer to the procedures in this chapter. If the new chain will be connected by a permanent master link, use the following procedure.

CAUTION
This procedure is for installing a chain with a permanently-staked master link. Master links that are secured by a spring clip are not recommended.

1. Remove the seat and rear fender as described in Chapter Thirteen.

2. Remove the drive chain guard (A, **Figure 64**) and cover (B).

3. Loosen the two axle bearing holder bolts (**Figure 65**) on each side of the holder.

4. Loosen the drive chain adjuster (C, **Figure 64**), then move the axle assembly forward to provide maximum slack in the chain.

5. Attach a chain breaker tool. Route a length of light gauge wire through the left (engine) side of the tool and chain, then attach the wire to the frame.

NOTE
After the chain is broken, the new chain can be attached to the wire and routed to the drive sprocket as the old chain is being pulled from the engine. If the old chain is not wired, its weight will usually pull it out of the engine when the ends are free.

6. Attach a chain breaker tool to the drive chain. **Figure 66** shows a typical tool. Follow the manufacturer's instructions for attaching and using the tool.

7. Drive the link pin from the chain.

8. Attach the end of the new chain to the wire and route the new chain over the drive sprocket. The engine must be in neutral for the drive sprocket to rotate.

9. Route the chain over the driven sprocket and secure the chain ends with the master link.

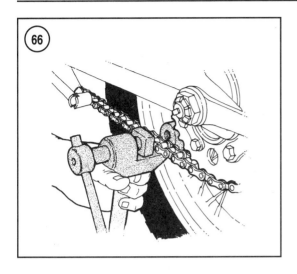

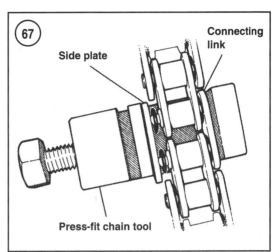

NOTE
Check that the O-rings are on the master link pins. Insert the link from the back side of the chain.

10. Place the chain link side plate on the master link. The identification marks must face out.

11. Stake the link pins using a chain riveting tool (**Figure 67**).

12. Adjust the chain as described in Chapter Three.
13. Install the drive chain guard and cover.
14. Install the seat and rear fender assembly as described in Chapter Thirteen.

TIRE CHANGING AND REPAIR

Refer to Chapter Ten.

Table 1 REAR SUSPENSION SPECIFICATIONS

	New mm (in.)	Service limit mm (in.)
Rear axle runout	–	3.0 (0.12)
Shock absorber spring free length	105.9 (4.17)	103.8 (4.09)
Drive chain		
Size	428, O-ring, endless type	–
Links	98	–
Drive chain free play	20-30 mm (3/4-1 1/4 in.)	
Drive chain length, 21-pin span		
Service limit	268 mm (10.6 in.)	
Shock absorber small spring direction	Down	–
Rear suspension	Swing arm type	–
Rear wheel travel	65 (2.56)	–

Table 2 TORQUE SPECIFICATIONS

	N•m	in.-lb.	ft.-lb.
Axle nut	60-80	–	44-59
Axle bearing holder bolts	90	–	66
Driven sprocket nut	40	–	29
Rear wheel axle nut	60-80	–	44-59
Shock absorber mounting bolts	25	–	18
Swing arm pivot bolt/nut	90	–	66
5 mm bolt and nut	5	44	–
6 mm bolt and nut	10	88	–
8 mm bolt and nut	22	–	16
Wheel lug nut	55	–	41

CHAPTER TWELVE

BRAKES

This chapter provides service procedures for the front and rear drum brakes. Replacement procedures for hub bearings, seals and brake cables are also included.

FRONT BRAKES

Removal

The following procedure details the complete removal of the front brake assembly. To replace only the brake shoes, perform Steps 1-6.

Refer to **Figure 1**.

1. Engage the parking brake.
2. Remove the front wheel as described in Chapter Ten.
3. Remove the cotter pin and axle nut from the axle (**Figure 2**).
4. Remove the collar from the axle (**Figure 3**).
5. Remove the brake drum from the axle.

> *WARNING*
> *Brake lining dust is hazardous and should not be inhaled. Before removing the brake drum, place a disposable container below the drum to catch the brake lining dust. After the drum is removed, wipe the dust from the parts with a disposable damp cloth. Do not use compressed air to clean the parts. Minimize the amount of airborne dust.*

Wipe the dust and grease from the brake panel (**Figure 4**). Do not get grease on the brake linings. Dispose of the dust and contaminated cloth.

6. Inspect the brake linings and drum assembly as described in this chapter. To remove the complete brake assembly from the steering knuckle, continue with the procedure.
7. Spread the brake linings and springs so they can be removed from the pivot (A, **Figure 5**) and brake cam (B).
8. Disconnect the brake cable end from the brake arm (**Figure 6**).
9. Remove the pinch bolt and nut (A, **Figure 7**), then remove the brake arm (B).
10. Remove the wear indicator (A, **Figure 8**) and return spring (B).

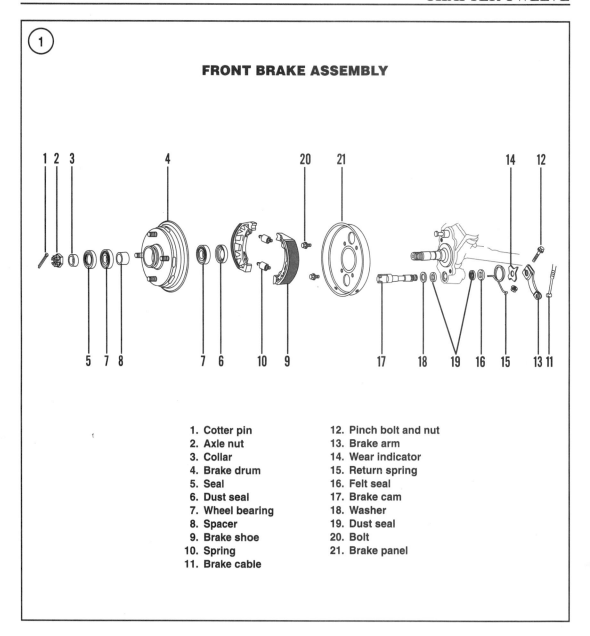

FRONT BRAKE ASSEMBLY

1. Cotter pin
2. Axle nut
3. Collar
4. Brake drum
5. Seal
6. Dust seal
7. Wheel bearing
8. Spacer
9. Brake shoe
10. Spring
11. Brake cable
12. Pinch bolt and nut
13. Brake arm
14. Wear indicator
15. Return spring
16. Felt seal
17. Brake cam
18. Washer
19. Dust seal
20. Bolt
21. Brake panel

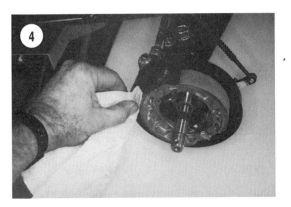

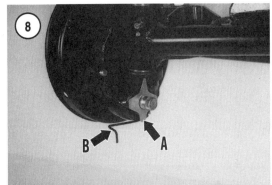

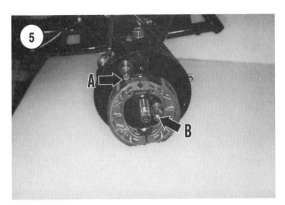

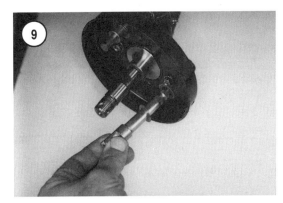

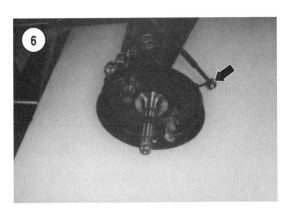

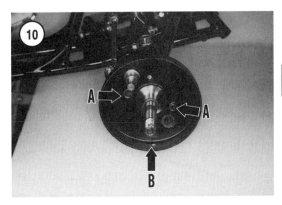

12

11. Carefully pull the brake cam and washer out of the brake panel (**Figure 9**). Account for the felt seal on the back side of the brake panel.

12. Remove the two bolts securing the brake panel to the steering knuckle (A, **Figure 10**).

13. Clean and inspect the parts as described in this chapter.

Installation

Refer to **Figure 1**.

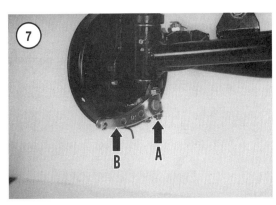

1. Install the brake panel to the steering knuckle. Tighten the bolts (A, **Figure 10**) to the specification in **Table 2**.

> *NOTE*
> *Install the brake panel so the drain hole (B, **Figure 10**) is down.*

2. Apply grease to the dust seals on both sides of the steering knuckle.
3. Apply grease to the length of the brake cam, then carefully insert the brake cam with the washer through the seals in the steering knuckle (**Figure 9**).
4. Apply engine oil to the felt washer. Slide it over the brake cam and seat the washer into the steering knuckle (**Figure 11**).
5. Place the return spring over the brake cam. Insert the straight end (**Figure 12**) of the spring into the hole in the steering knuckle.
6. Place the wear indicator on the brake cam splines.

> *NOTE*
> *Align the master spline on the indicator with the master spline on the brake cam. The spline on the indicator is slightly wider, and the spline on the brake cam is marked with a dot on the end of the shaft (**Figure 13**).*

7. Align and install the brake arm on the brake cam splines. Align the dot on the brake arm with the dot on the brake cam shaft (**Figure 14**). Tighten the pinch bolt and nut to the specification in **Table 2**.
8. Engage the return spring with the brake arm (**Figure 15**).
9. Attach the brake cable to the brake arm.
10. Spread the brake linings and springs so they can be installed on the pivot (A, **Figure 5**) and around the brake cam (B).

> *NOTE*
> *Lightly grease the pivot and brake cam where they contact the brake shoes.*

11. Apply grease to the dust seals on both sides of the brake drum, then install the brake drum.

> *NOTE*
> *If the brake drum will not fit over the shoes, adjust the cable at the brake equalizer. Back off the cable adjuster*

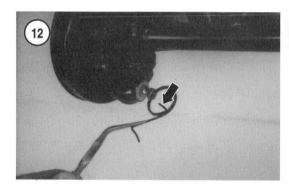

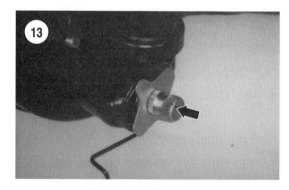

nut so the brakes will retract. If necessary, refer to Chapter Three for cable adjustment procedures.

12. Insert the collar into brake drum seal (**Figure 16**).
13. Install and tighten the axle nut to the specification in **Table 2**. After the correct torque is reached, if necessary, continue to tighten the nut until the cotter pin hole is visible.
14. Insert and secure a *new* cotter pin into the axle.
15. Adjust the brakes as described in Chapter Three.
16. Install the front wheel as described in Chapter Ten.

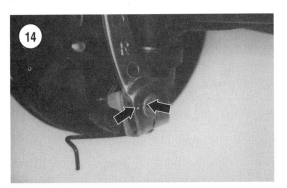

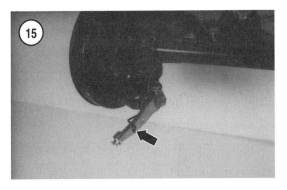

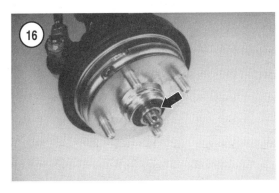

REAR BRAKES

Removal

The following procedure details the complete removal of the rear brake assembly. To replace only the brake shoes, perform Steps 1-12.

Refer to **Figure 17**.

1. Engage the parking brake.

2. Remove the right rear wheel as described in Chapter Eleven.

3. Remove the cotter pin and axle nut from the axle (**Figure 18**).

4. Remove the lockwasher from the axle (A, **Figure 19**).

5. Remove the right rear wheel hub from the axle (B, **Figure 19**).

6. Remove the inner and outer locknuts from the rear axle as follows:

NOTE
*The following procedure requires the special tools shown in **Figure 20**. Order the 41 mm axle-nut holder wrench (part No. 07916-9580200 or 07916-958020B) (A, **Figure 20**) and the 41 mm axle-nut torque wrench adapter (part No. 07916-9580400 or 07916-958010B) (B, **Figure 20**) from a Honda dealership, or use equivalent tools on hand.*

a. Place the axle-nut holder wrench on the inner locknut and the axle-nut torque wrench adapter on the outer locknut. Attach the adapter wrench to a breakover bar, as shown in (**Figure 21**).

b. Remove the outer locknut.

c. Remove the inner locknut. Use a standard wrench (**Figure 22**).

7. Remove the lockwasher (A, **Figure 23**) and drum cover washer (B).

8. Remove the six bolts from the perimeter of the drum cover (**Figure 24**), then remove the cover, dust seal and rubber seal.

9. Remove the seal ring (**Figure 25**) from the brake drum.

10. Disengage the parking brake.

WARNING
Secure the vehicle so it will not roll or fall when the parking brake is released.

11. Remove the brake drum from the axle.

WARNING
Brake lining dust is hazardous and should not be inhaled. Before removing the brake drum, place a disposable container below the drum to catch the brake lining dust. After the drum is removed, wipe the dust from the parts with a disposable damp cloth. Do not use compressed air to clean the parts. Minimize the amount of airborne dust. Dispose of the dust and contaminated cloth.

12

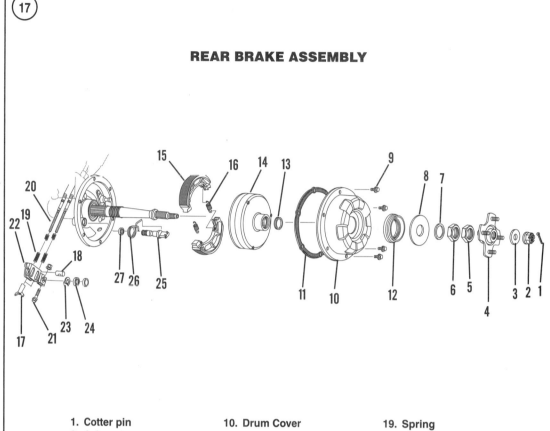

REAR BRAKE ASSEMBLY

1. Cotter pin
2. Axle nut
3. Lockwasher
4. Wheel hub
5. Outer locknut
6. Inner locknut
7. Lockwasher
8. Drum cover washer
9. Bolt
10. Drum Cover
11. Rubber seal
12. Dust seal
13. Seal ring
14. Brake drum
15. Brake shoe
16. Spring
17. Brake adjusting nut
18. Joint piece
19. Spring
20. Brake cables
21. Pinch bolt and nut
22. Brake arm
23. Wear indicator
24. Felt seal
25. Brake cam
26. Return spring
27. Dust seal

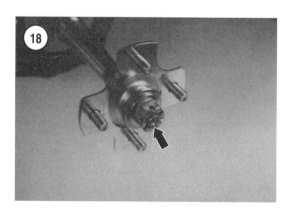

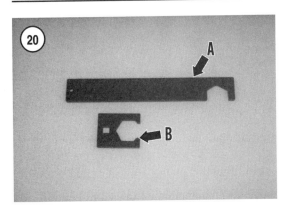

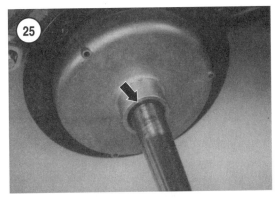

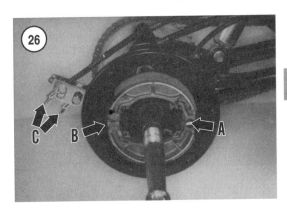

12

12. Inspect the brake linings and drum assembly as described in this chapter. To remove the complete brake assembly from the axle, continue with the procedure.

13. Spread the brake linings and springs so they can be removed from the pivot (A, **Figure 26**) and brake cam (B).

14. Remove the adjusting nut, joint piece and spring (**Figure 27**) from both brake cables (C, **Figure 26**). Remove the cables from the brake arm.

15. Remove the pinch bolt and nut (A, **Figure 28**), then remove the brake arm (B).

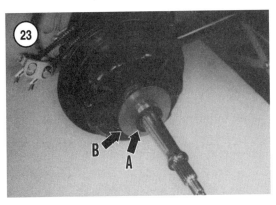

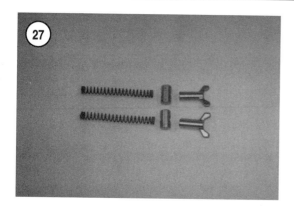

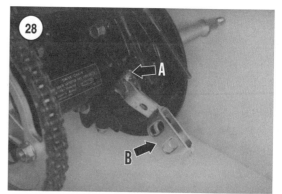

16. Remove the wear indicator (A, **Figure 29**) and felt seal (B).

17. Carefully pull the brake cam and spring out of the housing (**Figure 30**).

18. Clean and inspect the parts as described in this chapter.

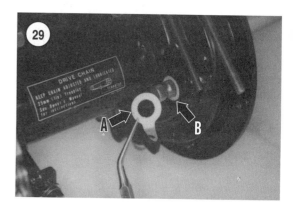

Installation

Refer to **Figure 17**.

1. Apply grease to the dust seals on both sides of the axle bearing holder where the brake cam is installed.

2. Apply grease to the length of the brake cam, then fit the short end of the spring into the hole in the cam.

3. Carefully insert the brake cam through the seals in the axle bearing holder (A, **Figure 31**). The spring must rest on top of the axle bearing holder as shown in B, **Figure 31**.

4. Apply engine oil to the felt washer. Slide it over the brake cam and seat the washer into the axle bearing holder (B, **Figure 29**).

5. Place the wear indicator on the brake cam splines (A, **Figure 29**).

NOTE
Align the master spline on the indicator with the master spline on the brake cam. The spline (A, Figure 32) on the indicator is slightly wider, and the spline on the brake cam is marked with a dot (B) on the end of the shaft.

6. Align and install the brake arm on the brake cam splines. Align the dot on the brake arm with the dot on the brake cam shaft (**Figure 33**). Tighten the pinch bolt and nut to the specification in **Table 2**.

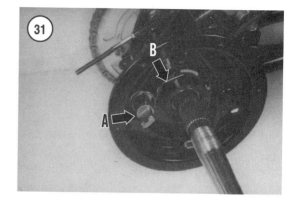

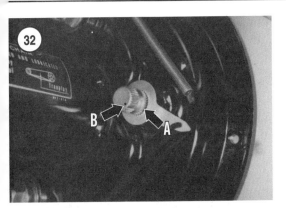

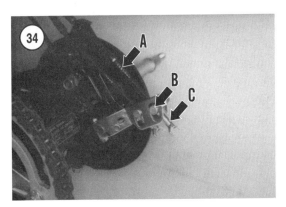

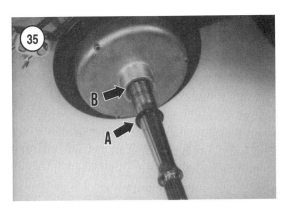

7. Attach the brake cables to the brake arm. Make sure each cable passes through the spring (A, **Figure 34**), pivot piece (B) and adjusting nut (C) correctly. Do not tighten the adjusting nut. The brake shoes must be completely retracted to install the brake drum.

8. Spread the brake linings and springs so they can be installed on the pivot (A, **Figure 26**) and around the brake cam (B).

> NOTE
> Lightly grease the pivot and brake cam where they contact the brake shoes.

9. Apply grease to the brake drum and axle splines, then slide the drum into place on the axle.

> NOTE
> If the brake drum will not fit over the shoes, adjust the cables. If necessary, back off the cable adjuster nuts so the brakes will retract. Refer to Chapter Three for cable adjustment procedures.

10. Lubricate and install a new seal ring (A, **Figure 35**). Seat it in the brake drum (B). Make sure the seal is flush with the brake drum bore.

11. Install a new, lubricated dust seal on the drum cover (**Figure 36**).

12. Place a new rubber seal on the brake cover, then bolt the brake cover into place over the brake drum.

13. Install the drum cover washer (B, **Figure 23**) and lockwasher (A) on the axle.

> NOTE
> The concave side of the lockwasher should face in toward the brake drum.

12

14. Install the inner and outer locknuts on the axle as follows:

a. Engage the parking brake. If necessary, adjust the nut (A, **Figure 37**) so the brakes engage with the brake drum. The drum must be held steady so the locknuts can be tightened correctly.

b. Finger-tighten the inner locknut (B, **Figure 37**).

c. Attach the axle nut torque wrench adapter to a torque wrench, then torque the inner locknut to the specification in **Table 2**.

d. Clean the axle threads so they are free of grease.

e. Apply threadlocking compound to the threads, then finger-tighten the outer locknut.

f. Hold the inner locknut with the axle nut holder wrench (A, **Figure 38**) and torque the outer locknut using the axle nut torque wrench adapter (B). Tighten the locknut to the specification in **Table 2**.

15. Slide the wheel hub onto the axle splines.

16. Place the lockwasher on the axle and against the wheel hub.

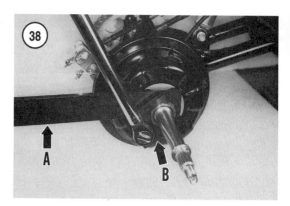

NOTE
*Check that the **OUT SIDE** (**Figure 39**) mark on the lockwasher is facing out.*

17. Lubricate the axle nut threads with grease.

18. Install and tighten the axle nut to the specification in **Table 2**. After the correct torque is reached, if necessary, continue to tighten the nut until the cotter pin hole is visible.

19. Insert and secure a new cotter pin into the axle.

20. Adjust the brakes as described in Chapter Three.

21. Install the rear wheel as described in Chapter Eleven.

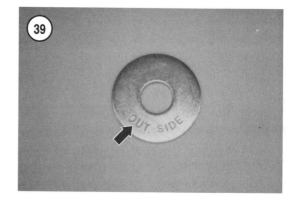

BRAKE INSPECTION

Perform the following checks for brake drums and linings. Checks specific to the front or rear brakes are indicated.

Brake Drum Check

1. Check the brake drum diameter as follows:

a. Measure the inside diameter of the brake drum using a vernier caliper (**Figure 40**).

b. Refer to **Table 1** to determine if the drum is still within the service limit. Replace the drum if necessary.

2. On front drums, check the condition of the rubber seal (**Figure 41**). If the seal is torn or missing, replace as follows:

a. Remove the old seal and any residue from the drum with solvent.

b. Apply adhesive, such as Gasgacinch, around the perimeter of the drum.

c. Install the new seal. Make sure that the alignment tabs (**Figure 42**) on the seal fit into the drum.

d. Allow the adhesive to dry before installing the drum.

3. On the rear drum, check the condition of the drum splines (**Figure 43**). Also inspect the splines on the axle. The drum should be a firm fit on the axle.

Brake Lining Check

1. Visually check the brake linings for contamination, breakage and scoring. If any damage is evident, replace the brake linings as a pair.

2. Visually check the brake linings for uneven wear. If the linings are worn at the ends, replace the linings as a pair.

3. Measure the lining thickness (**Figure 44**) at several points. Refer to **Table 1** to determine if the linings are still within the service limit. Replace the linings if they are not within the specification.

SEALS AND BEARINGS

Seal Replacement

Several dust seals are used throughout the brake system to prevent the entry of moisture and dirt in critical areas that rotate. Dust seals are used on the brake cams, brake drums and brake pedal. Install new seals whenever the brake system is overhauled. Always install new seals when wheel bearings are replaced.

1. Pry old seals out of their recess with a wide-blade screwdriver. Place a shop rag under the screwdriver to prevent damage to the part (**Figure 45**).

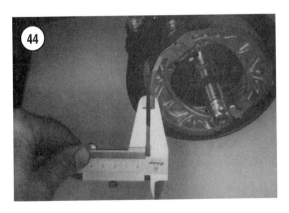

12

2. Pack grease into the inner lip of the new seal.

3. Clean and lubricate the bore in which the seal will be installed.

4. Place the seal *squarely* over the bore (**Figure 46**). Make sure the manufacturer's number or mark is facing out unless specified otherwise.

5. Place a suitably-sized driver or socket over the seal (**Figure 47**). The driver should seat against the outside diameter of the seal (**Figure 48**).

6. Press the seal into place, flush with the housing.

Bearing Inspection

The front brake drums are each equipped with two wheel bearings.

1. Turn each bearing inner race (**Figure 49**), and check for roughness, noise or binding. The bearings should turn smoothly and quietly.

2. Check for axial and radial (**Figure 50**) play. Replace the bearings if worn or damaged.

> *NOTE*
> *Always replace hub bearings as a pair.*

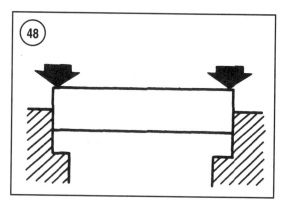

Bearing Replacement

1. Remove the dust seals as described in this section.

2. Remove the outer hub bearing as follows:

> *NOTE*
> *The tools shown in this procedure are part of the Kowa Seiki Wheel Bearing Remover set (**Figure 51**). The set is distributed by K & L Supply Co., Santa Clara, CA and can be ordered from Honda. The set is designed so a*

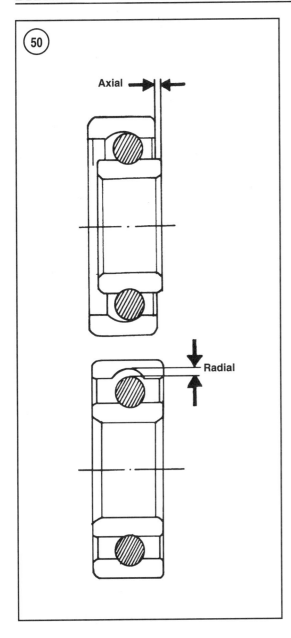

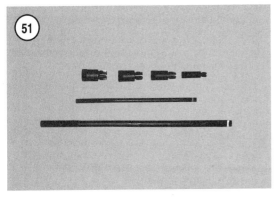

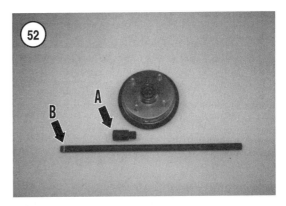

properly-sized remover head can be wedged against the inner bearing race. The bearing can then be driven from the hub.

a. Select the appropriate-size remover head (A, **Figure 52**). The small, split end of the remover must fit inside the bearing race.

b. Insert the small end of the remover head into the outer bearing (A, **Figure 53**).

c. Insert the tapered end (B, **Figure 52**) of the driver through the back side of the hub (B, **Figure 53**). Fit the tapered end into the slot of the remover head.

d. Position the hub so the remover head is against a solid surface, such as a concrete floor.

e. Strike the end of the driver so it wedges firmly in the remover head. The remover head must fit securely against the inner bearing race.

f. Reposition the assembly so the remover head is free to move, and the driver can be struck again.

12

g. Strike the driver to force the bearing and remover head from the hub.

h. Remove the driver from the remover head.

i. Note the direction of the spacer, then remove it from the hub.

3. Drive the inner hub bearing out with a bearing driver or a large socket that fits on the outer race.

4. Clean and dry the hub and spacer.

5. Before installing the new bearings and seals, note the following:

a. Inspect the new bearings and determine which side faces out. This is usually the side with the manufacturer's marks and numbers. If a shield is on one side of the bearing, the shield faces out.

b. Apply grease (NLGI#2) to bearings that are not lubricated by the manufacturer. Work the grease into the cavities between the balls and races.

c. Always support the bottom side of the hub near the bore when installing bearings.

6. Place a bearing *squarely* over the inner bearing bore.

7. Place a suitably-sized driver or socket over the bearing. Seat the driver against the outside diameter of the bearing (**Figure 54**).

8. Press or drive the inner bearing into place and seat it in the hub.

NOTE
Do not press or strike the bearing directly. Bearing damage will occur.

9. Turn the hub over and install the spacer.

10. Press or drive in the outer bearing and seat it in the hub.

11. Install the seals as described in this section.

REAR BRAKE PEDAL

Removal/Inspection/Installation

Refer to **Figure 55**.

1. Remove the seat and rear fender assembly as described in Chapter Thirteen.

2. Remove the return spring from the pedal.

3. Remove the cotter pin from the pivot.

4. Remove the washer.

5. Tilt the pedal back so the rear brake cable can be removed.

6. Remove the pedal from the pivot.

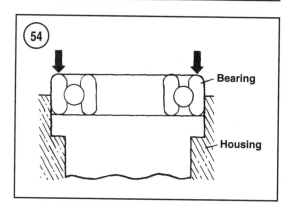

7. Inspect the assembly as follows:

a. Inspect the pedal and pivot for signs of debris passing around the seals. Replace the seals if necessary.

b. Inspect the return spring for fatigue. Replace the spring if the coils are not tight. The spring must be strong enough to raise the pedal after releasing the brakes.

c. Inspect the washer for wear. The washer miminizes lateral play of the pedal. Replace the washer if necessary.

8. Reverse these steps to install the brake pedal. Note the following:

a. Lubricate the pivot, dust seals, cable end and pedal bore with grease before assembly.

b. Install a new cotter pin.

c. Check the pedal for proper operation and adjustment after assembly. Refer to Chapter Three for adjustment procedures.

BRAKE PEDAL CABLE

The rear brake is cable-actuated. The cable ends are attached to the foot pedal (**Figure 56**) and rear brake arm (A, **Figure 57**). When the brake pedal is applied, the cable tightens and pulls on the brake arm, which engages the brake shoes with the brake drum. The cable needs to be in good condition and adjusted properly for maximum braking capability. Refer to Chapter Three for adjustment procedures.

Inspect, and if necessary, replace the cable following the procedures in this section.

Inspection

1. Inspect the cable housings for splits, corrosion and kinks.

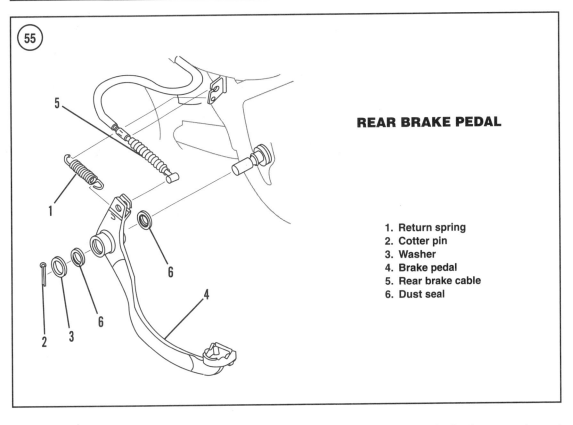

REAR BRAKE PEDAL

1. Return spring
2. Cotter pin
3. Washer
4. Brake pedal
5. Rear brake cable
6. Dust seal

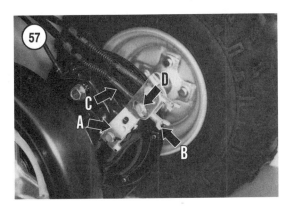

2. Inspect the cable ends for fraying, corrosion and kinks.

3. Check the cable for drag and binding. Operate the brake pedal while observing the brake arm at the rear wheel. The arm should move smoothly.

4. Replace any cables that are damaged.

Removal/Installation

1. Remove the seat and rear fender assembly as described in Chapter Thirteen.

2. At the brake housing:

   a. Remove the adjusting nut (B, **Figure 57**) from the cable housing.

   b. Slide the rubber boot down so the cable housing can be removed from the support bracket.

   c. Remove the cable end from the brake arm.

   d. Remove the spring (C, **Figure 57**) from the cable housing and account for the joint piece (D) in the brake arm.

3. At the brake pedal:

   a. Slide the rubber boot down so the cable housing can be removed from the support bracket.

b. Remove the cable end from the pedal (**Figure 56**).

c. Lubricate the new cable end with grease, then attach the cable to the brake pedal.

d. Slide the rubber boot down so the cable housing can be inserted into the support bracket.

4. At the brake housing:

a. Slide the rubber boot down so the cable housing can be inserted into the support bracket.

b. Place the spring over the threaded portion of the housing.

c. Check that the joint piece is in the brake arm.

d. Insert the cable end through the joint piece, then thread the adjusting nut onto the housing.

5. Refer to Chapter Three to make final adjustments to the cable.

6. Install the rear fender assembly and seat.

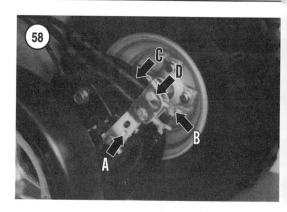

PARKING BRAKE CABLE

When the parking brake is not engaged, it is also a hand-operated rear brake. The brake is cable-actuated. The cable ends are attached to the left hand lever and rear brake arm (A, **Figure 58**). When the hand lever is applied, or locked, the cable tightens and pulls on the brake arm, which engages the brake shoes with the brake drum. The cable needs to be in good condition and adjusted properly for maximum braking capability. Refer to Chapter Three for adjustment procedures.

Inspect and, if necessary, replace the cable following the procedures in this section.

Inspection

1. Inspect the cable housings for splits, corrosion and kinks.

2. Inspect the cable ends for fraying, corrosion and kinks.

3. Check the cable for drag and binding. Operate the brake pedal while observing of the brake arm at the rear wheel. The arm should move smoothly.

4. Replace any cables that are damaged.

Removal/Installation

1. Remove the fender assembly and handlebar cover as described in Chapter Thirteen.

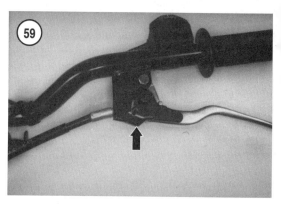

2. At the brake housing:

a. Remove the adjusting nut (B, **Figure 58**) from the cable housing.

b. Slide the rubber boot down so the cable housing can be removed from the support bracket.

c. Remove the cable end from the brake arm.

d. Remove the spring (C, **Figure 58**) from the cable housing and account for the joint piece (D) in the brake arm.

3. At the left handlebar lever:

a. Pull the lever (**Figure 59**) back, then release the cable end from the lever.

b. Remove the cable from the frame clips.

c. Apply grease to the cable end, then attach the new cable to the handlebar lever.

d. Route the new cable to the brake housing, but do not clip the cable to the frame.

4. At the brake housing:

a. Slide the rubber boot down so the cable housing can be inserted into the support bracket.

b. Place the spring over the threaded portion of the housing.

c. Check that the joint piece is in the brake arm.

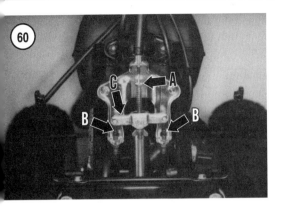

d. Apply grease to the cable end, then insert the cable end through the joint piece. Thread the adjusting nut onto the housing.

5. Adjust slack and clip the cable to the frame.

6. Refer to Chapter Three to make final adjustments to the cable.

7. Install the fender assembly and handlebar cover.

FRONT BRAKE CABLES

The front brakes are cable-actuated. The primary cable (A, **Figure 60**) is attached to the right handlebar lever and controls the action of two secondary cables (B). A secondary cable goes to each front wheel. The ends of all cables attach to the equalizer plate (C, **Figure 60**). When the brake lever is pulled, the primary cable pulls up on the equalizer plate, which then pulls on the secondary cables. The secondary cables need to be in good condition and adjusted identically so that braking forces are equal at both wheels. Refer to Chapter Three for adjustment procedures.

Inspect and, if necessary, replace the cables following the procedures in this section.

Inspection

1. Inspect all cable housings for splits, corrosion and kinks.

2. Inspect the cable ends for fraying, corrosion and kinks.

3. Check the cables for drag or binding. Operate the handlebar lever while observing the brake arms at each wheel. The arms should move smoothly.

4. Replace any cables that are damaged.

Primary Cable Removal/Installation

Refer to **Figure 61**.

1. Remove the front fender assembly and handlebar cover as described in Chapter Thirteen.

2. At the equalizer assembly:
   a. Remove the adjusting nut (A, **Figure 62**) from the cable housing.
   b. Remove the cable housing and spring (B, **Figure 62**) from the equalizer. Account for the joint piece (C) in the equalizer.
   c. Remove the cable housing from the top of the equalizer.

3. At the right handlebar lever:
   a. Pull the lever (**Figure 63**) back, then release the cable end from the lever.
   b. Apply grease to the cable end, then attach the new cable to the handlebar lever.

4. At the equalizer assembly:
   a. Seat the cable housing into the top of the equalizer.
   b. Place the spring over the housing threads.
   c. Pass the cable end through the equalizer joint piece.
   d. Thread the adjusting nut onto the housing.

5. Refer to Chapter Three to make final adjustments to the cable.

6. Install the front fender assembly and handlebar cover.

Secondary Cables Removal/Installation

Refer to **Figure 61**.

1. Remove the front fender assembly and handlebar cover as described in Chapter Thirteen.

2. At the equalizer assembly:
   a. Loosen both cable adjusting nuts (D, **Figure 62**).
   b. Remove the cable end and housing from the equalizer assembly.

3. At the wheel:
   a. Remove the cable end from the brake arm (A, **Figure 64**).
   b. Remove the cable from the support bracket (B, **Figure 64**).
   c. Route the new cable through the support bracket.

4. Apply grease to the cable end, then attach the cable end to the brake arm.

5. At the equalizer assembly:

12

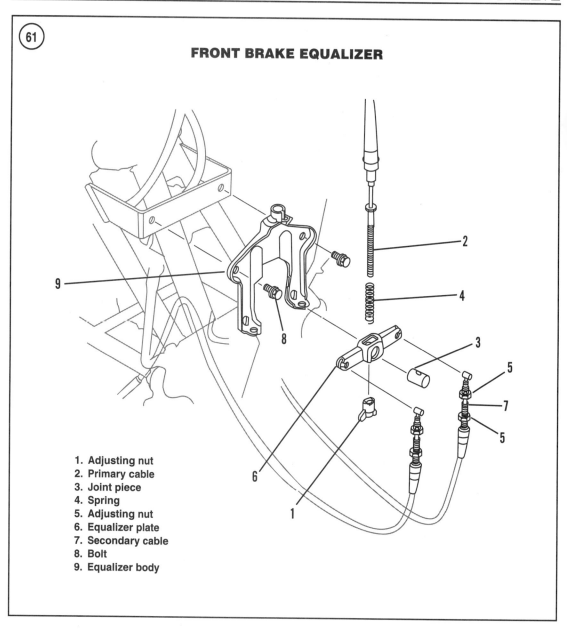

FRONT BRAKE EQUALIZER

1. Adjusting nut
2. Primary cable
3. Joint piece
4. Spring
5. Adjusting nut
6. Equalizer plate
7. Secondary cable
8. Bolt
9. Equalizer body

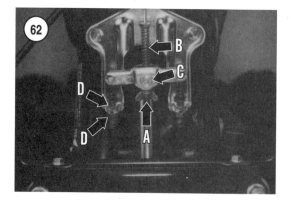

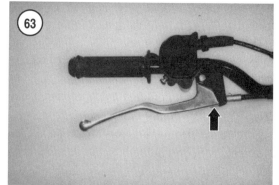

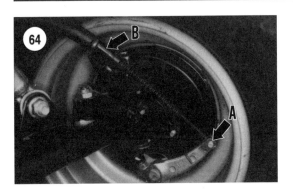

a. Pass the cable housing threads through the equalizer. One locknut should be below the equalizer and the other locknut should be above.

b. Apply grease to the cable end, then attach it to the equalizer plate.

6. Refer to Chapter Three to make final adjustments to the cable.

7. Install the front fender assembly and handlebar cover.

Table 1 BRAKE SERVICE SPECIFICATIONS

	New mm (in.)	Service limit mm (in.)
Front brake		
Drum inner diameter	110 (4.3)	111 (4.4)
Lining thickness	4.0 (0.16)	2.0 (0.08)
Rear brake		
Drum inner diameter	140 (5.5)	141 (5.6)
Lining thickness	4.0 (0.16)	2.0 (0.08)

Table 2 TORQUE SPECIFICATIONS

	N•m	in.-lb.	ft.-lb.
Front brakes			
Brake arm pinch bolt	10	88	–
Brake panel bolt	12	106	–
Brake cable stay bolt	12	106	–
Front wheel axle nut	70-90	–	52-66
Rear brakes			
Axle outer locknut	130	–	94
Axle inner locknut	45	–	33
Brake arm bolt	10	88	–
Brake drain bolt	25	–	18
Rear wheel axle nut	60-80	–	44-59
Parking brake lever pivot screw	9	80	–

12

CHAPTER THIRTEEN

BODY

This chapter contains removal and installation procedures for the body panels and seat.

> *NOTE*
> *When removing the bodywork, be careful to not break or damage the tabs and slots.*

SEAT

Removal/Installation

Refer to **Figure 1**.

1. Pull up on the seat lock lever (**Figure 2**).
2. Lift the seat from the vehicle (**Figure 3**).
3. To install the seat, insert the prongs at the front of the seat into the recesses (A, **Figure 4**) in the body.
4. Insert the rear seat prongs into the holes (B, **Figure 4**) in the storage compartment.
5. Press down on the seat to lock it in place.
6. Lightly lift at the rear of the seat to ensure that it is locked.

REAR FENDER ASSEMBLY

Removal/Installation

Refer to **Figure 1**.

1. Remove the seat as described in this chapter.
2. Disconnect the mudguards from the footpegs by removing the nuts and screws from both footpegs (**Figure 5**).
3. Remove the screw (**Figure 6**) from both fenders.
4. Remove the four bolts attaching the bodywork to the frame (**Figure 7**).
5. Lift the complete fender and mudguard assembly from the vehicle. Carefully disengage the tabs from the front fender (**Figure 8**) during removal.
6. Remove the mudguard stays from the frame and footpegs (**Figure 9**).
7. If the mudguards are to be removed, carefully pry the pin from each trim clip (**Figure 10**). Remove the complete clip from the hole after the pin is removed.
8. Reverse these steps to install the rear fender assembly.

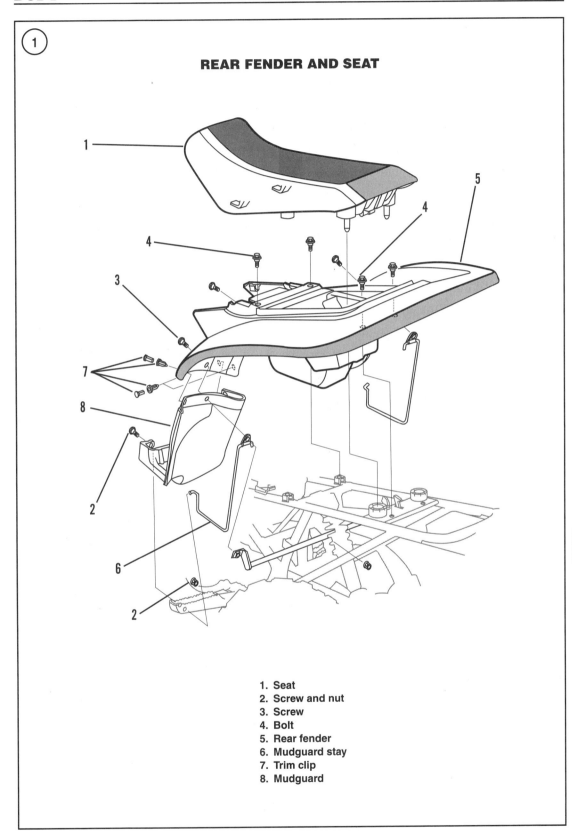

REAR FENDER AND SEAT

1. Seat
2. Screw and nut
3. Screw
4. Bolt
5. Rear fender
6. Mudguard stay
7. Trim clip
8. Mudguard

13

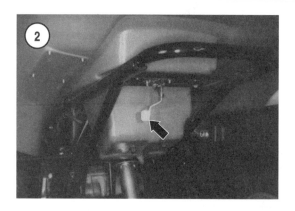

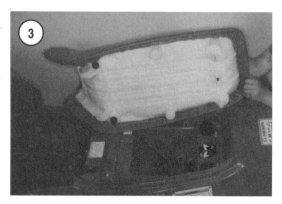

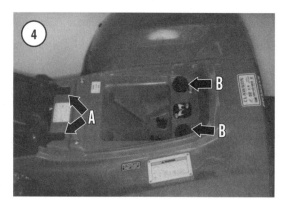

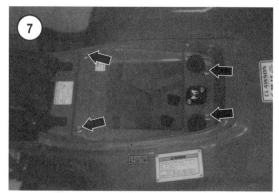

FRONT FENDER ASSEMBLY

Removal/Installation

Refer to **Figure 11**.

1. Remove the seat as described in this chapter.

2. Carefully pry the pin from each trim clip (**Figure 12**). Remove the complete clip from the hole after the pin is removed.

3. Slide the front cover up to disengage the tabs in the slots (**Figure 13**), then remove the cover.

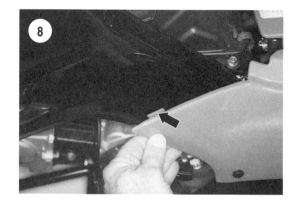

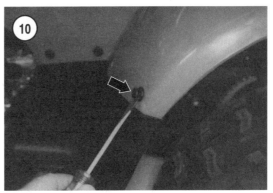

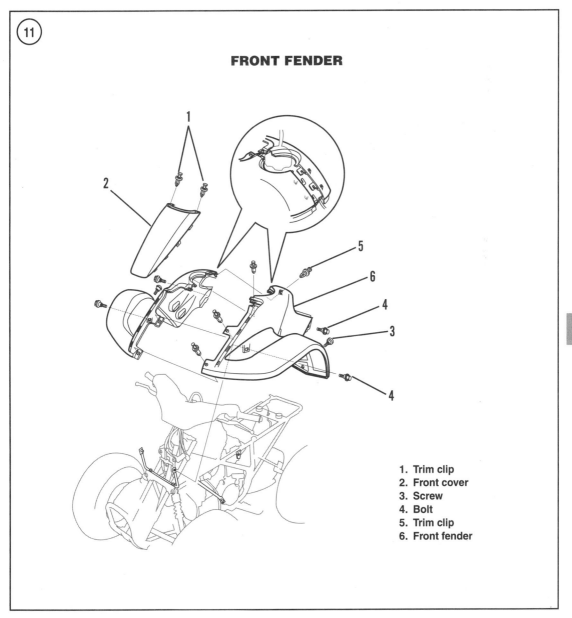

FRONT FENDER

1. Trim clip
2. Front cover
3. Screw
4. Bolt
5. Trim clip
6. Front fender

13

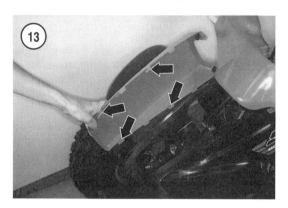

4. Remove the screws (**Figure 14**) from the rear of both fenders.

5. Remove the four bolts attaching the bodywork to the frame (**Figure 15** and A, **Figure 16**).

6. Carefully pry the pin from each trim clip at the front and rear of the fender (**Figure 17** and B, **Figure 16**). Remove the complete clip from the hole after the pin is removed.

> *NOTE*
> *On 2000 models, the front fender assembly can be removed without removing the two clips nearest the front of the vehicle.*

7. Reverse these steps to install the front fender assembly.

HANDLEBAR COVER

Removal/Installation

Refer to **Figure 18**.

1. Remove the handlebar cover caps (A, **Figure 19**).

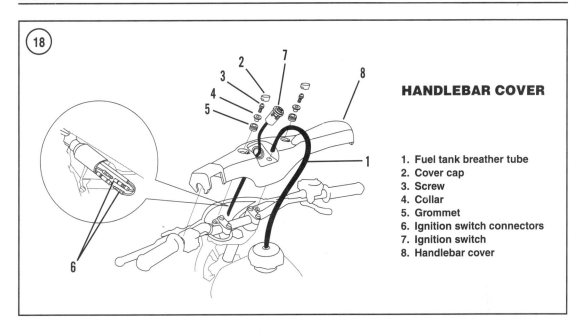

HANDLEBAR COVER

1. Fuel tank breather tube
2. Cover cap
3. Screw
4. Collar
5. Grommet
6. Ignition switch connectors
7. Ignition switch
8. Handlebar cover

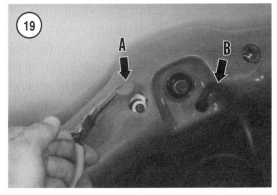

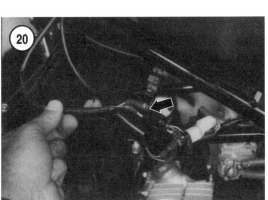

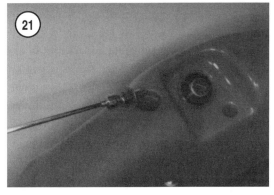

NOTE
Make sure the proper wires are disconnected. The black/white and green wire combination is also used for the engine stop switch.

4. Remove the screw, collar and grommet from each hole in the handlebar cover (**Figure 21**).

5. Lift the handlebar cover from the vehicle.

6. Refer to Chapter 9 for ignition switch replacement and testing.

7. Reverse these steps to install the handlebar cover. Note the following:

   a. Route the wiring so it is not pinched or near hot surfaces.

   b. Apply dielectric grease to the ignition switch connectors to prevent the entry of moisture.

2. Remove the fuel tank breather tube from the steering shaft (B, **Figure 19**).

3. Disconnect the ignition switch wires (black/white and green) below the fuel tank (**Figure 20**).

INDEX

14

IGNITION SYSTEM

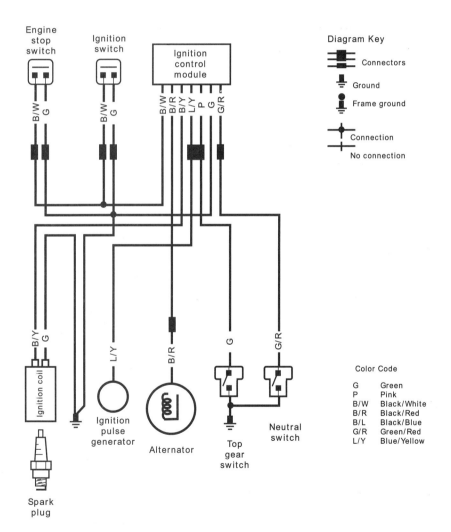

Diagram Key

Connectors

Ground

Frame ground

Connection

No connection

Color Code

G — Green
P — Pink
B/W — Black/White
B/R — Black/Red
B/L — Black/Blue
G/R — Green/Red
L/Y — Blue/Yellow

15

MAINTENANCE LOG

Service Performed	Mileage Reading				
Oil change (example)	2,836	5,782	8,601		